DAVID T. KYLE

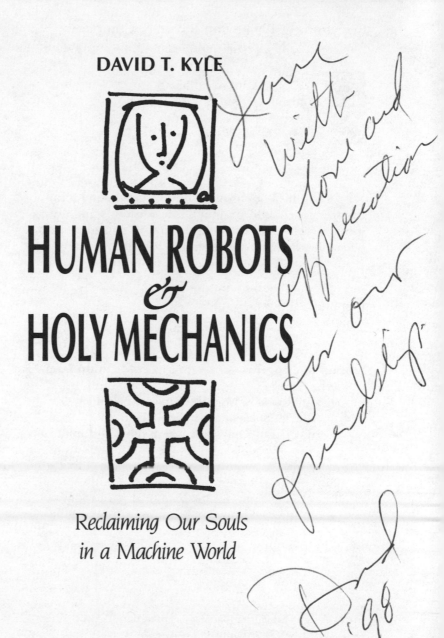

HUMAN ROBOTS
&
HOLY MECHANICS

*Reclaiming Our Souls
in a Machine World*

Swan/Raven & Company ■ Portland, Oregon ■ 1993

1427 N.W. 23rd Ave, Suite 8
Portland, Oregon 97210

(503) 274-1337

First printing: February 1993

Library of Congress Cataloging-in-Publication Data
Kyle, David T.
Human Robots & Holy Mechanics: Reclaiming Our
        Souls in a Machine World
Social criticism, Organizational psychology, Spiritual
        pp. 300

ISBN 0-9632310-0-6
1. Social criticism. 2. Organizational psychology.
        3. Spiritual.

LC # 92-93334

Cover design and illustration: Marcia Barrentine
Book design by Gary Hardin and Marcia Barrentine

This book was set in 11 point Garamond typeface
Printed in the United States of America

CONTENTS

ACKNOWLEDGMENTS 7
FOREWORD: Malidoma Somé 9
INTRODUCTION 13

PART I
ROBOTS IN THE MACHINE

LIVING IN A MACHINE 21
- The Message of the Machine
- Encounter with the Sacred
- The Machine Economy
- Doing Business in the Machine
- The Machine Protects Its Own
- Art as Advertising Consumption
- Worker Needs and Machine Needs
- The Purpose of the Worldwide Machine

THE GOAL OF THE MACHINE:
FINANCIAL POWER AND CONTROL 49
- The New World Leaders
- The Money Game

SERVING THE MACHINE 59
- Birthing the Modern Machine
- High-tech and High-touch Oiling

THE FAILURE OF OILING THE MACHINE....................67
- Why We Don't Challenge the Machine
- People as Parts in the Machine
- Work Addiction
- Women and the Machine
- People: Dispensable Assets

THE RISE OF THE MACHINE WORLD 79
- Nature as a Machine
- The Rush toward Free-market Capitalism
- Developing America's Machine
- The Machine Runs On Addiction
- The Perfect Addiction: Television

PART II
BECOMING HOLY MECHANICS

INTRODUCTION 99

THE MAKING OF AN AMERICAN ROBOT 103
- America: Dream and Reality
- Trying to Save the New American Dream
- The Old/New American Dream

LEADERS IN THE MACHINE 115
- Male Executives and the Abuse of Power
- Men Maintaining the Power
- The Struggle of Women Executives

CHANGING THE CONTEXT OF OUR MINDS 127
- Competition and the Scarcity Assumption
- Being a Resource Rather than a Victim

THE EPIPHANAL COMMUNITY...135
- The Breath of Inspiration
- Inspiring Epiphanies
- Bandit Organizations
- "Aha" Conversations
- Epiphanal Action
- The Loving Resistance Fighter

WHAT TO DO AS THE MACHINE BREAKS DOWN....................155
- How Possible is the Breakdown
- The State of the World
- From Fear to Hope
- At the Threshold of Changing State
- The "End of the World"
- The Economy
- Don't Face the Change Alone
- Messages From Planet Earth

PART III
RECLAIMING OUR SOULS

INTRODUCTION 187

REJECTING THE MACHINE: A RETURN TO THE SACRED.........191
- The Luddite Tradition
- Remembering Where We Made Wrong Turns

THE TRANSITION: LIVING FROM THE INSIDE OUT 199
- Between Two Worlds
- Living From the Inside Out

RECONSIDERING THE SACRED 205
- The Absence of the Sacred
- The Voice for Sacredness in the World

A CALL FOR ELDER-LEADERS...217
- The Elder Stage of Life
- Initiation with the Dagara of West Africa
- Initiation is Remembering
- Myth, Ritual and Power
- Initiating Elder-Leaders
- Old and New Forms of Leadership

OUR ESSENTIAL UNIQUENESS...233
- Finding Our Iron
- The Male-mother and the Crone
- Woman's Sacredness and Her Body
- Crying Out for Our Gift
- Elder Initiators
- Elder-leaders to Awaken Us from the Trance
- The Sound of Our Soul

THE WORLD OF IMAGINATION 251
- The Wyrd
- Dreamtime
- Pilot Rutters
- "Imaginal" Cells

REAWAKENING OUR SOULS......................................,........267
- A Turn on the Spiral
- The Teaching of Indigenous Peoples
- "Remembering" to Be Radical
- Radical Acts
- The Dance of Mirrors and Shadows

AFTERWORD — David Spangler 281

BIBLIOGRAPHY AND SOURCES...................................285

INDEX 291

ACKNOWLEDGMENTS

As with all projects, this book is the result of many people's input and effort. For the belief and encouragement to continue writing and make some ravings on paper into a readable book I express my appreciation to David Pond, Scott Taylor, Tom Pinkson, Divi Williams, Denny Berthiaume, J'aime Schelz, Chris Thorson and to the people of the Performance Edge. Thanks to Robert Gilman, Bill Bridges, and Hal Bennett for their helpful comments and criticisms of the manuscript. For the great care and dedication in editing, I thank Myrna Oakly for a superb effort. To my senior editor and book designer, Gary Hardin, my sincere thanks for constantly challenging me to make this a better book. Special thanks to Malidoma Somé for writing the foreword, and David Spangler for writing the afterword. I am indebted to both for our long discussions about the ideas presented in this book.

I dedicate this book to my family who are exploring with me the sacred journey: my partner, Patt, who by her love encourages my feelings and honesty; and Shellie and Christopher who have been important touchstones to grounding my life.

FOREWORD

by Malidoma Patrice Somé, Ph.D.
Spokesman for the Dagara Ancestors

Our post-modern world has successfully completed the conversion of man as prisoner, slave and servant of the Machine. The worst enslavement is the enslavement of us by our own machines. Trapped in the prison house of a mechanized consumer-driven society, we suffer silently, deeply and consistently in a terrible aloneness while an unfeeling Machine expects us to continue giving to it. It is absurd to give our lives to something that will never live. It is absurd to die empty.

David Kyle points to the source of the problems that ail our urban corporate cultures. Through a detailed presentation of the strategy of the corporate world to enslave the person and a comprehensive proposal for a mature retaliation, Kyle takes us into and out of the Machine. With his vivid and poignant arguments, he guides our eyes and our attentions toward ourselves, not as outsiders watching the corporate world at work, but as insiders and participants in the service of the corporate world that only feigns to serve us.

We are the robots of the Machine David Kyle speaks about, and we are the artisans of our spiritual impoverishment. This testimony invites each one of us to reconsider our position with the Machine and the daily contradictions it pours into our lives. He invites us to reconnect with the wisdom of our ancestors instead, and to allow our initiation to be complete. David Kyle invites us to turn back and allow ourselves to be remade by Mother Nature so that we can be fulfilled by her primal word.

A machine-made person simply cannot be taught to love. The Machine is, by its outward boundedness and stiffness, incapable of love and compassion. Whatever we get from the Machine, serves its own purpose, not our purpose. The crime of the Machine is that it makes us forget. To remember includes rebellion against the tyranny of the Machine, and David is encouraging us to awaken, to say no to it, and to come together as a society that values the powers within. May we listen and surrender to this timely call to liberate ourselves into life.

Human Robots &
Holy Mechanics

Introduction

*I*n the fall of 1991 I was stuck. I had spent several months working on a novel and suddenly came to a point where I didn't know how to continue. After struggling for several weeks with different scenarios I decided to stop writing. In contemplation one morning, the obvious came to me. The story couldn't resolve itself because I was unresolved in a major part of my life. The feeling was that I had to gain some kind of insight before I could understand what to do with the characters in the story.

I wrestled with this idea for a few days, until one morning I realized that the blockage I was experiencing, in continuing to write the novel, was tension about my relationship to the business community that I had been part of for 12 years. The story line of the novel had developed into a future scenario in which science, technology and business were causing enormous personal and collective changes in the country. How the business community had developed technology was a major sub-theme in the book. Over the year I had been writing the novel, I struggled with the idea of whether to stay with consulting or to do something else. It dawned on me that particular morning that the internal struggle I was having wasn't the question of continuing to do consulting or not. Rather, the issue was to comprehend the small part I was playing as a consultant in a structure that was negatively affecting me and everyone else on the planet.

My impulse was to write about this issue and to try to understand what I was feeling. From time to time I sent drafts to friends. They kept encouraging me to write more. The result is this book. My hope for you, as the reader, is that my reflection and thinking will encourage you to consider whatever is the core question of your life right now. I urge you to write about it, to talk with friends, and to be quiet and listen to the voice of the Sacred within you. Struggling honestly and fully with our personal questions is the basis of engaging in, and contributing to, an in-depth response to the larger cultural and environmental questions that are affecting all of us.

This book is divided into three parts. The first part explores what I call the corporation-economy, or the Machine. I voice what many of us intuitively know about this Machine's world we now live in. I began to recognize that my role in the Machine, as a management consultant, has been to oil it, and keep it going. But I also realized that *we all are a kind of robot in the Machine* by our participation and living in it. My intent in this section is to challenge the assumptions and attitudes that many of us hold about being part of this monolithic entity. In challenging and criticizing the Machine, I am also probing the part I play in it and the strange paradox of criticizing it from the inside while fully participating in it. The reality is that there is no place for any of us to completely get outside of the Machine. I acknowledge my own myopic view and the danger of not seeing the beauty in the individual tree because of my focus on the poor condition of the forest. In focusing on the forest I am sharply critical of the leadership of this worldwide Machine. In laying out my views, I want to underscore that there are people who are the exception within the Machine power structure. These people hold many views similar to mine. These individuals are applying sincerely, in their own way, creativity and knowledge to many of the issues I raise. However, my position is that the Machine culture (as a term for describing our present world system), cannot be tweaked or modified to make our lives work better. Our current view of the world and this system must change. The Machine must change, and we as individuals must start to change the Machine from the inside out. This first part of the book gives context and information about how we got into the Machine's culture and what it is doing to us. This may help some of us take the next step of asking some different kinds of questions of ourselves and responding to the corporation-economy Machine in alternative ways.

The second part of the book addresses the transition we are experiencing at the end of this last decade of the 20th century. Five-hundred years ago the view that life worked like a machine was conceived by our forebears. Through 20 generations, the developing of this collective imagination made concrete the world economy we live in today. The imagining of life as a machine has turned many into human robots that now at the end of the 20th century serve the Machine, rather than the Machine serving humanity. This second part also examines the process of how and why we are beginning to turn our backs on the Machine. Our direction is not to arrive at some finite solution for our social and environmental problems. Rather, our challenge is to discover in ourselves the capacity to make choices and shift from being victims of the Machine to becoming resources within it. If we can individually make this shift to a new place of inner resource we can learn to draw from some deeper intuition and insight that will help us access new directions for family, friends, and associates in our communities.

In the third part of the book, I assert that the Machine has cut us off from our souls and the Sacred — from the most meaningful relationship in human existence — the connection with an otherworld of reality that comes to us through nature. My belief is that we must somehow find a way to restore the Sacred in our lives in order to reclaim our souls. I hold the view that life is optimally experienced as an integrated whole when the individual is nested within a self-conscious community of like-minded people. I believe that this kind of community holds as its primary value a conscious connection and relationship with a transcendent Reality. A community connected to this larger reality views all of created life as equal and important.

The other assumption I hold is that the natural world is and always has been, for our species, the mediator and connector between this physical world and the non-physical world that is just beyond our normal perception. Both the physical and non-physical together combine to make the spiritual dimension. This spiritual dimension is what many traditions call the Otherworld.

I also believe that native peoples and our archaic ancestors hold some fundamental perceptions, beliefs and ways of relating to the physical and non-physical world that we have lost in the Machine culture, and that we need to regain these fundamental concepts. I believe that such indigenous peoples can provide insight and pathways of action that can help us bridge the dead-end we are coming to as a species. I believe these native peoples hold the genetic memory of how to access a deeper imagination than we currently live within. These *old ways* mixed with an earnest and bold exploration of our own interior topography of imagination provide a promise of new possibilities for community and personal relationships.

Besides a call for a return to a new sacred imagination, I believe we must rediscover and reinitiate older women and men into what I call elder-leaders. In our youth-driven culture we have lost the important role older men and women must play in a society in order for it to be healthy and balanced. It is the natural ability of older men and women to initiate young people in our culture, and to take on a spiritual wisdom and healing role for our communities. By engaging our elders I believe that we will increase our possibilities of finding ways to circumvent the doomsday apocalypse we are now creating on this planet.

My suggestions and proposals toward the end of part III are to consider the ways that we can reclaim our souls and return to the Sacred in order to survive the destructiveness of the Machine's monoculture. This discussion will offer different ways that we can reconceive and reimagine an alternate future for ourselves, for our children and for our planet.

This is not, however, a book of answers. It is an attempt to look again at the history and condition of our current dilemma as it affects us today in this machinelike culture in which we all play a part. It is also a book that attempts to have us remember what we know about the mystery and sacredness of the natural world. And it is a book that attempts to point to some simple pathways within us where we can reexperience a renewed relationship with the Sacred, with ourselves and with one another.

Our dialogue with each other is critical and important at this time. The choices we are making to live differently, and the support we give to each other to be thoughtful and creative about what we do with our lives, will enable all of us to participate in developing a different kind of world. I hope this book contributes to the growing worldwide dialogue.

Portland, Oregon
September, 1992

PART I

ROBOTS IN A MACHINE WORLD

People are not machines, but in all situations where they are given the opportunity, they will act like machines.

LUDWIG VON BERTALANFFY
THE INVENTOR OF GENERAL
SYSTEMS THEORY

Living in a Machine

*T*he Machine is now the world. Nature is something we visit on vacations. The Machine's values of a consuming monoculture with its powerful teaching tool, television, have taken away our independence in making personal and collective decisions. The leaders of the Machine proclaim that every new product is progress and that every culture, every part of the world, must have and buy what these leaders choose to supply. Diversity in the world is quickly being lost. Whole species are becoming extinct daily. Cultural traditions and identities are being lost. Yet, in the despair and loss there are pockets of resistance, of growing seeds of change and hope among us even as the situation becomes more depressed and crazy-making. Most of us are like human robots in service to a monolithic Machine. And we are in need of holy mechanics who will help us reclaim our humanity.

In 1909 E.M. Forster, who wrote *Passage to India*, created a prophetic science-fiction story that portrays the ultimate destructiveness of a machine-world culture. In the story, "The Machine Stops," he describes our future, one in which machines have totally taken over the running of the world. Humans have gone underground away from the toxic world above, where nothing can live any longer. They dwell in individual rooms, rarely traveling out into the maze of tunnels, pipes and wires. The people interact by viewing one another on their flat-screen TV plates. All their physical needs are provided for by the Machine.

The plot of the story concerns a woman who has a son whom she has not seen in the flesh for years. He keeps requesting that she travel to visit him in his cubicle. She resists for a period of time, but then finally consents to see him by taking a difficult journey through the underground mechanical labyrinth, and then by an airship from Australia to the Northern Hemisphere. When they finally meet face to face, the son tells his mother that he has traveled to the surface of the planet. He describes both the wonder of ferns and grass, and stars and moon. But the Machine finds out that a hole has been opened to the surface and sends its repair unit to both fix the hole and bring back any human that has reached the surface. The son describes the terror of being pursued by a wormlike tube that coils around his legs and drags him back down the ventilation shaft he had opened. Brought back to his room he is threatened by the Committee with "homelessness" — toxic death through banishment to the surface without the Machine. His mother scolds her son for going where no human now lives. But he responds that he saw people. A woman, he tells her, came to help him as he screamed and ran in terror from the worm tube. But the woman, he reports, was killed as the worm pierced her throat with a metal probe. The mother is shocked by his description and strange views. She leaves him and returns quickly to the safety and comfort of her own room. Time passes, but a day comes when the TV and other communication and service devices in her room slowly begin to break down. Music has static in it, and is not as clear when called up by a press of a button. Air becomes stale. Food grows moldy. But even with the complaints, people still revere and quietly pray to the Machine for help. Suddenly, one day the Machine stops. Of its own weight and decay the Machine begins to die, a kind of mechanical suicide. As electric power stations go silent and valves burst, the Machine progressively destroys itself and the humans who are buried in its mechanical bowels. The incomprehensible words of the son keep coming back to the mother as the Machine falls into darkness: "The Machine stops." In the darkness the mother flees her room into the passage where people are dying. The son, who has been traveling through the mechanical maze in order to reach his mother, calls out to her. When she answers him, he wades through the dead bodies telling her in great triumph, that they are dying, but that they can finally talk to each other directly, and touch each other without the mediation of the machine. As an airship falls into the metal city and explodes, the mother asks the son if there are really people on the surface of the earth. The son responds by saying, " I have seen them, spoken to them, loved them. They are hiding in the mist and the ferns until our civilization stops. Today they are Homeless — tomorrow . . . ." And the mother responds, "Oh, tomorrow — some fool will start the Machine again, tomorrow." And the son says, "Never. Humanity has learnt its lesson."

Forster, 85 years ago, sensed the power and rapaciousness of the newly released industrial Machine. He sensed its capacity to take control of the world very rapidly, and somehow put humans into a deep trance with its constant movement of turning wheels and humming motors. From 1900 to today the industrial world has given way to incomprehensible speeds of information and connectivity. We live now in a world that is rapidly being connected by fiber-optic cables and satellite transmission, by mobile telephones and notebook computers, by virtual reality and nanotechnology.

Everyday people around the world do almost exactly the same things in the same way. On a given day I will get into a steel and plastic vehicle, travel on miles of asphalt and concrete, work in a huge steel and concrete structure whose air is constantly recirculated; leave in the afternoon to travel in a titanium jet that deposits me at an airport that is identical to most any in the world, and rent a temporary vehicle that will take me to a hotel that is interchangeable with one found almost anywhere else in the world. No matter where I live in our country I can read the same newspaper, watch the same

TV programs at the same time of day, eat the same processed food, sleep in the same type of bed with the same furnishings found in all hotel rooms, meet in the same kinds of office complexes and watch the same kind of movie entertainment.

At whatever socio-economic level one lives, one has the comfort and security of sameness almost anyplace in the world today. As a people, we complain of our isolation and alienation from each other and from the natural world. We fear growing crime and the threat to our economic security. We complain about the constant work and the hectic pace of living. Politically we seem confused and cynical, we lack the will to solve fundamental problems in our societies. In my view, Forster's vision of a Machine-driven world is more than a metaphor, and is growing daily in our experience. His story reveals the emotional reality of our daily experience in a Machine world. And like the mother in his story, we find ourselves chanting the same mantra of denial: "Tomorrow, no matter how difficult our problems, the Machine will continue, the Machine will save us."

The Message of the Machine

Recently when people asked me about my practice as a management and organizational consultant, I told them, "I am tired of oiling the Machine." This phrase has become my metaphor for supporting a structure, a system and a way of living that is emotionally, spiritually and, in many ways, physically killing a vast majority of us who work and live in our post-industrial-information-economic society — what I call the corporation-economy Machine.

Although not all of us work in companies that we think are machinelike, all of us live in the Machine's corporation-economy. We all are affected by the Machine's cultural force that influences such things as our ideas and values, the food we eat, what we do for entertainment and recreation, our relationship to the natural world, what kind of interactions we have with people, and what scientific or technological gadgets we use. Some of us try to resist and reject parts of this Machine's monoculture. But the reality is that no one escapes the Machine's full embrace. The Machine's culture has been created through a consistent set of messages sent and received over the past 100 years: continued economic growth is the basic good of society; use of all natural resources for the benefit of humans is our right; technology creates a better and happier life for all; and the consuming and buying of things is the natural way to live life. The Machine has trained us like robots to serve its ends and purposes. Like any slave, we long to be free, and at the same time we are frightened to break the bonds that enslave us. Our escape isn't in some rebellion to tear down factory buildings or burn cars. Rather, it lies inside our minds. This robot slavery that is ingrained in us comes out of our own imagination.

We have created and accepted this machine culture within our minds. The only way to change it is through a deeper and more powerful imagining of who we are and what we want to be. Aboriginal peoples teach us that the doorway to a clearer and more powerful imagination is in nature. Indigenous societies, past and present, are organic cultures. They are cultures that live and grow naturally from some deeper and more mature perception of the balances needed in life. These ancient cultures provide hints about how we may enter through the doorway of nature into another way of conceiving reality. Entering a new imagination for how we want to live is still possible for us today. Many of us know this doorway and have entered and experienced the promise of its beauty. My earliest and most direct encounter with this doorway occurred some 20 years ago.

Encounter with the Sacred

I had been sitting for several hours at the edge of the medicine wheel I had constructed. I was fascinated by the chipmunks as they moved closer to me while running in and out of the circle of stones. My hours of stillness allowed the chipmunks to lose their fear of me. One golden-backed chipmunk became so bold as to run across my legs, stop on my knee, raise up on its hind legs and chatter at me. I tried to suppress a laugh, but my stifled chuckling scattered them all back to the nearby juniper tree.

I was camped above timberline among the granite rock and gnarled juniper trees in the Sierra Nevada Mountains of Northern California. Earlier in the week, as I hiked cross-country over several 11,000-foot ridges, I had stumbled upon the small meadow and campsite high above an alpine lake. I had built the 30-foot-wide medicine wheel in the meadow.

The medicine wheel is an old shamanic ritual circle that has been used for thousands of years by indigenous people around the world for meditation and ceremony. Constructing the large circle of stones, and then placing a cross of stones inside the circle, had been an exercise for remembering different parts of my life and personality that I was trying to understand. I had been teaching for several years, and each summer I spent some time backpacking alone in the Sierras. I used this time by myself to focus on becoming aware of deeper parts of myself as well as attempting to connect with the mysterious and sacred in nature.

The wind had begun to bluster toward the end of the day. A weather front of dark clouds moved toward my location from the west. After the chipmunks retreated to the juniper, I got up, stretched, and decided to get into my tent as rain began to spatter in the granite dust. I was hungry. I had fasted for two days to heighten my sensitivity. I had walked and sat within the circle of stones for many hours each day. The purpose of this activity was to keep my concentration and focus on the pattern of the stones in the medicine wheel as well as on the surrounding environment of trees, animal life and changing weather conditions. In the Native American tradition the use of the medicine wheel and nature in this way is a method to understand how one's interior experiences and images reflect the outer world and vice versa. I had learned to

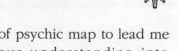

use the wheel and nature as a kind of psychic map to lead me beyond the edge of self-conscious understanding into exploring new emotional, psychological and spiritual terrain within myself.

With the dark clouds moving in fast and the light dying, the temperature dropped quickly. I crawled into the tent and into my down sleeping bag. Both were welcome comfort and warmth. When I closed my eyes I was startled by the almost psychedelic images of weird, nightmarish demons and animals. I knew I could put myself into a deep fearful place if I let myself battle with this interior world. I decided to get out some food, break my fast and change my mental focus. I did this and quickly went to sleep.

The storm had slowed its arrival during the night. When I got up the next morning there were snow flurries in the air. I made the decision to break camp and move down to a lower altitude before the snow storm gathered in intensity. I had breakfast and packed my gear. I squatted over my cat-hole latrine to relieve myself before starting the day hike out of the wilderness.

While squatting I began to hear music. At first I was confused. I got up and looked down toward the lake to see if someone was playing a radio. No one had been there all week, and I couldn't see anyone now. I walked around the campsite but couldn't identify where the music was coming from. As I concentrated more on the sound, I could distinguish the general pattern of the music as being a large a cappella choir singing in complex harmonies. I sat down on a rock and felt both awed and a little frightened by it.

The sound was distinctly outside of me. I noticed that it was a little louder when I turned to one particular direction. As I listened, I felt that I was at some invisible threshold, a gateway into some other world. I moved to the medicine circle and felt some kind of container around me. Within this container I could hear the music more clearly. Inwardly, something seemed to invite me to surrender and open myself to some sort of doorway. It wanted me to move through the threshold to where the music was originating.

The rational, logical part of me resisted what was happening. It argued that I was getting mentally unstable. It told me that I shouldn't be having this experience. I wasn't meditating or fasting. I had broken the ritual space I had created for the week, eaten food, prepared myself to go back to my "normal" life, and was sitting over my make-shift latrine when this strange music intruded on me. My rational mind said this wasn't how or when a spiritual experience was supposed to happen!

As I struggled with my internal logic, the music continued to slightly fade in and out. I knew I was at a critical decision point. Something inside me said I could make a choice to go through into another dimension — or turn off the music and hike down the mountain.

But I couldn't decide. I put on my pack and began to walk out of the campsite to test if the music would stay with me. It did. I stopped walking. I stood for a long while listening to the music and finally told myself I would stop it. Immediately the music fell silent. And immediately I regretted this decision. Then a very clear voice said, "another time will come when you are ready."

Nature, ritual, celestial music, voices, dreams, thresholds, otherworlds — these are the experiences of the Sacred. These take us back into an earlier time in our history. They reveal a different consciousness, a different perception, and a different experience of reality. Indigenous peoples, however, still live daily with these sacred elements. Unusual as my experience may seem it is not that unique.

Julian Jaynes, the behavioral psychologist, in his original work on the two brain hemispheres and consciousness, *The Origins of Consciousness in the Breakdown of the Bicameral Mind,* describes how most normal adults have heard exterior music, or voices, or have seen visual images at some point in their lives. Our problem in the contemporary Machine world is that we don't have a context to interpret the significance of these experiences, nor have we been taught what they could mean or how they could fit into our daily lives. We generally store these seemingly unusual experiences away and forget the deeper knowings they may have opened in us.

When people sat quietly on the farm porch a hundred years ago listening for hours to the night sounds, they must have had this experience of music and voices, just as native people do today as they speak of otherworld contact with spirits when doing their ceremonies and vision quests. Jaynes' methodical account demonstrates that our ancestors lived in this sacred world of the gods and spirits, but we in Western cultures lost this deep personal connection over the past 2,000 years. It is this loss of personal connection to another dimension that has created the growing separation from Nature and from each other. Yet today, it is our reapproaching of the Sacred through Nature that is fundamentally needed to challenge our robotic lifestyles in a world of increasingly complex and mechanical existence.

This acknowledgment and experience, by many of us, of the deeper realities that coexisted in the world of our ancestors, and that still exist in the lives of present day native peoples around the world, offers not only hope but possibilities as well that we can know and experience a different pathway into the future. For us to explore and create an alternative imagination that moves away from the Machine we need to understand what drives and reinforces the reality of our present world. The most basic determiner of maintaining this world, past and present, is a particular type of economics.

The Machine Economy

The Machine's economy has developed through a particular technological-industrial growth pattern. From almost total agriculturally-based societies, that existed up into the mid-1850s, Western European and American societies moved into cottage industries. From there they moved into a textile manufacturing economy that created the basic structure to support the emergence of light industrialization. From small factories producing clothes, furniture, and pots and pans came the introduction of coal and steel manufacturing to support the transportation industry of steam engines and steel ships. With the discovery of the refining of oil for gasoline we embarked on heavy industry as we moved into the 20th century. In the middle of the 20th century, technology made rapid and significant shifts as vacuum tubes gave way to transistors and silicon chips. With micro-computer chips came the age of miniaturization and the onset of the ability to mimic the functions of the human brain.

Now, at the end of the 20th century, electronic industrial manufacturing has revolutionized the older industrial segments of the economy. Electronics has introduced information as *the* product that has connected all parts of the planet together. This information product has created the new revolution that science, technology and business are birthing today in such areas as bio-engineering and nanotechnology. Both of these new industries have huge implications for how humans will exist in the future.

At the center of the biotechnologies revolution is genetic engineering. Genetic engineering works at the basic creation level of organisms in designing genes that will do such things as create cattle that will always produce a superior flavor in their meat, develop micro-organisms that can eat up oil sludge in the ocean, or mass produce identical superintelligent children by introducing genes into sperm cells that are designed for this purpose.

Nanotechnology moves machines into biology. Nanotechnology goes beyond gene creation by going to the smallest level in an organism — the molecule. This technology has developed microscopic machines the size of a molecule that can go into the atomic structure of organic or inorganic materials. These molecular machines rearrange the molecules so as to create new forms of plants, animals and materials. Technologists have designed theoretical nanomachines that can do such things as enter the blood stream and eat fat, repair blood vessels, or regenerate a new kidney. The claim of these bio-engineers is that they will solve all the food, resource and disease problems. The nanotechnologists assert that the human organism is now an interchangeable suit of clothes. They believe they are on the threshold of creating a technology that would download one's brain activity into a biological robot so that one could live forever. In this rapidly growing and government-protected technology is the future dream of an utopian world in which individual human awareness will never die.

These two technologies comprise a radically new type of industrial revolution that will move us into the real-life science fiction of human robots and into the Nazi ideal of a potential superhuman race. It is here, in these two emerging technologies, where humans will become part flesh and part robot, and where the machine ideal will become the primary value. Our technology has outpaced both our concepts of what it is to be human and our relationship to the natural world. Values, philosophy, religion and ethics are being lost in the wake of a technology that plows into a surreal future. (Later in part III we will consider some of the implications of technological tools that no longer serve us.)

Because of rapid acceleration of technology in the past 150 years, this industrialized-electronic-information Machine has moved swiftly from Europe (particularly England), to the United States. Then, 30 years ago it moved from the United States to Japan, and spread throughout Southeast Asia and the rest of the world. Now this monolithic Machine is felt and experienced culturally as a particular way of perceiving the world.

Some of these widely held perceptions include that industrial machines are a better way to create work for people than subsistence living and agriculture; that it is better for people to live in urban centers than to spread out in the rural countryside; and that the natural world of trees, rivers and minerals are merely the fuel to keep the industrial machine-style economy growing. Even stronger is the belief that economic growth is the most important survival value of the industrial Machine.

What the Machine also bestows on us is a bland monoculture of fads and image-oriented behavior. It has taken the old 1950's notion of "keeping up with the Joneses " to a worldwide level. We are taught to want the latest model car, the biggest television screen, the next step up in a new house, the lowest calorie soft drink, or the widest or narrowest suit tie. Constantly we are motivated to buy more things even when we have a closet full of them, or urged to believe that it's trade-in time for the car or kitchen appliance. Whatever our level of personal awareness or resistance to consumer buying, we are confronted with its bewitching appeal daily.

Even in our personal resistance to consumerism we are all subjected to propoganda daily by billboards, newspaper ads and via radio and TV commercials. American corporations alone spend more than $100 billion a year on advertising. David Riesman's classic study, *The Lonely Crowd,* describes the 20th-century transition from what he and his co-authors described as a middle-class movement from "inner-directed" (internalization of societal values) to "other-directed" (susceptible to passing fads because of no internal values) social characteristics. This study was written in 1950 at the beginning of the television era. In the 1961 revision, Riesman notes that in the 10 years since they completed the original study, TV was having a bigger impact on "other-directedness" than they had anticipated. But Riesman makes an interesting comment based on Alex de Tocqueville's observations of early 18th century U. S. citizens. He says in a footnote to his discussion about the mass media, "Even before the rise of advertising," Tocqueville saw Americans ". . . as competing with each other in the race for and display of possessions. Americans were ready for the mass media even before the mass media were ready for them." Something in our national character, Riesman argues, seems to have predisposed us to be leaders of worldwide consumerism.

Doing Business in the Machine

The economic Machine described here is made up of specific little machines — corporations and companies who produce the things we consume. What makes these individual machines potentially destructive to individuals who work in them is that they only survive by serving the greater Machine. If this mega-Machine is not creating more things, and in fact starting up more and different kinds of companies to create products, something is "wrong with the economy." Every year thousands of companies are started to provide the products and services to keep other companies functioning. For example, we all know that IBM, Apple, Microsoft, and a host of hardware and software computer companies produce so-called productivity tools to be used in other companies. These tools give dimension and complexity to the next generation of products that are created at ever faster rates, and consume natural resources at accelerating speed.

The evolving dominance of multinational corporations in the United States, Europe and Japan over the past 25 years linked various company machines together to create dominance and control over the world's natural resources. Oil in Alaska, trees in Indonesia, coal in Siberia are mere numbers on a computer printout for the leaders of these multinational companies. Decisions are made in New York, London, or Tokyo that destroy whole ecosystems, villages, or ages-old ways of life. Natural and human systems and ways of life are decided upon by people who don't see the results of their decisions. And when companies are forced to see the results of their actions, as in the case of the Alaskan oil spill, they rationalize the destruction as a regrettable but small cost of "progress." Progress is rationalized in these circumstances because these corporations own these natural resources, and often care little about the impact that resource harvesting and manufacturing has on the local people or on the environment. Classic examples of the lack of *real* concern by the Machine's companies for people and the environment are demonstrated by both Union Carbide and by Exxon.

In the 1986 Bhopal, India, Union Carbide chemical disaster that killed 2,000 people and injured over 200,000 others, the company, after initial pronouncements of sympathy and public-relations statements that they would do everything they could to help the people, fought in court from paying damages and reparations. In the Exxon Valdez oil spill in Alaska in 1989, the company advertised extensively on television that the company was fully committed to the cleanup. When environmental costs began to mount significantly, Exxon rapidly backed away from its promises to make everything right and stopped the clean-up within six months.

This basic rationalization of "it's the price of progress" by these corporate decision-makers over the fate of the resources of the planet is rooted in the ethic of greed. A contemporary example of this greed is the resistance of the Reagan-Bush administration to any government regulations that limits the profits of corporations, no matter what their effect is on people or the environment. Regulations cost businesses money. Businesses want to get rid of regulations in order to make more profit. Corporations want cheaper ways of doing business even if this hurts the health of workers, creates toxicity on the planet, or creates human diminution.

An example of the exploitation of deregulation that deeply affected our children was the Reagan-Bush administration's efforts in 1984 to get the Federal Communications Commission (FCC) to eliminate the restrictions on the number of minutes per hour that advertising would be permitted on children's television programming. These FCC controls were to assure quality programming for children and mandated that the content of a program was more important than advertising. By changing the composition of FCC commissioners, the administration was able to get a ruling to deregulate these programs. Taking away the restrictions that protected children from being subjected to sophisticated advertising then permitted companies to market and advertise toys or any other product as part of the *content of a program.* The Ninja Turtle cartoon program, for example, was designed to sell Ninja Turtle dolls.

In the book *Who's calling the Shots? How to Respond Effectively to Children's Fascination with War Play and War Toys,* authors Nancy Carlson-Paige and Diane Levin present startling statistics of how toy manufacturers made huge sales increases after deregulation, and how they got into the business of producing children's TV shows. "The profit in toy sales were enormous, and some toy manufacturers began to share the wealth with television stations that carried their shows. By December 1985 all of the 10 best-selling toys had television shows connected to them. And in the fall of 1987, 80 percent of all children's television programming was produced — literally paid for — by toy companies. Sales of TV-linked toys skyrocketed after deregulation, growing from $7 billion to $14 billion between 1980 and 1988. . . . Because of the TV and toy linkup, children increasingly were made to feel that they had to have certain toys in order to play."

Over and over the cases of deregulation during the Reagan-Bush era have been for the benefit of the corporation-economy, not for the best interests of people, the environment or natural resources. In the entire worldwide community of nations, the United States and Liberia are the only two nations that have not signed the agreement to reduce chemicals that destroy the ozone layer of the atmosphere. The Reagan-Bush administration resisted new regulations in order to protect the huge chemical industry in the United States that doesn't want to stop selling these products to unsuspecting people in the Third World.

A classic example of speaking out of two sides of the mouth by the Bush administration was in first promoting and then denying federal regulations to the 1990 Clean Air Act. President Bush resisted the Act and pushed hard in congressional legislation to get pro-industry measures included in the Act that were detrimental to the environment. At the same time Bush made the claim of being the Environmental President for signing the Act. But the story of the administration's resistance to clean air does not stop at the creation of the Clean Air Act.

The environmental lobby hoped that after the act was signed, by focusing on regulations from the Environmental Protection Agency (EPA), the Clean Air Act could be fulfilled even though it favored polluters. The Bush administration, in an action calculated to make sure that industries would not have to meet regulated standards, set up Vice President Dan Quayle's Council on Competitiveness. This council was set up under White House direction through the Office of Management and Budget (OMB). The prime purpose of the Council was to oversee the EPA as it drafts regulations from new environmental laws such as the Clean Air Act. Its mission was to be an advocate and protector of industry even when the favoritism could negatively affects the health of the population. The EPA brought a series of regulations to the Council which were either shot down or modified in favor of industry lobbyists. The Council did such things as reject an EPA proposed regulation to ban incineration of batteries that would eliminate 65 percent of atmospheric lead emitted by municipal incinerators. The Council simply said (without public evidence) that the regulation did not meet financial cost-benefit guidelines. But one of the most notable battles was to force the EPA to let industries alter their permits to emit pollutants into the atmosphere without notifying the public. The EPA's administrator, William Reilly, used legal positions to oppose the Competitiveness Council's permit proposal. In the conflict between Quayle and Reilly, Bush backed industry lobbyists and Quayle. As W.K. Burke wrote in the weekly newspaper, *In These Times*, "Now that Quayle's Council on Competitiveness has won its first confrontation with Reilly, it seem the Bush administration has given industry virtual veto power over EPA decisions." And also the veto power over the air we breathe.

The resistance by our own government and by companies to regulations that protect people and the natural world is a strange conflict of personal and professional values. Most decision-makers in the corporation-economy hold a mindset that asserts that they must make a profit at any cost. As individuals, they want to protect and keep safe their families and the immediate environment in which they live. But "over there " where they don't live, in some other part of the country or world, it doesn't make any difference. Built into their financial reports is a perveted rationalization in which people in these companies con themselves and those around them into believing that their destructive actions to our world and the future of our children is somehow OK. Immediate jobs and profit somehow rationalize away consequences to these actions. And "over there" also has a built-in racism and a fascism that keeps the affluent, white First World leaders in control.

The Machine Protects Its Own

The culture of the Machine teaches that, by definition, the corporation is a living entity. Legal systems and tax structures recognize that a corporation is like a person. Boards of directors, presidents and employees come and go but the corporation continues on. The corporation has a life of its own, separate from human beings. The health of a corporation and its continuance as an entity depends on its capability to sustain itself financially. Because of this fact, the Machine's leadership asserts that the corporation must be protected and preserved. A secondary assertion is that the Machine will survive best when the leaders and managers of the organizations protect their own positions. These people assure the survival of the company by doing those things that perpetuate the company's existence. Those closer to the top of the hierarchy have more power to protect their positions at the expense of those lower down in the Machine's company.

For example, while the economy was in recession in 1991, with hundreds of thousands of people being put out of work, Wall Street executives got huge compensation increases. For example William Schreyer, Chairman, Merrill Lynch & Co. received $3.9 million in salary, bonus and stock options in 1990. In 1991 he received an incredible increase in pay to

$16.8 million. In a March 23, 1992, *Wall Street Journal* article, people outside the brokerage community questioned whether these individuals were worth what they were getting paid. Allen Greenberg, Chairman of Bear Sterns Cos., who was paid $4.2 million in 1990 and $5.3 million in 1991, responded to this questioning, "I don't know if Michael Jackson is worth what he gets, and I don't know if a [baseball player] who hits .250 is worth $2.5 million, which is what he gets," Mr. Greenberg said. "I'm not a philosopher." Those who hold the executive power, particularly in the financial community, don't need to philosophize. These CEOs are at the pinnacle of personal power and influence, and their salary and bonus reflects the intention of the corporation to make sure it both survives and prospers. Within the value system of the corporation-economy large salaries need no justification.

When a company that supports and perpetuates the Machine is threatened, senior management will often publicly rationalize that they are taking certain actions to protect the Machine for the "good of the stockholders." But in practice it boils down to the fact that senior management and boards of directors are often only protecting and preserving their own pocketbooks and prestige. Even in non-profit and educational institutions, actions taken by the institution — in the name of public-interest concerns — often simply reflect the needs for survival and prestige of the board and top management. Leaders in most of our economic-based corporations are not making decisions that effect "the good of the whole." They are making personal decisions that will further the power of the organization and their own careers and income.

One non-profit organization that I consulted for brought in an outsider as Chief Executive Officer (CEO). This individual had no experience in their area of service. The organization had a strong old-boys network. The board of directors felt, given the economic and demographic changes, that someone with a strong business background was needed to get them on track again. The CEO took the board at its word and began to make business decisions that changed efficiencies of operations, eliminated people that had been unproductive for years, and generally began to rearrange the furniture of the organization. After 18 months in the job the new CEO was forced to resign because he "moved too fast." Senior management, underneath the outsider, convinced the board of directors that the new CEO was threatening everyone's position and power base — including the board's. All agreed that the best decision was for the CEO to be replaced so that the organization could become "stable" again. Neither the board nor senior management were concerned about the best interests of the organization; they were concerned with protecting themselves and their positions of power and influence.

Art as Advertising Consumption

The leaders of these corporate machines learned in MBA schools — and through the general inoculation we all get from the machine culture — to accept as fact that expanding and increasing the supply of any kind of goods and services is what is both needed and demanded by the population. And further, like all of us, these leaders are hypnotized into believing that the corporate business Machine provides the primary "good" for a worldwide society of consumption. The method of convincing us that we need all these things comes through the mass media — particularly television. The power of television in influencing us to consume products is overwhelming. For example, the average American watches 21,000 commercials a year. Billions of dollars and thousands of people are employed in the production of this commercial creativity.

The basic propaganda message of our post-industrial-information-economic culture asserts that creativity and innovation are connected directly to economic consumption. Something new and different must be marketed and a profit made on it. There is little questioning or testing of the value, purpose or general good of the "new thing" created for individuals or the society. The only principle that rules is whether consumers accept or reject it. But consumerism is a larger issue than just accepting or rejecting a particular product. Consumerism has become a right for us in the United States.

Michael Jacobson, of the Center for the Study of Commercialism in Washington, D. C., asserts that the cultural impact of consumerism now controls the basic choices of our society. "We're raised," he says, "to be consumers, not citizens — to build our lives around things. If the choice is having a $25,000 car and the homeless, versus a $12,000 car and no homeless, American consumers would prefer the fancy car. Consumerism is selfishness." It is the use of our inbred selfishness of consuming, that drives the Machine to devise new things for us to buy.

To assure acceptance by the population for the "new thing," propaganda and behavioral conditioning are employed through the advertising arm of the Machine to stimulate people and companies to accept and buy the newest creation. To assure that we continue to buy, the advertising industry spends more than $500 a year on every woman, man and child in the country. The billions of dollars that are available co-opts our cultural values, particularly in the arts.

The combining of artistic creativity and advertising is now all pervasive in our culture. What is the artistic expression and what is an ad has all but merged in the popular culture. Deborah Baldwin writes in *The Hard Sell of Advertising* about corporations' infiltration of schools with "educational" materials and video programs that promote a corporate viewpoint. These corporations push Saturday TV with what amounts to half-hour cartoon commercials.

Corporations pay moviemakers to include name-brand products in their films. Products are then written into movie scripts as if they were a character in the movie.

Baldwin states, regarding artistic endeavor and our consumer culture, "So symbiotic are commercial and creative interests that well-known actors, producers, and filmmakers frequently 'cross-over,' lending their talents to Madison Avenue and further blurring the line between merchandising and the arts." All art becomes economics and investments. From paintings that sell for millions of dollars for their long-term portfolio strategy to the promoting of a new painter, playwright, author or filmmaker because of his or her potential value to the promoters, creativity becomes one more commodity to stimulate the economy. More creativity and money is put into the 30-second commercial than the 30-minute sitcom. Programming exists so that we can watch the commercial.

Worker Needs and Machine Needs

Since 1990 Sears, Roebuck and Co., the third-largest retailer in the country, has eliminated 42,650 positions, and plans to continue eliminating jobs up through 1993 in an effort to improve its profitability. Some 3,200 sales clerks who work on commission quit their jobs rather than accept reduced commissions that were announced in February of 1992. Sears announced that the reduction of commissioned personnel and their commissions saves Sears $60 million annually. The next target for reduction they proclaimed would be in regional human resource and finance offices. One analyst who tracked Sears for the financial community said, "I think it shows that they're serious in continuing to lop off overhead" (read people). And another analyst said, "Nobody likes being laid off, but for Sears to survive, they must be more efficient. They got that message some time ago and they're carrying through with it."

The Machine's message comes through loud and clear. Sears, the corporate entity, is more important than the people who make it up. What Sears is doing is probably good business sense. This corporation may have hired too many people, or are not competitive with other retailers because of its overhead. But the point is, when the survival of the corporate entity is at stake, the concern for the worker immediately takes second place. In all ways we work *for* the Machine. The Machine as it now functions, doesn't work for us.

But beyond the cosmetic attempts of companies to promote Quality of Work Life task forces and the latest management sensitivity seminar, it is the basic nature of the corporation environment itself that has the devastating impact on the people who are working in it. The ways in which companies and organizations are structured creates a forced rhythm and speed of activity that generates tremendous psychological and physical stress on the people who are a part of these machines. Because of the hierarchical structure, pressure moves downward through the management layers with little direct influence from individuals at the lower levels over the choices of what they do daily. A daily put-down by supervisors over their subordinates for work-related mistakes often becomes part of the company culture. All these accepted stressful behaviors and norms contribute to a work environment that does not take into account or celebrate individual differences.

Books like *The Addictive Organization, Work Addiction* and *Working Ourselves to Death* describe how our contemporary work organizations emotionally and physically disable the majority of people working in them and create dysfunctional settings. The continual changing of time lines, fitting into assembly-line sequences and the pressure of daily deadlines tends to accumulate negative psychological energy and push the body into a state of chronic stress. Displacement of anger or emotional discharge on people from one level of supervision to the next level below in the organizational structure is often accepted (and excused) as a means to relieve the "normal" business pressure. To accept as normal these kinds of organizational settings is to be willing to accept that we live in an insane world.

In a little-known book called *Eupsychian Management,* by Abraham Maslow, the father of the human-potential movement, describes his experience as a scholar in residence at a California electronics plant. The book is a journal of his observations while spending time at this company. The book was first published in 1965 and expresses Maslow's confidence in the potential of enlightened management that many of us as consultants hoped could spread throughout the whole of the industrial Machine. However, one of his observations about the negative aspects of industrial life, I believe, holds truer today than when he wrote it. "How can any human being help but be insulted by being *treated as an interchangeable part, as simply a cog in a machine*, [my emphasis] as no more than an appurtenance to an assembly line . . . . There is no other human, reasonable, intelligible way to respond to this kind of profound cutting off of half of one's growth possibilities than by getting angry or resentful or struggling to get out of the situation."

Maslow's top need in his famous hierarchy of needs is called "self-actualization." The structure and environment of our machine companies by definition inhibit the creativity, individual uniqueness and inner exploration of people who seek to become self-actualized. Over the years, the constant discussion in business settings has been how to get more innovation and creativity into the organization. Methods and techniques for team brainstorming, are taught, "skunk works" that allow a small group to operate outside of company "rules" are initiated by management. Self-directed teams are formed; quality circles are organized. And in many companies there are continuous proposals for encouraging and stimulating creativity and innovation within the organization. Sometimes there are short-term breakthroughs, but generally the innovation process is based on an individual who by force of personality, comes to the surface of an organization, creates excitement, through creating some new product or innovation. But after this event the person then gets promoted and swallowed up into management. This person will most often be co-opted and even discouraged from being creative in the same way again. Their perceived potential management talents because they were successful will be deemed more important than their creativity.

My view is that Machine-organized cultures do not support innovation by definition. Hierarchical structure inhibits the democratic and chaotic way in which innovation, creativity and change work. What often passes for creativity and innovation in a company is problem-solving. Companies like problems solved because it makes them more efficient and saves them money. Get a team or an individual to solve a production problem and the team and management are happy. But to get people in an organization to be truly creative and innovative, or even eccentric, is to disrupt procedures, policies, and cut across functional boundaries, as well as to raise ethical, moral and spiritual questions about what they are doing. Facilitating or even encouraging entire groups to make decisions together could take away hierarchical control from managers. This tends to be messy, non-efficient and community centered. It also encourages people to explore their personal lives in the context of the business setting. This creative norm is clearly not what the Machine wants, and it is the reason why so little innovation among workers and mid-level management is ever encouraged or sustained.

The Machine predominantly plays on the lower needs of "safety and security" in Maslow's hierarchy. To satisfy this need to be secure, we are not to question authority, and we must serve the needs of the institution in which we work in order to protect our paycheck and our position. In this implicit pact with the organization we end up submitting to passiveness as well as to the repression of our feelings, our desires and our creativity.

For a period of time unionism provided an outlet for some of this anger and outrage toward the Machine mentality of corporations. But what unionism did in the last part of the 20th century was to try to strike the best deal with the devil, rather than challenge the Machine and its power over the individual.

Today, unions pride themselves in the fact that they sit on the boards of corporations and support and encourage the Machine in their control of the "mutual" interests of labor and management. But the issue is not just union interests in working conditions and money, it is the sublimation and reduction of individual diversity that happens to human beings becoming interchangeable parts and cogs in a machine.

Because the leadership buys into the Machine model, unionism, in trying to protect its own interests, becomes a smaller and smaller influence in our country. At a practical level, unions are unable to accept the fact that heavy industrial lines as well as the new electronics factories and assembly lines have moved west to Asia and south to Latin America. Nor are unions able to accept their own irrelevance as new industries like electronics firms figured out ways to convince employees that they don't need unions.

In the early 1980s I was a part of a team that gave seminars on how to keep unions out of high-tech companies. The view by management was that they didn't want economic control taken away. It was easy to convince workers that they didn't need an outside group telling them how to work. In those days it was easy to stop unions, and we believed we were doing so in the best interests of workers and management. In hindsight, it was just one more event that solidified the power of company management to control employees.

The Purpose of the Worldwide Machine

At the heart of this Machine complex of interrelated companies and countries, is the drive to control how people will live economically. What industries are important, what technologies to promote and research, and what products to get populations to buy is the strategic goal of the corporation-economy controlled by the World Bank, the International Monetary Fund and the Bank of International Settlements. It is no longer politics that rules the world, nor individual nation-states. Rather it is the interconnected financial markets and multinational corporations that become the medium for these markets to function. These corporation-countries are not interested in gaining political power (although this becomes a by-product of their control). The power that the corporation-economy wants is financial. The corporation-economy is rooted in money. It is the game of money and the power of money that the leaders of the corporation-economy want to play.

Today, at the beginning of the 1990s, the goal of the Machine's corporation-economy has been achieved. The achievement has been to create a worldwide integrated economy based on consumerism. The World Bank, The Trilateral Commission, the finance ministers of the seven democratic countries who meet quarterly, and multinational corporations in general, have a basic philosophy of creating a one-world integrated financial community.

Holly Sklar, the editor of the book, *Trilateralism: The Trilateral Commission and Elite Planning for World Management,* describes heads of multinational corporations proclaiming a vision where people from every nation are "enthusiastically" all eating exactly the same foods, listening to the same music and buying the same clothes. Sklar describes the members of the Trilateral Commission as the elite of corporations, financial institutions, government agencies, foundations and the media. From former President Jimmy Carter to David Rockefeller, former chairman of Chase Manhattan Bank, this elite group cuts across the political spectrum. "Corporations," Sklar says, "not only advertise products, they promote lifestyles rooted in consumption, patterned after the United States." What the Commission is after is to get Western values of capitalism, democracy and consumerism as *the* world values for all other countries. The message of Trilateralism is that all national economies should be part of "transnational corporate capitalism." And with a great deal of inferred racism, the Commission's stance is that "The Western way is the good way; national culture is inferior." This is the ultimate corporation-economy view. The same people who belong to the Trilateral Commission are part of the World Bank, the IMF, U.S. AID and presidents of the large multinational corporations. This attitude is guided by money. Its goal is to bring 5 billion people into one homogenized market that can be easily controlled and guided toward their elitist ends.

This integration of a one-world financial community is going forward at a rapid pace today. However, the imbalance in who controls the world wealth is very clear. Alan Dryer of the United Nations reported that the top 20 percent of the world population (First World countries) have 83 percent of the world's wealth. He pointed out that very little of this wealth is being shared with the 80 percent of the world that has so little. A startling fact is that the United States is next to the bottom of Western countries on per capita foreign aid giving. Ireland is the last on the list.

Although Japan, the United States and Europe wrangle over trade issues, the reality is that the tactics of competition between countries and companies do not diminish the agreement on the fundamental strategy that all have agreed to in creating a mono-economic culture that is based on the growth of worldwide consumer products. The appeal and willingness of Western countries to provide large loans to Eastern Europe and the states of the former Soviet Union have been that, in time, these former communist countries will be a great supplier of natural resources. The former Soviet Union, and the Russian Republic in particular, is the last huge natural-resource area in the world that hasn't been fully developed. Besides being a new wellspring of resources, these countries are a consumer market for products from the West. The materialism of communism failed, but the planned worldwide consumerism of capitalism has succeeded to the point that we have all become slaves to it. In some way or another all of us in the West have become "oilers" of the Machine. By both participating in consumerism and getting our money from working in it, we keep it going. We hope the corporations we work for and the country in general does well selling to other countries so that our economic style of life will continue.

The Goal of the Machine:
Financial Power and Control

While traveling across the 11 time zones of the Republic of Russia in 1990, I would ask my hosts in the cities I visited if they knew people who worked with folk medicine. I had heard from friends in the United States that "folk medicine" was one of the code words for those who were practicing alternative explorations of belief systems from the traditional Communist dogma. In the Pacific city of Vladivostok, I was led through an interesting chain of men and women to get to such a group. I learned later that I was tested by each group of people or individual before I was passed on to the next. I endured hours of black coffee and discussions until I was finally introduced to a woman who was bringing folk healers together from all over the former Soviet Union, Northern China and North Korea to teach interested Russian people both the traditional plant-based healing methods as well as spiritual healing methods. She had brought together some 30 healers with over 300 people who were learning from them. This group is tolerated by the government because the health-care system in Russia has fallen apart, and there are no medical supplies available. Anyone who has traveled to the country knows to avoid going to a Russian hospital.

Yet this group was more than a bunch of weird occultists. They were a community that supported each other and reached out to individuals in the city around them. They were happy. The woman who was the leader of this group told me that it was all right that the Soviet Union was falling apart. They were being affected by it, but they weren't concerned. Their vision, she said, was to reclaim the older traditions, the spiritual heart of the Russian people, and together build communities which could live in balance with nature once again.

As I also talked to business people in Vladivostok about moving from a production economy to a free-market economy, I heard an echo of the folk-healing group in another way. These businessmen and women would readily tell me that the economics of communism had failed. But they were afraid of simply embracing capitalism. As much as they wanted the things we had in the West, they didn't want to lose the fundamental values of economic equality, of making sure everyone had the basics of food and shelter. And they wanted to return to a protection of their natural resources. They were afraid that the Germans, the Japanese and the Americans would not give them a chance to shape their own destiny and direction. This group, like the folk healers, wanted to preserve and create a different type of community and society rather than simply copying ours.

Communism fought the Western-style Machine as they tried to build their own kind of economic system. Their Machine didn't work. Ours did. So our Machine bears down on them now. Who will survive in the former Soviet Union? The folk-medicine community or the new free-market business people? My hope is with the transformation of both concerns into a vital new system, perhaps even a new model for the world.

The New World Leaders

In 1992 as the former Soviet republics try to hold back their economic collapse, Western Europe, the United States and various international organizations like the International Monetary Fund (IMF) try to nurse these former production economies into the Western Machine's version of the "good life." The new country of Russia applied to the IMF to get financial assistance to meet the challenge of growing inflation, joblessness and social disruption. By borrowing, Russia and the other former republics are in a catch-22 situation. To borrow money, Russia must contribute 3 percent of the Fund's overall total of $125 billion. This means that almost $4 billion in hard currency must be deposited into the IMF before Russian businesses can borrow any money. Then, like the Third World countries that had to dismantle social programs and clear rainforests for multinational corporations in order to get money, the IMF tells the Russians on what and how they can spend this money. It also determines the type of government programs the Russians must implement, and sets the time frame for repaying the IMF.

No longer do the political leaders of countries control the destiny of world events; rather, the controllers are the financiers and the bankers of the Machine. They are the magicians who are creating the "new world order." They meet in world summits, set the values of currencies and manipulate world industries and markets. For the countries they represent, their financial decisions determine political, military and ecological decisions. For example, it is economic survival and opportunity that is creating a new political entity in the "United States of Europe." However, the struggle to create the Common Market will be difficult. Even though nationalist tendencies will resist the change, political and cultural borders will give way to common currency and an economic force that will challenge the 40-year dominance of the United States as well as the 15-year dominance of the Japanese. The Common Market is determining political alignment and restructuring not only for Western European countries, but is also realigning the balance of economic power, and therefore political power worldwide. With the demise of communism in Eastern Europe and the former Soviet Union, it will be a growing Common Market that will be the most aggressive and generous in bringing these cultural groups into the Western economic fold.

The German government is spending one trillion marks to integrate the former East Germans back into a unified Germany. It is offering many billions of dollars in aid and trade to the new governments of what is now central Europe and the former Soviet Union. Germany is leading the way in the "new world order." This action indicates the seriousness of the Europeans in forging a new economic unit as a competing force to the United States and Japan. The U.S. response to a united Europe is a united North America with the trade agreement that will open all economic borders between Canada, Mexico and the United States. The Japanese are formulating a response in terms of some kind of Asian Common Market.

As important as merging political units are to the Machine, the forces of cultural leadership have come through the emergence of worldwide television and popular music to shape basic values and attitudes of billions of people. The Machine's leaders use TV and music to create continuous images and sounds that promote the necessity of acquiring consumer goods. These two media have promoted this "primary value" of life in our world today. Whether we are in New York City or in the jungles of Indonesia we can watch the same sitcoms and hear the same rock'n'roll and get the same consuming message. Promoting this value and the importance of consuming is what drives the engine of the Machine's corporation-economy. Over 50 percent of the U.S. economy is based on people buying consumer products like TVs, VCRs, cars and the like. To keep this consumerism growing, products are designed to be throw-aways and consumables. Growth, as our leaders urge us, is "shopping more to keep the economy going." The volume of worldwide business is enormous. The three largest corporations in the world — Royal Dutch Shell, General Motors and Exxon — each make over $100 billion a year. To keep this volume of buying going takes ever new products and new creative strategies to influence consumer buying.

Politically, Western leaders promote preparation for war as a vital necessity for not only sustaining peace, but for our economic survival as well. In this post-communist era our leaders struggle to find new enemies to direct our war making. We keep military spending and armament production going both to fuel the economy and to bribe Third World countries to follow our policies. We sell arms to small nations and keep political and military conflict going so that the economic war machine runs easily alongside consumerism in order to make sure the economy is always being fueled. For all our rhetoric about peace in the world, the United States is the largest seller of killing machines to the rest of the world. Worldwide, the yearly military expenditure is $1.5 trillion. This is an enormous waste given the global problems of hunger, overpopulation, resource depletion and the like. But the reason why this price tag for military spending grows yearly is that it is another consumable that can allow corporations to continue making money. The prime value for the corporations and governments is not morality and human conditions, but rather keeping businesses profitable. With the Cold War over and government military budgets declining, the Machine is now pointed directly at underdeveloped nations to feed the world economy and fuel profits.

Resources, human and material, in underdeveloped nations are used to provide goods for developed nations. The United States and Japan, for example, support the Indonesian government's wanton destruction of indigenous people on one of its islands where there are vast stands of ancient forest, oil, and minerals. Thousands of these natives are being killed by government troops because the natives don't want their traditional lands destroyed in this way. The Machine cares little for the rights of people if those rights interfere with its economic plans. The destruction of the natives of Indonesia repeats our own western movement in the United States in the mid 1800s and the destruction of the Native American tribes. As in past eras, little is said by Western political or religious leaders to challenge the actions of the Machine's financial leaders and power brokers. In the corporation-economy, religious and political leadership becomes subservient to economic and financial leadership. The game becomes for them "Lets Make a Deal" on a grand worldwide scale. By supporting the goals and values of the Machine, political and religious leaders get part of the power, influence and wealth, just as they did in the 1800s in our country.

In the West, our political and religious leaders stand mute or join in with approval urging that financial progress must go on for the good of all. But in different cultures throughout the world, and in different ways dissent grows. Many people question whether the god of economic progress is enough for the human spirit. The loud cry through the centuries has been that humankind does not live by economic bread alone. Today many are beginning to cry out that our leaders cannot continue to rape the earth for short-term profit. The growing chaos and the deteriorating conditions of so much of the world's fragile resources are fostering movements and groups that want to resist and make a change in this Machine we've created. Some of the groups that are attracting converts advocate religious fanaticism and political absolutism because the Machine's corporation-economy has passed them by or has operated in a manner that doesn't permit them to be part of the money game.

Fascism and hatred are growing daily in the world. Dogmatism grows in the religious fundamentalism of Islam, the Christian fundamentalism of the United States, the right-wing religious fundamentalism in Israel, and the Sikh extremists in India. As with all fascists, these religious groups want control. Leaders of these groups urge a puritanical purging of consumerism while at the same time trying to gain control of large sums of money to support their cause. As with the Machine, these groups cry out to people to "give money so that we can succeed." Money — the fuel of the corporation-economy — does not control just business. Money also influences and controls religion, politics and the arts. The Machine makes commodities of them all. Actually, it is the money from the Machine that determines whether any of them will exist. In turn, each must bow down and worship the Machine's values and methods if they are to survive. This transnational, independent Machine is confident that it can control these extremist groups. It has been shown by the Reagan-Bush administration in the Iran-Contra affair, for example, that our government and the so-called "secret government" that is supported by our own multinational corporations, will make deals with individuals, corporations, and governments world-wide to accomplish their financial ends.

The Money Game

The new major financial "game" that is the focus of the world's elite is international money. Stewart Brand in his book, *The Media Lab: Inventing the Future at M.I.T.*, reports an interview with Peter Schwartz about this game. For a number of years, Schwartz ran the business environment section of strategic planning for Royal Dutch/Shell Oil. In 1987 he was hired by the London Stock Exchange to consider different future financial pictures for the world financial markets.

Schwartz' analysis is that as a result of worldwide telecommunications and high-speed computing, the almost instantaneous exchange of money is the most profitable of trades. The money game becomes an obvious and simple way to make profit when financial transactions are taking place somewhere in the world 24 hours a day. Schwartz describes the global money game this way: "Back when the dollar moved a tenth of a penny over three weeks, currency arbitrage was no game to play. But when the dollar moves three or four cents a day, and you've got a billion bucks here, five billion bucks there, there's good reason to move money from Tokyo in the morning to Paris in the afternoon. You're talking really serious money — tens of millions in profit absolutely risk-free." So huge is this game that in 1986 these international "risk-free" transactions totaled $87 trillion. Schwartz points out that $87 trillion was 23 times the United States Gross National Product for that year. This is big "free" money that exists, like electronic ghosts, in a reality that has no relationship to real goods, services or usefulness to anyone on the planet except for the elite who have the money to play in this gigantic world poker game.

Schwartz points out that the implications for the world economy in this money game are highly consequential. No one country (even the United States or Japan) can influence the game. It moves too fast. Rates change in minutes. The managing of domestic economies becomes more difficult because the "game" influences rates of exchange and affects trade balances (a big part of what is going on in our economy at this time with our trade imbalances). Schwartz warns that a worldwide credit collapse could happen, but it would start without us even knowing it. This he says is what happened to the banks loaning money to Brazil and other Third World countries in the 1980s. Because complex transactions were being done by computers nobody in the financial community knew for sure who was loaning what to whom.

This world money game is essentially computers talking to computers. Like the stock market when it is going up, everyone in the money game is trying to make as much money as they can before some kind of crash occurs. (This is one reason why major corporations aren't interested in investing in plants and products. They can make more playing the money game.) About this, Schwartz warns, "People innovate new mechanisms, and these mechanisms are tried, and they're commercially viable — coaggregating money and reselling it in a different way, and so on — but nobody knows what the consequences of that are. Nobody knows how to regulate that, nobody knows what the meaning of money is. And every time in history, *the thing which precipitated a depression was the collapse of the meaning of money* [my emphasis]. When these mechanisms evolve that way, completely out of control, there is enormous danger."

Schwartz points out that the U. S. government failed to support international control over how the game was played until recently. But the majority of the $87 trillion in transactions are done in dollars. By having the dominant international currency the United States holds the leverage in the money game and is beginning to use it. The control of the money game governs not only access to capital and interest rates but also who gets the money. Leaders of the world financial community are maneuvering to gain the power, and thus, control over this global money game.

The corporation-economy and the money game is now bigger and more autonomous than any set of human individuals. These "leaders" of the world financial community have become servants to an entity that is bigger than any one government or one company. The combined power of the technology and the ideas that foster and drive the technology have created *a mechanistic approach to reality that affects everyone on the planet.* We have set the Machine in motion and it has grown beyond our control. E. M. Forster's image of a machine that takes over the world is happening. For the majority of us to survive and live we will have to serve and be participants in the Machine game in some way.

Serving the Machine

*G*iven the power and the way the Machine's corporation-economy works, I observed that as a consultant my role, and the role of all consultants, is to oil the machine. Different consultants have different kinds of oil. There are a variety of cans: generalist, organizational, management specialist, expert and the like. The oils are as thick or thin as the experience and the integrity of the consultant.

The lubrication that consultants squirt into the machine attempts to reduce the stress and friction internally within corporations. Consultants provide this oil by developing strategies for future growth, by giving stress-management seminars, by negotiating conflict-resolution sessions, by introducing Wellness programs, and by helping to coach people out of the organization who "don't fit into the company culture." These kinds of oiling may contribute positively in some immediate sense for specific individuals or situations. But oiling in the long run simply helps to maintain a structure and an environment that doesn't support a healthy human work community.

In practical terms, oiling the Machine means that an external, short-term consultant tries to help the company or organization survive and move forward with as little chance of economic failure as possible. In this role consultants are called the "company shrink" and the "surgeon", as well as the "expert" and the "authority."

In serving the Machine, consultants struggle with dysfunctional executives, top-heavy management structures, stressful company cultures and rapidly changing markets. Companies look to consultants and training specialists for the latest fads of one-minute techniques and group-empowerment processes. In our fast-food, throwaway culture the newest gadget and the promise of the fastest results get the strongest hearing and the largest consultant fees. The sales role of the consultant becomes not only doctor but priest in assuring the organization that its financial health will improve and that its managers will manage better if they bow to the altar of the latest human interaction technique and the hottest management practice.

The theory of indeterminacy, from Nobel physicist Werner Heisenberg, asserts that there is no objective scientist. His theory holds that the perception of the scientist merely viewing the experiment influences the outcome of it. So too, with consultants. Our attempts to be objective, impartial and separate from the companies for whom we consult, are lost in our acceptance of the fundamental assumptions of sustaining the corporation-economy Machine. In our honest intentions to transform companies into humane workplaces and evolving human cultures that serve the good of humankind, we are really contributing to the growth of something else. When we consult we really serve the growth and the power of the Machine. In this way consultants have been one of the midwives in birthing the modern Machine.

Birthing the Machine

Historically there have been some significant consultants as oilers of the corporate Machine in our country. Of great importance is Daniel McCallum, who in 1855 introduced management hierarchy and the techniques of management methods to the Erie Railroad. By the turn of the 20th century McCallum's management structure had spread to most manufacturing and distribution companies thereby reducing the power and influence of the individual craftsman to communicate and interact with others in the organization about the creation of goods. The new management structures focused on planning and communication control. This meant that managers planned and the workers executed the plans. Communication changed from interactive and two-way to one way. Because of the pyramid structure of the new hierarchy, communication moved downward in an authoritative, telling mode from management to workers. Workers were parts, cogs, in a machine that could easily be replaced if they created problems or wore out. The role of workers was to simply do what they were told. Much worker abuse and the resulting rise of unions in the late 1800s onward happened from the disempowerment of those workers. They no longer could participate or have the legitimate right to communicate back up the pyramid, influence how the work was to be done, or negotiate the conditions under which they were working.

In the early 1900s, Frederick Taylor brought the stopwatch into the manufacturing plant. His theory used the new management structure to remove independent worker decision-making and control over the process of the work, and moved all decision making into the hands of management. This management power was achieved through time and motion studies of a worker's activity. Taylor's idea was to control every detail of the work flow in order to transform the workers into unthinking "parts," or cogs in a specific manufacturing process. Taylor argued that removal of worker influence over *how* things were made would result in both greater productivity and greater efficiency in producing goods. By separating the various work tasks into small units, arranging workers in assembly lines and then teaching them to move and work in specific repetitive ways, modern factories were initiated. Now it was easier to train any person to do a simple repetitive task than to depend on hiring those individuals who had the skill or talent to do the complete job.

In the early 1940s Kurt Lewin, the eminent social psychologist, introduced his three-part model of change for business organizations. His "unfreeze" concept (changing the current pattern) and "refreeze" concept (reinforcing new behavior patterns) were used in bringing new direction or new plans to organizations. These concepts were based on the notion that after a period of time trying to do things differently, people in organizations return to their traditional pattern of behavior. To solve this tendency to regress, Lewin proposed his "force-field theory." This theory held that an organized and analytical approach to change needs to happen because any behavior in an organization is the result of both driving and restraining forces. Restraining forces could be bureaucratic bottlenecks, driving forces might be meeting a project deadline and receiving a bonus. A program of planned change is directed toward weakening or removing restraining forces and strengthening the driving forces that exist in an organization. The purpose of using these models and theories is to improve both performance and productivity of employees.

Lewin's social behavioral theory and model is the taproot from which today's organizational development theories and techniques grow. Lewin, with his theory and behavioral approach, also launched the consulting business. Companies wanted to be more competitive and successful, and the organizational development model rapidly evolved into a variety of concepts, theories and techniques that could make planned change more predictable, productive and ultimately create more profit for the corporation. With Lewin and the birth of organizational development, the corporate profit-driven Machine rapidly evolved. The organization then evolved into a living entity separate from the individuals working in it. It now had "doctors" (consultants), diagnostic tools (like employee surveys) to determine its problems and remedies — known as interventions — to cure it. There were also a variety of growth specialists (expert consultants) to help the corporation through its growth and life cycle.

Fast on the heels of Lewin, Abraham Maslow, Robert Tannenbaum and Douglas McGregor brought in human-relations manipulation into organizations. McGregor had been influenced by Maslow's hierarchy of human needs. As an academic, McGregor understood that the history of management control had taught many managers to view workers as lazy, unable to learn, and unproductive unless the boss was always on them. This view is what McGregor called the "X" theory of human worker behavior. He then said if managers viewed workers as responsible, wanting to do a good job, and eager to learn (his "Y" theory), managers would get better results from workers. The assumptions of both theories is that the expectations one holds about people is how they will actually behave.

Robert Tannenbaum was the head of the behavioral science group at UCLA's Graduate School of Management. Through the 1950s this group developed fundamental ideas about human behavior in organizations and the uses of sensitivity training for managers. The wide variety of human relations training programs marketed to companies today emerged from Tannenbaum's research and McGregor's theory "Y."

The work of these two men, and many others who followed them, has spawned methods from basic supervisory training, to the building of manager self-esteem to cultural-sensitivity seminars, to one-on-one conflict-resolution negotiations. Although consulting and training fads continue to come and go such as manager encounter groups, ropes courses, assertiveness training and wilderness team building sessions, the constant drive to "oil the people" in the corporations is a perpetual preoccupation by senior management. Management spends money on human relations because they worry about the unpredictability of how the "human" factor interfaces with the hierarchical machine. What is clear is that management technology seems to improve the efficiency of the Machine's functioning, at least in the short term. And today, as the machine continues to roll on, we have the new consulting gurus in people like Tom Peters and Ken Blanchard cheerleading and motivating us with "thriving on chaos", and educating us with the latest "situational leadership" assessment.

High-tech and High-touch Oiling

The new high-tech and high-touch techniques that emphasize human-interaction strategies and personality feedback to employees are actually intended to systematize the management process with "better," "more integrated" people into a company culture. Human beings always have been perceived as the most difficult variable in companies' working most efficiently. It is thought that teaching people about themselves and about the psychological dynamics of others makes it easier to "oil" and reduce the human friction in the system. Given the monolithic nature of the larger corporations, employees are more than willing to go to training sessions to learn about themselves and others in order to find better ways to cope and survive in the corporate environment.

Both middle management and employees hunger for techniques and methods that will make a difference in solving human-interaction problems at work. People issues are what lower much of productivity — and where a vast majority of management time and energy is spent. In highly competitive business environments, senior management is more than willing to try any strategy that increases the competitive edge. Educators in management schools rush to fill this need. The increase of MBAs graduating each year reinforces a common corporate viewpoint. But the variety of books on how to survive business schools suggests how strongly they teach the lockstep approach to business that even many corporations find too rigid. However, it is not just business management that is the educational focus of corporations. With the growing failure of our public school system to prepare people to work in the new-technological Machine, companies have had to create their own educational and training systems to give employees the basics in math, reading and computer skills in order to do the corporation's work.

The result of developing this training system is a new multibillion-dollar educational business that is separate from our public system, one in which there is no public discussion on either its value or its purpose to the larger society. There is a lack of discussion because the Machine is now the definer of cultural values and education. Because of these available education dollars, consulting and training has evolved into a new growth industry. In many ways this growing number of consultants and training companies — because of the amount of money available — have become symbiotic with American organizational life and norms. What was pioneered as management and organizational consulting in the '40s and '50s here in the United States is now occurring worldwide. The major consulting firms like McKinnsy & Co., Arthur Anderson, Booz Allen and The Boston Consulting Group are the garages to the multinational corporations. Individual consultants and training specialists are the mechanics who keep the Machine oiled and running. Whether constantly working with people or working with the design of a new product, the consultant's role is to oil the Machine so that it runs smoothly, so that it grows bigger and makes more money. Consultants then, have have become robot nannies who have helped the Machine take on a life of its own.

In giving a critique of the role of consulting in the build-up of the Machine's culture, I do not wish to denigrate the many sincere and dedicated women and men who serve as consultants. Many of these creative individuals are bringing new alternatives to complex problems and are attempting to mitigate the negative impact of the Machine's values and behavior on individuals and groups within organizations. But, as a profession, we must recognize our role in the Machine and ask challenging questions about the system that we are supporting.

The Failure of Oiling

*I*n a 1991 *New York Times* article, Tom Peters wrote about his frustration as a consultant and teacher of practical management. He describes how, after his years of promoting *Excellence* and encouraging *Thriving on Chaos* in organizations, he didn't see many managers or companies actually using or implementing what he had written or taught over the years. When I look at my own consulting practice, I believe that my best contribution has been in helping a number of individuals with their personal growth and process of change, as well as simply coping with their hierarchical organizations. Probably my best success has been in encouraging many of these people to leave their organizations in order to be more creative and fulfilled doing something on their own.

For all the strategy sessions, visioning work, and cultural-change projects that consultants have done at the organizational level, I see little or no impact on intentional long-term and on-going organizational growth or change in companies. There are, however, a number of very serious-minded executives and leaders in these business communities who want to create a different kind of workplace. Many of them want an organizational environment that provides a community of healthy and balanced people who are doing interesting and positive things in their industry, and who contribute to the good of world society. These executives put in time, money and considerable effort to bring about their vision of change. But in the end they fail. And in the short term we as consultants fail.

We fail because all of us — consultants and executives alike — don't challenge the fundamental assumptions of the economic system that have evolved throughout the globe and originated from Western culture. Yes, to challenge the assumptions of a Machine-dominated, consumer-oriented world culture is to also challenge the fundamental way our personal life is structured.

Such a challenge questions the primary rationale for meaning and purpose in our society, and (most importantly) pokes deeply at the conditions of our own personal economic survival. How do we make a living, how do we interact with other people if we don't go along with the established cultural norm, and the consumer economic pattern? To challenge any or all of these assumptions scares us in some fundamental way. To consider these ideas intellectually is one thing, but to do something about them is another.

Why We Don't Challenge the Machine

Challenging our economic assumptions would change how most of us live our daily lives. Our corporation-economy has made us dependent on and vulnerable to the Machine. In the urban areas of the United States where 75 percent of us live and work, most individuals spend two to four hours a day commuting. This is usually done alone in a single automobile while being mesmerized by news or music. Both husbands and wives must work to survive credit-card bills and general day-to-day living. When there are children that need child care, the majority of the mother's income often goes to keeping a child in an understaffed facility that gives little personal attention to the child.

This lifestyle with its resulting tensions in the home — with little time and energy for family cohesiveness — produces a variety of sublimations and addictions: from TV to shopping, from overeating to taking prescription drugs, from using illegal drugs and alcohol to pornography and sexual abuse.

With this internal and external craziness in our lives, we turn to the messages and images from the Machine's voice to advise us how to cope. *Its message is to pleasure ourselves through buying something.* In a word, the fundamental practical assumption of this culture for our lives is materialism — the acquiring and using of things which increasingly separate and insulate us from the natural world.

We are flooded daily with consuming images. Some 95 percent of households in America have television sets. More than half that number own VCRs. The U.S. film industry makes $9 billion a year from movies. Half of the income comes from theaters and the other half from the sale of videos of movies. Between broadcast television, movies and VCR watching we spend a large percentage of our time as a population staring at film or electronic images to give us some kind of pleasure. Over and over these images promote our machinelike culture. We initiate few ideas of our own as we spend the majority of our time having ideas and images fed to us. There is nowhere in the culture that the message of materialism is not preached around the clock.

Even the exploring of spiritual alternatives gets laced with this drive for the materialistic. In our churches we pray for the President and business leaders to guide us in the right economic direction. New Age groups proclaim their spirituality through prosperity affirmations as the way to gain abundance in the material world. But the New Age message, like so much else in the culture, becomes another commodity. To prove this marketing abundance, sales of New Age related products for 1991 was over $1 billion. These products include books, goddess statues, shaman drums, tarot cards, subliminal tapes, and healing conferences.

When it comes to our education system the materialist message is "get an education to get a better job." With the basic value of education primarily encouraging people to get a better-paying job, young adults have little experience with solid thinking skills, values, history, ethics, questioning of authority, philosophical consideration or learning good communication skills. Formal education has become a process of learning to have good marketable technical skills in order to apply for the highest paying job.

Education programs within companies are another form of oiling that is used to keep the robots functioning. Practical psychology and human-relation skills are often included in the corporation training program because they are not taught in schools in such a way that workers can interact effectively on the job. The company is willing to "oil" us in this way so that the Machine can be more competitive in the marketplace by not having interpersonal problems detract us from efficient productivity.

The Gross Domestic Product is keyed on keeping people consuming for the sake of buying, not because there are genuine needs. President Bush echoed the Machine's philosophy before Christmas 1991 when he urged everyone to buy more to help the economy — buying not saving; spending resources, not conserving them; creating products that we throw away or that are created for built-in obsolescence so that we will have to buy more. The resulting imbalance, craziness and illness of our society, and Western culture in general, are mirrored in the TV commercials that attempt to convince us to buy sleeping potions and indigestion products. "There is no sleep for the wicked" goes the old saying. At some deep level of our collective psyche can we no longer sleep through nor stomach what we are doing to ourselves, to others and to the natural world?

People as Parts in the Machine

The machine world is a foreign environment to the fundamental needs of humans. As human beings we have different rhythms and cycles of mental, physical and emotional patterns that change and fluctuate on a daily basis. For the corporate-economy to make us into human robots is to kill us. The grind of the machine culture and the structure of organization in the places we work are not healthy or supportive to the human body or psyche.

In the early 1930s Dr. Rexford Hersey, an industrial psychologist, began doing studies on workers that showed how mood changes in employees in manufacturing plants went through a regular and predictable cycle. Hersey found there was a high and low point to worker moods. In the high part of the cycle men in the factories would be cheerful, have positive interaction with their co-workers, and be full of energy. In the low part of the cycle, efficiency went down in production, workers became moody and developed a variety of physical symptoms.

Research done in Denmark and Japan confirms that the hormonal changes in both men and women demonstrate that forcing humans into an unchanging pattern of behavior produces both stress and illness. For example, studies on individuals who work with computers all day show increasing cases of carpal tunnel syndrome (stress to the wrist and forearm), as well as health problems resulting from radiation emitted by the computer screens.

Current studies in chronobiology show that fluctuations in body temperature, hormonal activity, circadian rhythms and blood pressure all go through significant changes in a 24-hour period. Chronobiological studies of workers in companies indicate that women are more sensitive to these physical and emotional cycles. Men may be sensitive as well, but they seem to override these biosignals. Psychiatrist Terry Kupers has described this tendency by men to disregard their natural cycles and rhythms as "pathological arrhythmicity." He sees this denial and overriding of inner impulses as the cause of personal and marital dysfunction, depression, and stress-related diseases like heart attacks.

Social critic Jeremy Rifkin, in his 1987 book, *Time Wars,* demonstrates the insidious power of our time-constrained culture. Our punching in and out of work, adjusting to rush-hour traffic, meeting production deadlines, making sales numbers, scheduling vacations a year in advance, getting the kids to soccer games on Saturday, all create a pattern of stress. This stress overrides the normal interaction between our body and psyche and the natural rhythms of the seasons, the sun, the moon and general daily weather changes. Rifkin says, "Lost in a sea of perpetual technological transition, modern man and woman find themselves increasingly alienated from the ecological choreography of the planet."

Because we are not encouraged to listen to our bodies, we override these internal messages, get sick, and do things out of phase with our personal growth cycle and body rhythms. The result is that we tend to remain in chronic stress, anxiety and even depression. Yet, our structured economic life foists a further three-pronged hoax on us. Our religious, educational and entertainment institutions teach us to disregard ourselves and our connection to our natural rhythms, as well as to nature itself. Our leaders assert that working in the Machine represents the highest personal and social value. Hard work and hard play, goes the cultural message, generate a meaningful life that will be rewarded here on earth with money to buy things, and rewarded in the hereafter from the money we've given to our favorite charity or TV evangelist.

Television and print media describe the human pain and triumph of accepting the coglike machine life. The message is clear: those who have the most money have the best chances, the most opportunities and greatest blessings from both man and God. Those who don't have the money are thrust to the fringes of society. In 1992, for example, of the more than 4 million homeless people, an estimated 40 percent were families with children, 45 percent were single men and 15 percent were single women. We've all heard the stories of educated men and women sliding into homelessness. All these people are not bums, drug addicts or irresponsible hippies. The number of homeless people grows in this machine-driven society and we do nothing to fundamentally change this situation. This points to our own fear and terror of falling in behind the outcasts of our communities. Because the problem is larger than any one individual, town or state; the source of the problem lies in the Darwinian-like economics of the survival of the "fittest." Do we turn our faces away and pretend that *they* are not *us*? Have *they* become the untouchables of American society?

Work Addiction

Most of us won't face homelessness. But we will face potential addiction problems because we override the natural rhythms and messages from our bodies. The largest growing area of self-help groups in the country are 12-step addiction programs such as Alcoholics Anonymous. There are programs for overeaters, shoppers, gamblers, cocaine users, child abusers, and on and on. An interesting one is Workaholics Anonymous. The pattern of this addiction relates to work.

Work addiction is linked to the release of large amounts of adrenaline in the body. Work addiction thrives on crisis and stress in the work situation in order to get the adrenaline high. This adrenaline high gives a sudden rush of excitement, body intensity and speediness. Bryan Robinson in his book, *Work Addiction,* concludes from the research on stress and adrenaline addiction in workers that, "work addicts require larger doses to maintain the high that they create by putting themselves and those around them under stress. . . . On-the-job work addicts' managerial style is to re-create an uproar that they must resolve. Crises, which require the body's adrenaline flow, are routinely manufactured and doused. Another way they create stress is by driving themselves and pushing others to finish designated assignments within unrealistic deadlines. While work addicts get high, co-workers and subordinates experience many of the same emotions as children of alcoholics, notably unpredictability, confusion and frustration."

For all our concern about the pressure of work and its effects on our body and minds, the Japanese are facing a significant crisis of a phenomenon they call karoshi. Karoshi means death from overwork. A nationwide survey showed that more than half the population worried about working themselves to death. The situation is so serious that the prime minister's office released a 1992 report called "A Portrait of Tired Japanese." In this report one study indicated that over two-thirds of the work population felt tired or weak. Karoshi activists in the country claim that 10,000 people a year die specifically from overwork. The government considers the situation so significant for Japan's long-term competitiveness in the world economy that the Labor Ministry is campaigning to reduce average work time from 2,009 hours in 1991 to 1,800 hours by 1993.

The stress of working coglike in the Machine has a direct relationship to the increase in such immune diseases as Chronic Fatigue Immune Dysfunction Syndrome (CFIDS), environmental allergies, multiple sclerosis, diabetes and various types of flu viruses. Medical costs, disability claims, and use of sick days by workers are all increasing yearly. Many companies are shifting the burden of medical costs over to the employees in partial payment plans. The growing message from our bodies is that the Machine is not a healthy place for human beings. The effect of the Machine on human bodies is increasingly taking its toll.

Women and the Machine

In a study entitled, "The Economic Predicament of Low-Income Elderly Women", Julianne Malveaux, a San Francisco-based economist, outlines the growing economic and survival concerns for women in our country. The study, commissioned by the Southport Institute for Policy Analysis, a non-profit think tank based in Washington D.C. and Southport, Connecticut, focuses on women and population aging. Today 2.4 million women over age 65 are in poverty. This figure is growing. Malveaux warned in the study that even though younger women work full time and most understand the need for retirement pensions, future generations of older women still face economic peril as they get older, divorced or widowed.

To go from poverty to wealth is to observe another discrepancy for women in our male-dominated society: Generally, the man — not the woman — will get the best, have the most, and be on top. It is notable that out of the top Fortune 100 companies there is not one woman CEO. Not only are women CEOs being ignored by Fortune 100 companies, but the impact of women-owned businesses in the country are being ignored as well.

In March 1992, Cognetics Inc., an economic research firm, and the National Foundation for Women Business Owners, reported on an 18-month study they had completed. The study compared Fortune 500 companies to women-owned businesses and found that 5.4 million business, or 28 percent of total U.S. businesses are women-owned. Fortune 500 companies employ 11.7 million people and women-owned companies employ the same amount. Fortune 500 companies are declining and laying off people, where as women-owned businesses are growing. The study notes that women-owned businesses have been stereotyped as fringe businesses, as if they were evening Tupperware parties. In reality, their industry mix is the same as men's. Julianne Malveaux, the economist and nationally syndicated business columnist cited above, said in response to this study that women are starting their own businesses because of "the glass ceiling women face and because corporations have been inflexible about their family and work policies."

It is not only glass ceilings that are keeping women out of the CEO and President's offices, but it is also glass walls. Women tend to be locked in staff positions such as human resources and public relations departments. The number of women who are in operations and line positions make up a small percentage of the women in the work force. The woman vice president of manufacturing or worldwide sales is the great exception in corporations today. The glass walls are also keeping women boxed in horizontally in organizations; woman are unable to be in the decision-making and implementation process across the range of company positions.

Without women having significant influence in our company machines we wonder why there is so little genuine concern for Mother Earth, for natural rhythms of work life, and for balance between material things and human relations. The politically conservative white, Anglo-Saxon men who dominate the corporation-economy have largely cut themselves off from feminine values, have lost contact with their own inner world, and tend to define and judge any meaningful activity by the reductionist phrase, "the bottom line."

People: Dispensable Assets

Employees are numbers on computer printouts. Workers are laid off if the "bottom line" doesn't look good. Yet, within organizations there is fostered a fragile belief that "human resources are our most valuable asset." This belief of workers as valuable human resources gets interpreted, however, according to business conditions. In good times companies don't want to lose workers to the competition and tend to value their "contribution." But, in bad times, companies seldom consider consulting with employees as partners. In most organizations human resources are a commodity; workers are a "set of assets" to be used and abused.

It is not the general good that is being served then, but rather a specific good for a few individuals who will not only survive these actions, but who will potentially profit from the action of adjusting the profit margins by removing employees, or by initiating other "corrective" actions. By living in the Machine, we are caught in a double bind. We are cogs in the Machine's well-oiled structure so we have to support its survival in order for us to exist economically. And we have also learned to support getting rid of people, perhaps ourselves included, in order for the Machine to survive. The ultimate catch is that we serve the Machine even against our own best interests.

The Rise of the Machine World

*D*olores La Chapelle, a deep ecologist, in her book, *Sacred Land, Sacred Sex and Rapture of the Deep*, outlines the historical influence of a Western culture that has destroyed the relationship to living things by supporting the notion of seeing everything as a substance (a "thing") to use and abuse. Or to put it another way, we in Western culture have broken the connection with a nature-based reality and let a materialistic reality guide our cultural choices and behaviors. Our Western European tradition evolved from a philosophy of being subjective and intimate with nature to one of being objective and impersonal toward the natural world.

The philosophical roots of our present-day Machine was shaped greatly by two English philosophers, Thomas Hobbes and John Locke. These two philosophers laid the foundation and the rationalization for technological civilization as we know it today. Hobbes, in his writings, proclaimed the natural right of individuals to use the world around them for the "supreme advantage of man." Locke declared that the proper study of man is not his political nature but his economic nature. Economic man, in Locke's view, was the end purpose of cultural activity.

One of Locke's infamous quotes reflects the effect of linking nature and economic man: "Land that is left wholly to nature, that hath no improvement of pasturage, tillage, or planting, is called as indeed it is wast [waste]; and we shall find the benefit of it amount to little more than nothing." These types of philosophical statements were gaining wide support in Europe when the vast new wealth of gold, silver, furs, fish and spices poured out of the New World of North and South America beginning in the 1500s.

It was the 17th-century philosopher Sir Francis Bacon who made the direct connection between the superiority of man over nature and a method to prove it as true. Bacon proclaimed *reason* to be the fundamental basis of truth. The scientific method became the new religion. Bacon initiated the scientist into a priesthood that preaches to this day the dominant belief in the objectivity of the scientific method for manipulating the physical world. The view of this priesthood is that the natural world is at the service of *man*. For example, to do experiments on animals, or to dig into ancient burial grounds is neither immoral to the animal nor a sacrilege to the tribal culture because it is for the sake of "knowledge." Doing something for science or knowledge is supposed to cover a multitude of sins. The fact that science could discover from this method such "magical" wonders as bacteria being the cause of many diseases, as well as how to split an atom, gave science credence and power over humankind as the centuries progressed. For all its seemingly helpfulness to the world, science (as a supposed neutral and objective force) also created in the German scientific tradition the tragic and twisted partnership with fascist Nazism. As any religion, science has its dogmatism, its blind spots and its vitriolic rejection of anything that challenges its position of power.

Nature as a Machine

Benedictine monks invented the mechanical clock sometime during the 13th or 14th century. What inspired this mechanical device was the desire by the monks to give precise regularity to the monastery routine, particularly to devotions and prayers proclaimed seven times a day. By the 14th century this mechanical wonder was located in the town hall clock tower and in the shops of merchants. The clock then created the pattern for specific work hours and production times for workers. This mechanizing of time into seconds, minutes and hours separated the experience of time from the natural world. The daily movement of the sun and the changing patterns of the seasons, as well as the rhythms of the body, were no longer held as the primary regulators of life. No matter what was happening in nature or to people, the clock began to dictate human activity and prescribe the patterns of day-to-day behavior. It was the philosopher Thomas Hobbes, in 1651, who used the clock image to reduce the body to mere mechanical parts. He said, "For what is the heart, but a spring; and the nerves but so many strings, and the joints but so many wheels, giving motion to the whole body." The clock, originally designed for spiritual purposes, actually provided the fundamental shift away from nature toward a machinelike view of reality.

But it was René Descartes, philosopher and mathematician, who had the greatest influence in changing the mindset of modern Western culture. This early 16th century Frenchman established dualism — the inherent separation between human being and nature — as the guiding principle for the modern age. Descartes' idea of separating humans from nature broke the long historical bond of our relationship with nature, where before we believed ourselves part of nature, not separate from it. Descartes' dualism placed humans outside of nature, as fully rational subjects, and placed everything else within nature as non-rational objects for humans to manipulate.

It is from Descartes that we have the conscious birth of what I term the Machine culture. Descartes' notion was that the universe operated like a giant machine. The mechanical motion of this machine ran according to mathematical laws, predictable much like a clock mechanism. Descartes applied this mechanical idea of the machine to all of nature. Because he saw plants and animals as machinelike, he believed they could be used according to the dictates of the so-called superior human mind.

The work of Isaac Newton, in the late 1600s and early 1700s, then extended the machine viewpoint to all laws of nature. Newtonian physics describes everything from the motion of stars to atomic particles as part of a mechanical structure. Newton and those who followed him in the scientific priesthood held that *man,* by discovering these laws, proves his superiority and natural right to be dominant over all matter (read "mother") in nature. It was *man* (or rather, men) who were championing the exploration of the natural world. The women who were knowledgeable about the natural world had been murdered in the great European witch hunts of the 12th and 13th centuries. Over 9 million women were put to death because they possessed knowledge of herbs, healing, midwifery and a connection to the goddess traditions of ancient Europe. The Catholic Church initiated a 200-year rampage to assure male dominance in the society. It was during this time that laws were passed that only men could be physicians.

Andre Gunder Frank, a contemporary Chilean economist, in his book, *World Accumulation*, points out that early scientists followed the philosophers in rationalizing that the development of wealth and the focusing on profit should be a chief determinant of what science should be used for. In this vein, Galileo Galilei, 16th century Italian astronomer, mathematician and physicist, used his research in telescopes to construct a more accurate clock for determining longitude of ocean-going merchant voyages. In this same period Englishman philosopher and statesman, Roger Bacon, argued in support of science that the purpose for the "mechanical arts" was to yield substance and profit.

In the 1650s came the founding of scientific societies funded by commercial companies. These were pretentious institutions such as the Royal Society of London that funded many scientific ventures. These societies operated similar to the way corporations today fund research in universities. At this time European governments began employing mathematicians and scientists to solve navigation and military problems. This marked the beginning of the military-industrial complex.

The Rush Toward Free-market Capitalism

When we move from these philosophical scientific positions to the practical historical conditions of this era, we notice another set of factors that moves us toward the philosophy of the Machine's corporation-economy. Once the accumulation of economic capital through trade began in Europe, market cycles of boom and bust began. In 1492 Spain was in a severe economic depression. Christopher Columbus came to Ferdinand and Isabella, the new monarchs of this newly founded country. The Spanish had just driven out the Moors and the Jews. The new king and queen responded eagerly to Columbus' promise of finding a new source of wealth for them. Although Columbus was addicted to gold, in his four voyages to the New World he brought little gold back with him. His promise of wealth, however, came true for these monarchs as other expeditions found the gold, silver and copper in South and Central America.

The year 1492 also marked a significant turn for the English and the French who had just ended the One Hundred Years War. This freed both countries to turn their attention and resources to the newly found riches in the Americas, in India and in Africa. The rest of Europe was coming out of the Black Plague and years of severe crop failure, due to a long period of cold climate during which glaciers had extended into the lower food-growing valleys. Finally, the religious crusades and witch hunts by the Catholic Church had left Europe in emotional and spiritual shambles. Out of this depressive long cycle, new frontiers permitted Europeans to turn away from these underlying problems — Europe reached out to restock itself through the rape and pillage of indigenous peoples and lands throughout the world. This action reflects much the same pattern engaged in today by our destruction of the rainforests and indigenous peoples through clear-cut logging and strip mining.

The monarchies of Europe began a huge capital accumulation of world wealth through the rape, enslavement, and pillaging of millions of native peoples and their natural resources. These ruling families turned the Europeans into consumers by developing in them a craving for new products. They promoted sugar, spice and opium addictions. The growing demand for these products also fueled slavery of native peoples, both in the Caribbean as well as in Africa. These addictions and slavery were then rationalized by philosophers, religious leaders and scientists on behalf of the ruling families.

Political and business leaders entered into a marriage that made capital wealth and consumption the fundamental political and economic means to rebuild the power base of a relatively few major families in Europe. For example, the Portuguese discovered gold in Brazil in 1697. There was so much gold in these mines that Portugal produced nearly half the total output of gold in the world for the rest of the 16th, 17th and 18th centuries. This gold provided the capital to set up sugar plantations, and enabled Britain to build factories in England, thus starting the Industrial Revolution. This wealth of gold, in turn, extended and financed trade to India, to Africa and also financed the exploration of the rest of the New World. After a thousand years, of no previous enslavement of humans in Europe, the sugar addiction was used to justify the capture of African and native peoples of the New World. These native peoples were forced to supply slave labor for not only sugar, but eventually for tobacco and cotton plantations as well.

With the expansion of trade came the dominance of colonialism, and the competition between the European states to carve up the world between themselves. With the power and influence gained from new resources discovered throughout the known world, capital accumulation through the trading and selling of these commodities came under the direct protection and influence of political and military leaders. These individuals were then co-opted and were allowed to increasingly share in the rewards that had previously been in the private control of the monarchical families. The modern deal-makers were born. But as is true of all capitalistic systems, the cycles of economic highs and lows that were driven by the vagaries of supply and demand for goods, created rolling depressions throughout Europe, and often other parts of the world.

Developing America's Machine

The depressions of 1762 and 1789 were major stimuli to both the American and French Revolutions. The background to our revolution was the result of a primary threat to the foundation of wealth for the revolutionary leaders-to-be in our country. The political/economic leaders in the colonies had built their businesses on the so-called Triangle Trade of sugar, rum and slaves. For many years, ships built in New England took barrels of rum produced there to Africa, where the rum was traded for slaves. These same ships then took the African slaves to the island sugar plantations located in the Caribbean. In trade, part of the profit was taken in molasses, which was delivered to rum distilleries in New England. One slave was worth 200 gallons of rum! Later, after the American Revolution was fought and won, these same ships were employed to bring slaves to the cotton plantations emerging in the South. Before the Revolution the colonies also supplied food to the Caribbean sugar plantations. Over half of the food production in the American colonies went to supply food for slaves on plantations.

England in the late 1700s was experiencing a deep economic depression because of poor management of trade between Britain and India. The Sugar and Stamp Acts were taxing schemes that the English government imposed on the

American colonies to get new capital to jump-start the faltering economy in the British Isles. These two ways of taxing the colonies threatened to limit the fortunes of the leaders in the colonies who were profiting from the Triangle Trade. The fight for independence was really a fight to keep and protect the wealth of a few Colonial political/economic leaders. Many people in the colonies who were not profiting from the Triangle Trade did not support the Revolution, and this is the reason why the Revolutionary Army had such a difficult time being funded and supported.

After the Revolution, American political and business leaders accelerated their accumulation of capital by initiating relentless exploration and movement across the rich landscape to the West. Native peoples were used as fur trappers for a while and finally were eliminated through European diseases and outright slaughter. The eastern half of the North American continent was almost completely denuded of hardwood trees, furs, fisheries and various kinds of ore. As topsoil was depleted, farmers simply moved westward. Entrepreneurs thought up new products as they discovered new resources to exploit. Whether it was the depletion of the beaver for hats or the slaughter of millions of buffalo for their tongues and robes, this westward movement left a pernicious wake of blood over this continent's indigenous peoples and creatures.

The Machine Runs on Addiction

The expansion of Western culture over these five centuries by capitalistic exploitation of the natural world has been based on addiction. Capitalism worked, Dolores La Chapelle argues, by "making a group of people addicted to some 'substance' and then selling it to them. Capitalism worked as long as we had an enormous source of cheap natural resources. But there are no more cheap resources. Continuing in its history of 'addiction,' capitalism is now relying more and more on addictive drugs to fuel its growth."

A root cause for why we have diminishing faith in our government grows with revelations about the Iran-Contra scandal, the laundering of drug money through banks in the United States and Switzerland, the financing by drug money for covert political operations, and the feeble results of the so-called War on Drugs. There is strong evidence that the multibillion-dollar drug trade is connected to the highest levels of business, the military and the government. Daniel Sheen of the Christic Institute, who was the attorney in *The Pentagon Papers*, *Silkwood*, and other public action cases, has documented evidence of this involvement and has brought suit against many of these individuals in "high places," only to be rejected or threatened with countersuits by Federal Court judges. What is increasingly clear is that addictive substances have always been used to fuel the profits and finance ventures of a relatively small group of wealthy people in the Western world. Enslaving people through drugs, poverty, or as workers in plantations or factories has been a 500-year tradition in Western society.

Alfred McCoy, in The *Politics of Heroin: CIA Complicity in the Global Drug Trade,* by using the Freedom of Information Act to get at CIA documents and interviewing CIA and other intelligence agents from around the world, concludes that American diplomats and CIA agents have been involved in worldwide drug trafficking for years. McCoy lays out three basic ways they've been involved. The first is *coincidental complicity* — covert alliances with groups directly involved in drug traffic (Noriega in Panama and Pot Pol in Cambodia). The second, *support of the drug traffic* — protecting drug lords as political and economic allies in local wars. This was true in the Contra involvement in Nicaragua and with the drug cartel in South America, as well as in protecting the heroin and opium lords in the Golden Triangle of Southeast Asia. The third type of involvement has been by *active engagement* — providing military and commercial transport of opium, heroin and cocaine in order to bring the drugs directly into the United States. For all the public relations and media hype about a

"War on Drugs" by our government, there is evidence that the so-called "secret" part of our government (glimpsed in the Iran-Contra mess) has been actively involved for over 25 years in the multibillion-dollar drug industry. The BCCI bank scandal, and the CIA use of the bank to launder drug money made this connection even more explicit.

In mid 1992, law enforcement and social agencies have concluded that the anti-drug policy and the billions of dollars spent on trying to stop the flow of heroin and cocaine at our borders, as well as the filling of our prisons with drug pushers and consumers is not working. The clear strategy that stops hard drugs is education and rehabilitation. Yet, the Bush administration actively rejected this view and continued to let hard drugs destroy people in the urban core of our cities.

Besides the problem of hard drugs in our society, the legal addictives of alcohol, tobacco and prescription drugs not only take a higher death toll on our population, they also create and rationalize a climate for escape and irresponsibility. A May 15, 1989, *Los Angeles Times* article by Dr. Peter Bourne, President of the American Association for World Health, stated that "An estimated 10,000 individuals die worldwide each year from the effect of illicit drugs. More than 2.5 million die from the effect of tobacco. . . . As if this were not bad enough the office of U.S. trade representative has threatened three countries with trade sanctions for refusing to open up their markets to United States tobacco products." Bourne further points out that just as in the opium wars of the 1840s in China, powerful economic interests are willing to exploit a large Third World market with total disregard for health concerns. Our government unremittingly supports the tobacco companies by threats to these foreign governments.

"The inevitable conclusion," Bourne states, "is that our drug policies are fundamentally determined, not primarily by health concerns, but by economic interests. As a rich and powerful nation we are determined to define as legal a drug we can export at immense profit to the rest of the world regardless of the health consequences." In 1990, for example, U.S. tobacco companies exported 160 billion cigarettes worldwide. This means there was over a pack of cigarettes for every person on the planet. To understand what we can expect in the coming years, exports in 1990 were three times higher than the five years previous.

The Perfect Addiction: Television

Over and over some form of addictive product has driven the economic interests of Western countries. Today, the most efficient "drug" the Machine has brought to its service is television. The average American spends five to six hours a day watching television. If someone spent five or six hours a day, everyday, sitting, ingesting, smoking, or staring blankly at an object, one would conclude that he or she had some kind of addictive problem. Yet, as with tobacco and other unhealthy products, the Machine's economy encourages and uses TV to convey one set of values and views to the population — that consumption of material things is good for us, for the country and the world. This is the same message that has been given to Western societies for 500 years. We've exploited the rest of the planet to fulfill the message of consumption. And in the mad, voracious desire for the Machine to grow bigger, these non-Western peoples, those whom we have exploited, now become a collective pool of new consumers. We turn our television satellites on these countries and hook them on the television drug so that they will become consumers as well.

Today 100 corporations control 75 percent of all advertising on television. Their paying for the content and the programming assures the continued promotion of their fundamental message. This message is now promoted everyday in our educational system. Public education and corporate advertising have been married in the new Channel One system. More than one-third of all middle- and high-school students (11,500 schools) view this commercial news channel in school everyday as part of their current events curriculum. News is sandwiched between lively, colorful, creative commercials featuring school-age-specific products. In a Wisconsin school when the teacher asked what the class remembered about the news broadcast the answer of one student was the Snickers candy commercial. Asked why the student remembered the Snickers commercial, the student said, "Because it's candy." A University of Michigan study of Channel One reveals little improvement in students' mastery of current events, but great improvement in product recognition. A 30-second commercial spot on Channel One sold for $120,000 in mid 1991, double the costs for commercials on network prime time news programs.

The impact of television on children, by conditioning them to a machinelike culture, is changing them both psychologically and physically. By the age of 18 the average child in the United States will have seen between 350,000 and 640,000 TV commercials. Our children are more secure and less anxious watching TV and playing Nintendo or computer games than they are exploring a field or woods near their home.

How the TV set functions technically is part of the addictive process. One aspect of the technical effect of watching the "tube" is that it induces passive alpha-brainwave trance effects. Brainwave pattern studies show that when we are emotionally down or physically tired and we decide to "zone out" on the tube, the flicker effect of the electronic lines that make up the TV image has a hypnotic and depressing effect on the human nervous system. Rather than becoming relaxed, we tend to become more tired and more irritable when we stop watching it. This hypnotic depression in turn can lead to more watching of TV in order to get the supposed calming effect. With this irritability-depression cycle, compulsion to watch in order to relieve the nervousness creates a strong addiction pattern. This growing addiction pattern to relieve irritability and depression may account for the increasing number of hours that people are watching television. Jerry Mander in his study of the TV phenomena and its effect on us from childhood through adulthood says,

"Simultaneously, it (TV) speeds up our nervous systems, making us too fast to feel calm, too fast to read, almost too fast to relate meaningfully to other human beings, and too fast for nature. From this alienation training , a new human emerges: speed junkie. " Like the workaholic high on adrenaline, we are creating a population hooked on the uppers and downers, the speed and depression of watching the television drug. The power of television to condition and train children is enormous.

The 1992 five-year study on television viewing, "Big World, Small Screen: The Role of Television in American Society," by the American Psychological Association, found that children watch on average 8,000 murders before they finish elementary school. The 195-page report, bringing together many different research projects, draws a strong link between the violent images on TV and the insensitivity of children to use violence in their interactions with others. One study confirmed that the deadliest felons had watched the most TV violence as children. The conditioning of children to a consuming culture is also apparent from the studies in this report. One finding showed that children up to the age of seven can't distinguish between commercials and programming. Most of us know from our own experience how the blending between programming and advertising in sitcoms is becoming as common as docu-news shows that re-enact (actually interpret) events as though they were just happening. If we, as adults, become blurred in our own perceptions by simulations, how difficult is it for our children to sort out the Ninja Turtle cartoon program from the commercials urging them to buy the toys? The reason that children find television more comforting than the natural world, the study cited, is that kids begin watching TV in infancy when parents sit them in front of the set to keep them quiet. Our children are being suckled at the breast of the TV mother, rather than Mother Nature.

Joseph Chilton Pearce, who has written such books as *Crack in the Cosmic Egg* and *The Magical Child,* notes that the damaging effect from sitting children in front of the TV is less the content of the programs and more the "pairing of imagery in synch with sound." To understand this pairing of imagery and sound, he cites the physiological brain research by Paul Mclean at the National Institute of Mental Health, Department of Brain Evolution and Behavior. Mclean found in his research that children who continuously view TV from an early age, hearing the sound linked with seeing the TV image, have limited the ability of their brains to create their own images when hearing language spoken in non-television situations. The reason this happens is that the constant reinforcement of TV images in the developing brain of the child creates a particular kind of neural structure that immediately gets stimulated when the TV comes on. These neural structures are set in what is called the old reptilian brain that governs our fight or flight syndrome. By the constant presentation of the images from TV, the higher neural structures in the child's brain don't get stimulated enough. Aural stimulation through storytelling and being read to develops internal imagery that stimulates brain growth in the higher neural structures of the neocortex.

With the increase in TV watching by young children, Pearce observes that the higher neural structures of the brain "simply lie dormant, and no capacity for creating internal imagery develops. Television, by providing all the action synthetically is handled by the same, limited number of neural structures regardless of programming, since the brain's work is already done for it [by television]. This is habituation. So neural potential is unrealized and development is impaired." Through the continual viewing of TV, our children's higher-brain development is being limited. The old part of the brain that is being constantly reinforced by television viewing is conditioned to be manipulated into fight or flight. Our children's brains are literally being wired to the television set. A deeply ingrained stimulus-response pattern is being developed and conditioned into the brains of our children to have them respond to the images and sounds of fear as their fundamental perception to the world.

The conclusion of Pearce and other researchers is that not only do messages in television programs and commercials affect us psychologically, but also the physical effects of the TV itself are physiologically destructive to our organism. Both the electronic technology of the television set and its content, is changing us as human beings.

What we can notice, then, in this 500-year history of creating the corporation-economy, is the selling of unhealthy and destructive products for short-term economic gain. Whether it is TV, cocaine, alcohol, sugar, coffee, chocolate or some new designer drug, we humans seem susceptible to the use of substitute substances to help us touch some unspeakable feeling deep inside. But the substitutes the Machine offers in finding this inner place don't work. In small amounts all of these products could be helpful in this pursuit, but rather than encouraging moderation, the Machine overwhelms us with them, making them dark mirrors that reflect back to us emotional, physical and spiritual death. In their temporary high or good feelings, in their sudden insights or in their rush of energy, they give brief moments of hope and relief. Then we fall back again into the trap of unfulfilled appetites. Our habits only cover up a deeper pain within us. We find we have to consume more and more of these substitutes to regain those brief moments of good feelings.

The Machine uses addiction in these difficult times because it knows, through advertising research, that we want to feel good. The way in which we currently live doesn't make us feel good any longer. Instinctively, however, we know there is a different, more natural way to live. But the Machine urges us to live in materialism. It pounds us with images from the outside, parading before us sexy bodies, high-fashion clothes, delicious food and exotic travel. All promises of its version of heaven on earth.

This, then, is the 500-year history that weighs upon on us, suffocating us, causing us also to become one of the endangered species. Each of us in the Western world, no matter what our status or position, is caught in the cultural web

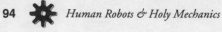

of this profit-driven Machine. Somehow, the deep, often unfelt pain that you and I hold within living the way we do, may eventually trigger us to react and respond in a rebellious way. Understanding the source of this pain and becoming conscious of our personal roots in serving the Machine can help us begin to break away from it.

PART II

BECOMING HOLY MECHANICS

Beyond living and dreaming there is
something more important: waking up.

ANTONIO MACHADO
SPANISH POET

Introduction

Becoming holy mechanics means to change our state of mind. It means changing the framework of our perceptions and the way we view ourselves and the world. This change is, first of all, a choice to move from the outer complexity as robots to the inner simplicity of our lives as humans. Because we don't know rationally what to do about the Machine, doesn't mean we lack personal power. Once we decide that we want to live differently, courage, insight and new opportunities come to us. The simple act of deciding to reconnect with nature, to turn inward to our own spiritual power will automatically bring to us the possiblity of *doing* something. The first step in being a holy mechanic is to know that *we are deciders not doers*.

When we decide to turn our psychic back on the Machine, something changes deep within us. Even as we still work and live in the Machine's culture, we can do so with a heightened sense of compassion and kindness for ourselves and others. We can grieve for the abuse to the land and to its peoples. We can be more honest about the role we've all collectively played in it. This grief can also move us to speak out and take actions in ways that we haven't done before. When we decide, we feel a compassionate stirring within us. We grow more silent and listen to ourselves and to the sounds of Nature's voice.

Like many others I've talked with, I have begun to stop the Machine's conditioning mechanisms by not listening to radio, not watching TV, nor reading the newspapers for long periods of time. (I now rarely watch television.) Without these external shapers of my consciousness I now get the information I need about the world in other strange and interesting ways. Someone suggests a book, a friend gives a call, a headline catches my eye, an intuition illumines a new thought or feeling in me. Over time I realize that I am being guided by an internal process that is teaching me how to learn and be in the world in some different kind of way. Strangely, as I practice this new listening to myself, I feel that my old interior beliefs, perceptions and feelings are continually being shattered. As these things shatter inside me I go through periods of confusion and anxiety. But the shattering of these culturally, Machine-based perceptions is opening up more space inside both my mind and my soul. Although, inside, I feel continually shattered, the paradox is that my outside life seems to grow stronger in focus and direction concerning what I do. If we are to respond in a new way, our inner world of imagination has to change rapidly so that the outer activity of our life can move in unexpected and freer ways.

The adventure of another kind of life and world that emerges from a new imagining is growing in many of us. As we choose a different way of living, and return to our imagination for the truth of what ancient peoples have always seen, we move away from the Machine's consumer-driven world while we are still living in it. It is similar to what Jesus said to his followers, "Be in the world, but not of it." Our task, while still in a machine world, is to find out how to be holy mechanics, how to "fix" ourselves, how to help ourselves as human robots in reclaiming our souls, particularly as the Machine begins to break down. The trick in this reclaiming is to first see clearly our robot condition, and at the same time rediscover that holy or soul part of ourselves that accesses knowledge in a way that is different than from what this machine world now offers us.

The Making of an American Robot

*T*he repeated message from my father as I grew up in the 1940s and 1950s was, "get a college education." He had wanted one, but couldn't have it because of family responsibilities, and he wanted me to get what he didn't have. In his view, for his son to have a college education was to get a ticket on a train that he could never ride.

The value that guided my father's generation was to push one's children at least one rung higher up the economic and social ladder than one had been able to achieve. For the majority of people in the first half of this century there was a general value that one sacrificed to make sure the kids succeeded. If children succeeded, they did so for the whole family.

At age 12, my father, the oldest of eight children, took on the role of provider and surrogate father. His father died when he was nine. His stepfather died when he was 12 years old. Starting at age 13, he worked with the grain threshing crews in the summer and fall, following the harvests from Canada to Oklahoma. In the winter he chipped the "dew" out of outhouses in sub-zero weather in North Dakota to earn money to feed the family. By the time he graduated from high school he was class president, a straight-A student, and captain of the state championship football and basketball teams. Scholarships from North Dakota State, the University of Minnesota, and even Harvard were all turned down, however, in order that he could continue providing for the family.

After marrying my mother he managed auto garages, traveled as part of the "white" team against the original Harlem Globetrotters, and, in 1930, invented a long-life battery. His patent mysteriously disappeared. Two months later one of the major battery companies announced that they held a patent very similar to the one he had applied for.

Two years later, in the midst of the Great Depression, my father, mother and baby sister set out for Oregon with their best friends and their infant daughter. They first lived together in a small travel trailer with the two babies and the men earned one dollar a day cutting trees. Later, my dad became the owner of one of the largest garages in downtown Portland by the beginning of World War II. Dad was moving fast, traveling up the ladder toward the American dream.

From the financial success of the garage, he bought a new manufacturing franchise that produced concrete roofing and split Roman brick. By the time I was 12 years old, I watched Ike being nominated for the presidency on our neighbor's television set. We later headed to California after dad sold the manufacturing business. My father had the idea to build and sell automated machines that would make roofing tile, bricks, patio blocks, and other concrete products. He and his partner went back to running gas stations by day to pay the bills, and by night, worked on building the new machine. Four years later they opened a demonstration plant for the machine's products. My father invented new color dye formulas for the concrete products, figured out how to make California slump stone on the machine (the hottest brick in Southern California at the time), and ran out of money to finance the next stage of building and selling the machines nationwide. Unscrupulous investors stole the business out from under him, and sold the machine and his formulas to Hazard Block Company, the largest brick and block company in Southern California.

After being financially and emotionally broken from the loss of his dream, a friend of dad's helped him buy a small garage and gas station at the Mexican border. My father started over, but now as a broken man with a crushed dream and with alcohol as his daily support. Fourteen years later, while selling the garage in order to retire, he bled to death on a hospital room toilet.

My father, born at the turn of the century, believed in the values of this country. The success and tragedy of his life (and many in his generation) is woven into the fabric of our culture today. My attitudes and beliefs were shaped by my father's self-determination, his willingness to work hard, his creativity and inventiveness, his skill with people, his constant reading, and his dreams to build something out of this life. In the late 1930s he attended Communist party meetings, as did many others who were intellectually trying to find a way out of the conditions of the depression. He died a Republican who felt the Democrats were selling out the American people to massive government spending. He was a complicated man, a lonely man, a driven man. Like so many fathers of my generation, he wanted me to go to college, to go beyond what he had done, to make a "mark on the world." My father lived the American dream, was part of building it, but in the end he felt that it hadn't played fairly with him.

By the time I finished high school in 1958, my beliefs were also rooted in this dream. But by the time I left the University of California in 1964, my view of the world had shifted in several ways.

America: Dream and Reality

My consciousness was shaped by both the culture of the 1950s (the American Dream values of my father) and the culture of the 1960s. In the 1960s I realized that I was among the "first fruits" of the American Dream and that this dream wasn't enough to satisfy some inner longing within me. The roots of my 1950s beliefs grew from individualism and progress, the fundamental beliefs of U.S. industrialization.

These beliefs came into full blossom at the end of the most bloody and destructive period of our history, the Civil War. A full generation of American young men were slaughtered in that war, just as a generation of English, French and German youth were slaughtered 50 years later in World War I.

My grandmother was born in 1871, six years after the Civil War ended. She told me of traveling by covered wagon from Minnesota to North Dakota and being chased by a band of Indians. She died in the early 1960s having witnessed the movement of 90 percent of Americans working for themselves in agriculture in 1900, to 75 percent of American workers being wage-earners by 1950. She was part of a worldwide population explosion, and witnessed humanity growing from 645 million people on the planet in 1800, to 1.5 billion in 1900, to 5.5 billion in 1990.

Starting from kerosene lamps and wood stoves, she finished her life cooking in an electric kitchen, watching television, flying in an airplane and driving on freeways. And she saw me, the first fruits of the American dream, go off to the university to experience the full blossoming of a middle-class-consumer society where Ronald Reagan was pitching the General Electric slogan on television in the 1950s, that "Progress is our most important product".

Throughout his tenure as governor of California and then as president in the 1980s, Reagan continued to preach the message of progress even though government statistics showed that the average income of the middle class decreased substantially and the average income of the very wealthy increased at an unprecedented rate by the time he left office.

James Steele and Donald Barlett from the *Philadelphia Inquirer* did an investigative series in November 1991, entitled "America: What Went Wrong?" The figures they cite on income during the Reagan era are astounding. They write, "Between 1980 and 1989, the combined salaries of people in the $20,000 to $50,000 income group increased 44 percent. During the same period, the combined salaries of people earning $1 million or more a year increased 2,184 percent. Viewed more broadly, the combined wages of all people who earned less than $50,000 a year — 85 percent of all Americans — increased an average of just two percent a year over those 10 years. Those figures are not adjusted for inflation, which cuts across all classes but hits the lower and middle classes hardest. Between 1980 and 1989, the number of people reporting incomes of more than a half-million dollars rocketed from 16,881 to 183,240 — an increase of 985 percent."

A study by the Center on Budget Policy put it simply. In the 1980s a major redistribution of wealth took place in the United States. By 1990 the top 5 percent of the population in the United States earned more money *total,* than the bottom 40 percent of the population combined. Real wealth moved from the poor, making them poorer, to the wealthy, making them wealthier. This movement of wealth from poor to rich occurred as the government cut social programs, cut food stamps, and altered distribution of federal taxes back to the states for mental-health facilities and the like. All these programs had helped the bottom 40 percent of U.S. citizens. This loss of human support systems put more people into the homeless ranks, and created a growing permanent underclass in our society, members of whom will never make it into the middle-class ranks. Many of these younger people in the underclass come from middle class families who, even though educated, will never be able to afford to own the kind of house they grew up in or have the luxuries and affluence of their parents.

The American dream of getting "rich quick" was fully demonstrated in the 1980s. But this in turn, was a death knell to the promise of a broad and prosperous middle class that had been preached and encouraged since the Great Depression of the 1930s. Reagan's preaching for General Electric on television and Eisenhower's domestic policies in the 1950s fueled the middle-class vision, but the 1960s opened the crack in the national psyche and attempted to break down this conformist dream.

As a product of both the 1950s and the 1960s, I rebelled from the so-called American dream by opening my mind with psychedelics, and by rejecting the middle-class acceptance of loyal and blind allegiance to religion and government. I helped shut down colleges, challenged the educational system, lived communally and like many of my generation finally turned inward to meditation, psychology and spiritual growth. After teaching for 12 years, and trying to influence the education system, I dropped out, traveled, and built houses for a couple of years. Through a series of serendipitous events I was offered work in the business world at the beginning of the 1980s. I worked in high-tech companies developing management programs, and then joined a consulting firm.

Trying to Save the New American Dream

With the same 1950s naiveté, I, along with other consultants, human-resource professionals, and training and development specialists, made "progress [of business] our most important product." We believed that business was somehow the means to change the planet for good. We said to each other in our conferences and newsletters that we could transform business into the instrument of universal salvation to create a new sense of community for people. Business was to be a place of personal growth for individuals and an arena where we would help develop a leadership that would respond creatively to the fundamental problems of the day.

Many other friends, as well as I, held our 1950s hopefulness with our 1960s change and growth experiences, and made one more attempt to change our world for the better. We came on-line at the beginning of the 1980s and rode the rocket of prosperity to the stars. Companies had money and they were spending it. Things were changing and people wanted to experiment. But by the end of the 1980s things weren't working well. We had been around companies long enough to notice the cycles of what companies really wanted. In the increasing difficulty of competing in a worldwide economy, executives were being hired for their ability to manage a company's downturn and lay-offs. The enthusiasm of executives for new ideas turned to gritted teeth and dark faces. The Machine wasn't doing well, even with all the promise of the Information Age as the latest economic savior. We consultants began to oil the machines, constantly trying to provide the right strategies, training change and transition managers, and, trying to facilitate the downsizing of companies without creating too much anxiety and fear.

Peter Drucker, the management teacher and elder statesman of business, says in his work, *Managing for the Future* (1992), that the latest reduction in the work force by large corporations is not just the result of our current hard economic times. Rather, he suggests, companies are attempting to change how they operate. He says, "businesses will undergo more, and more radical restructuring in the 1990s than at any time since the modern corporate organization first evolved in the 1920s. . . . Large American companies have cut management levels by one-third or more. But the restructuring of corporations — middle-size ones as well as large ones, and eventually, even smaller ones — has barely begun." The overall cause of this massive restructuring is the worldwide development of the corporate-economy. What Drucker sees driving these efforts are world trading blocks like Asia and Europe, business alliances like IBM and Apple, reducing of clerical overhead to outside contractors, the influence of large pension funds and mutual trusts influencing how companies manage themselves, as well as the challenge of integrating the Third World countries into the world economy.

My own experience in corporations the past few years confirms Drucker's view about downsizing. The early 1990s economic down cycle has forced companies to re-evaluate how they manage and work. People being laid off in these large corporations are finding it difficult to go to work for similar types of companies. Many of the workers in these companies will fall lower down the economic scale into lower paying service jobs. The full force of the Machine's effort is to automate and take the human factor out of the Machine as much as possible. The small amount of capital investment that is going into manufacturing plants is used to automate jobs with robotics equipment. The other strategy companies are using, as they lay people off, is to send jobs offshore or across the border into Third World countries where labor is cheap, and environmental constraints are minimal. The great desire of American corporations to implement the North American Trade Agreement is that Mexico will become a bonanza of cheap labor for manufacturing. But in our global, machinelike economy any Third World country that offers the cheapest labor is where corporations are heading.

Large billion-dollar corporations like Nike roam the Third World to find the cheapest labor. Nike, who owns no manufacturing plants to make their products, licenses factories to make their shoes in Southeast Asian countries like Thailand and Indonesia where wages are extremely low and work conditions match the U.S. sweat shops of the early 1900s. Through nearly slave-labor conditions Nike has very low overhead costs per pair of shoes. Use of cheap labor enabled Nike to make 39 percent in profit in 1991. To make this profit Nike spent $180 million in advertising to promote the themes of health, fitness and self-empowerment with the slogan of "Just Do It!" The First World, mainly white consumers, "Just Buy Them!" at the expense of both Third World workers and the unemployed in our own country.

The Old/New American Dream

Are we really just robots in a machine? Has the addiction of consumerism infected us too deeply to change? Is the world-corporation/finance-driven economy running on its own? Are we and the "leaders" of these companies now simply servants to it? These are not simple questions. Nor are they abstract questions. How each of us struggles to answer them determines the meaning, purpose and direction for our lives into the future. To answer these questions we each have to examine our personal historical roots in a machine culture. Like any good gardener, knowing the condition of the root system helps us determine how to transplant the tree and how to keep it alive as it goes through the transition of being uprooted and transplanted.

My father pushed me up a rung on the cultural ladder, but it wasn't what he imagined it to be. My generation became a bridge between our parent's materialist American Dream and a new dream. Our parents' dream — the American-consumer dream — was finally more powerful than communism's materialism. But our dream became a different one with several interconnecting strands. Our dream of the '60s was a spiritual dream that had been quietly streaming through the American psyche from the time of Ralph Waldo Emerson and Walt Whitman, and the other transcendentalists of the 1800s. This was the dream of bringing Eastern and Western spiritual traditions together, of honoring the earth as a sacred being, and reclaiming intuition and the body as the basis of experience and learning. It broke into our national psyche in the 1960s as a deep response to the materialist consumer dream of our parents, and because of a deep desire to live our lives differently.

The popular media of the Machine have chewed up the '60s period and has made it into a caricature of love children, psychedelic posters and Camelot. But the eruption of this collective psychic energy brought forward a number of new ideas — from John Kennedy's Peace Corps and Martin Luther King's non-violent civil rights resistance to Berkeley's free-speech movement and the Chicago Democratic Convention reaction; from community living and a vision for nature to the resistance to the war in Viet Nam and the human-potential movement. All these collective energies opened up a generation of men and women to a different set of ideas, beliefs and values that are still being struggled with today in the underground of our souls. The legacy of the 1960s for the 1990s includes civil rights, feminism, environmentalism and a widening of our spiritual viewpoints.

Many colleagues of my generation did not "tune in, turn on and drop out." But they were affected by the explosion of this collective 1960s energy. And many of us from that generation carry this strange schizophrenia of an old/new dream deep inside. Although, during the 1970s and 1980s this dream got buried within us, somehow, it is now time for many of us to go back and find the source of that dream within us. It is time to begin to re-create it in a new way, in the 1990s. Perhaps the dream now has a life of its own and will offer us an interdependent strand of new cultural threads that will weave the dream together as we move closer to the turn of the century.

Leaders in the Machine

*B*oth men and women seem to have different triggers that raise challenging issues about metamorphosing into a different leadership role as an older person in our society. However, there is little guidance, support or articulation, particularly by our youth-oriented culture, to help older people journey through this important and significant passage of life. The lack of both personal understanding and cultural clues about how to approach this stage in life has far-reaching implications for the kinds of leaders we are producing in politics, education, religion and business. One study found, for example, that 45 percent of career professionals (both women and men) suffer from work-related emotional problems. Among these problems are extreme stress with high blood pressure and heart attacks. Other symptoms include job burn-out with resulting chronic health conditions such as continual colds and flus. Low productivity can then happen due to low physical energy and debilitating physical conditions like Chronic Fatigue Immune Dysfunction Syndrome (CFIDS), Epstein-Barr virus and mononucleosis. I believe physical and psychological problems often arise because there is emotional and moral conflict between organizational values and ethics, and the personal values and ethics held by the individual. Individuals who work for companies like Nike that use Third

World slave labor to produce their products often find their internal conflict and attempts at intellectual rationalizations very difficult to cope with over time.

Male Executives and the Abuse of Power

When a male executive "hardens his heart" and becomes a human robot in service to the Machine, he has great difficulty hearing his moral and spiritual voice. If a male executive between the ages of 50 and 60 doesn't know how to listen to his inner, intuitive voice, he will often not hear what others are trying to say to him about the condition of the organization and of his response to it. He is unable to hear new internal messages that are trying to bring to the surface a new awareness in him.

Rather than letting this psycho/spiritual pressure break open the defensive shell that protects his true feelings, beliefs and moral standards, this man often will experience a growing defensiveness and an anxiety that lingers and eats at him. Then, ultimately, some form of physical, emotional or spiritual sickness will overcome him and cause him to stop — and finally listen, or perhaps, even die. An example of this pattern is the growing rate of high blood pressure and fatal heart attacks in executives.

Men crossing the age of 60 who have not heeded the internal message to listen and to change their underlying views of themselves, will not only get more depressed, but will often turn away from others. Or they may try to rejuvenate their lives as if they were in their forties by seeking relationships with younger women. Learning, growth and change seem to consciously stop for these executive men. Life seems to atrophy. Environments for meaningful learning for them become impoverished. They are reinforced by the same people, do the same activities, go to the same places they've gone to for years. As tension between this familiar old pattern and the new inner impulses intensify, anger and rage often determine the behavior of the executive. And this frustration gets played out in the workplace.

Time and again I am called into companies to work with CEOs or senior managers who are abusive with their employees. The tragedy is that until confronted by their actions, these men are not fully aware of their abusive behavior or their impact on all levels of the organization. The unconscious power of the anger and rage of both CEOs and senior managers can be terrorizing to those who work for them. The power of this rage creates a collective energy that produces a negative atmosphere throughout the entire organization. They fail to see the stress they displace on their employees, the demands for perfection that they themselves cannot meet, or the biting sarcasm that hurts self-esteem and professional worth in their colleagues, co-workers, and subordinates.

The problem with most executives is that they often do not identify or see their own negativity at work. What we might call abusive they may simply call being tough. In the drive for these executives to get results they often will excuse the devastating effects they have on people.

Fortune magazine periodically runs an article on "America's Toughest Bosses". In the February, 1989 issue some of America's toughest bosses are quoted. Here is a sampling of what subordinates say about them, and how the boss (in these male examples) sees himself:

Richard J. Mahoney, Chairman, Monsanto
> *How others see him:* "He has a big ego . . . subordinates have to stroke him a lot . . . listens to others but doesn't understand . . . little empathy with subordinates. . . can't believe he is wrong.
> *How he sees himself:* "I am demanding, not mean. Forgiveness is out of style, shoulder shrugs are out of fashion. Hit the targets on time without excuses."

Hugh L. McColl Jr., Chairman, NCNB Corp.
> *How others see him:* "We sit on the edge of our chairs . . .

he manages with aggressiveness and perfectionism, and he expects us to cope with the tension."

How he sees himself: "I expect the Herculean. There's no golf in the middle of the day, no coasting to retirement. If you're not leading, you're out of here."

Harry E. Figgie Jr., Chairman, Figgie International

How others see him: "From horrendous to delightful, from idiotic to brilliant . . . working with him was a nightmare . . . really abusive . . . the Steinbrenner of industry."

How he sees himself: "You don't build a company like this with lace on your underwear. We bought small companies with no management depth. There is no room for error."

Robert L. Crandall, Chairman, AMR Corp. (parent of American Airlines)

How others see him: "His toughness is very visible . . . has a towering temper and swears a lot . . . focuses all his energy on the issue and sees everything in black and white. Those who have been with him for years learn tocounter his faults with logic and reasoning."

How he sees himself: Declined to be interviewed.

Frank A. Lorenzo, Chairman, Texas Air

How others see him: "He thinks he's a great manager, but he's not . . . incredibly impulsive . . . not trusted inside or outside the organization . . . good dealmaker though."

How he sees himself: "I have to be tough but fair. Webuilt this company from businesses that were failing. We didn't just take over a big company and blow out the cobwebs."

The writer of the article, Peter Nulty, after describing in more depth these and other highly placed business leaders, concludes by giving some observations:

- Tough bosses have difficulty identifying constructive toughness from the destructive kind of toughness.

- The tough bosses believe that their power to fire someone is the hardest thing for a subordinate to handle. Some subordinates say getting fired can be a relief.
- While toughness may consist of abuse, it is usually unrelenting pressure and tension that causes the problem for subordinates.
- Tough bosses eventually find people who can handle their rage and terror. Or to put it in psychological terms, are co-dependent to them.

Nulty concludes: "As global competition heats up and turmoil rocks more industries, tough management should spread. So look for more bosses who are steely, super demanding, unrelenting, sometimes abusive, sometimes unreasonable, impatient, driven, stubborn and combative. And have a nice day."

All of the bosses quoted above display the problem of not recognizing the difference between their negative qualities and other parts of their personalities. What their subordinates saw as very negative, these bosses believed were elements that contributed to their success. These men may be very kind and loving to their children, be generous of time and money to their community, but in their leadership role in corporations they have built their success around negative leadership that is unrecognizable to them as different from the "nicer" parts of themselves. In this splitting and unconscious disassociation of themselves these executives have become unfeeling robot leaders in a machine culture.

Men Maintaining the Power

My experience is that there is both suppressed and overt anger in most men who are caught in company machines. Much of my encounters with sexual harassment in companies seems to be suppressed anger towards women. In their attempt to prove their own competency and capability, women get relegated into being a sexual object. Making the woman a sexual object deflects the professional challenge, but also maintains the male role of dominator in the Machine's corporations. The Machine's values are masculine. Women who introduce into the business world a different set of values — a stronger ethical and relationship style of communicating and decision-making — threaten these kinds of male leaders and the Machine's patriarchal value structure.

Men in leadership positions easily assume the dominant role in the hierarchy because the values of the Machine encourage it. Feminine values are usually rejected. Professionally, many men may commit unethical or compromising acts for the sake of the organization, that go against their own personal values. This inner conflict between being committed to the company and moving upward in one's career while suppressing and rationalizing one's own personal values, creates deep tension and a form of sickness in the person.

With increasing dissonance between machinelike values and his personal values, a man will often become a drone at work and increase his workaholism. As a result he will continue to get the outer rewards of money and position as a rationalization and justification for his ultimate betrayal of himself. He has been swallowed up by the Machine's values — co-opted with the promise of power and influence, money and status. These so-called rewards, however, cover up intense grief and pain that I find grow to dramatic outcomes in these executives. As the high negative health statistics for executives show, all too many of these men die of heart attacks or cancer, or they become alcoholics. My view is that there is a direct relationship between this self-betrayal and disease to the resulting addictive behavior to alcohol, sex and other drugs. To resolve the tension and inner conflict, a man may retire as quickly as he can with his "golden egg" retirement plan and pour his energy into golfing, watching TV, and drinking. Or, he may try to escape into traveling and photograph sorting. Often these men come out of retirement and go back into some business venture because they are so deeply addicted to the old machinelike work pattern.

Men detached from the Machine seem to deflate. Their only purpose outside work is their reward of retirement, which often ends with an early death. Life without purpose evaporates quickly. And lives that have been connected only to the outer world and to masculine machinelike values and behaviors die even quicker, even when their bodies may be alive and active.

One high-tech executive who was a founder of a successful company, retired early with millions of dollars to escape a pattern of conflicting personal and organizational values. Eventually, however, he returned from living aboard his boat in the Caribbean and, to prove his worth and value to himself, was driven to create another start-up company. He like many other executives conditioned by the machine, failed to heed the call of his inner, intuitive voice. Rather, he retreated from the struggle of awakening to an inner life and returned to the familiar call of the Machine.

The Struggle of Women Executives

The women executives that I've worked with seem to respond differently than their male counterparts to the challenge of a machine world. Many of these women are as strong and forceful of character and personality as are male executives. But overall, the executive women I've worked with seem to be willing to listen to themselves more. They are ready to focus on interpersonal relationships and support others rather than compete with other executives for power and prestige. Many of these women, however, take on a particular professional role that my partner, Patt, has termed the man-made woman. Like her male counterpart, the man-made woman is continually proving to others in the organization that her intelligence, competency and ability to function are on an equal footing with men. In her younger years she wears the business uniform, semi-copies of men's suits, right down to the red bow tie. As she grows older she will work longer hours, push herself to complete the project perfectly and will show little emotion. This last characteristic of showing no emotion becomes the test of hardening into the man-made woman. Men fault women in the workplace for crying and having emotional outbursts of anger. The man-made woman learns to suppress her feelings.

One woman who was an elected official of a large U.S. city describes the extremes of men's rejection of emotion in the work setting. When Patt interviewed this women in a study, the woman described an evening meeting where a verbal encounter with another political office holder was particularly contentious. After the meeting she went back to her office, shut her door and while sitting at her desk had a "good cry." She then composed herself, and left for home. The next morning when she returned to her office there was an anonymous note on her desk that read, "Don't cry in your office." Since she was the only woman at the meeting, she had to assume that one of the men had stood at her door and listened to her cry. Clearly, from the assertiveness of the note, he believed that crying was totally inappropriate for an elected official. The labels of "temperamental," "bitchy" and "emotional" come quickly to women if they display their feelings strongly in a business meeting, or in private, with a good cry. The fundamental message for women in our society is that *to get at the top, she has to be like a man.*

Men in a machinelike company can get angry and rage (but not cry), while women are not allowed to express any feelings. The man-made woman learns to turn off her feelings and prove that her emotional strength is equal to a man's so-called emotional toughness. Not only is a professional woman damned if she does express feeling, she is damned if she doesn't exhibit toughness. A clear example of the contrast between men and women having a different standard of expressing anger was seen in the Anita Hill, Clarence Thomas Supreme Court hearing on network television in 1991. Anita

Hill, holding in check her emotions in order to be "professional" as she testified about sexual harassment from Thomas, was castigated by the committee and the press as being cold, calculating and unbelievable. But Clarence Thomas in venting his anger and rage at Anita Hill, was viewed and applauded as righteous, personally genuine, and believable in his position as Supreme Court candidate.

Patt describes in her work, *When Sleeping Beauty Wakes: A Woman's Tale of Healing the Immune System and Awakening the Feminine,* that the tragedy for professional women trying to survive in a machine world is that they slowly begin to lose something fundamental about their basic femininity. With a high percentage of working women getting auto-immune diseases, something is beginning to die emotionally, spiritually and physically in these women.

Ann Wilson Schaef, in her work, *Women's Reality: An Emerging Female System in a White Male Society,* says that the white-male system (what I've been describing as the Machine culture) is death oriented. She calls it a White Male System because it dominates in education, economics, politics and in religion. White males have the power, they are the decision-makers and control everything below them. This system, Schaef argues, is killing not only women, but the planet and men themselves. Her book focuses particularly on what the Machine's White Male System does to women, and how women need to "re-member" their own feminine systems once again. Women of all colors are suppressed by the White Male System. But white women have been the supporters of the White Male System, and therefore it is this group of women that can have the greatest influence in changing white male dominance. "White women", Schaef asserts, "believe that they get their identity externally from the White Male System and that the White Male System is necessary to validate that identity. Therefore, challenging the system becomes almost impossible." This is why, in Patt's view, we have so many man-made women in the Machine. Since they won't challenge the system, they are co-opted into it. And they try to be better than men at the man's own game. Schaef says that since white women have done better than other ethnic groups "they have to hide and/or unlearn their own system and accept the stereotypes [don't cry, don't be the bitch, but be sexually desirable] that the White Male System has set up for them." Schaef goes on to describe what she calls four basic male myths that keep the White Male System going, and that women buy into. She argues that these myths are largely unconscious in white males, but that they project these myths onto everything: to women, to people of color and to nature itself.

•Myth one is that the only thing that exists is the White Male System. Any other system is not normal, it is crazy, bad — in a word, threatening. Therefore, this system, the Machine culture, is the only one to adopt and follow.

•Myth two is that the White Male System is innately superior. Everyone in the world must follow the white, Western, capitalist form of reality, because it is simply the best.

•Myth three is that this male system knows and understands everything. By naming anything as "so," it then is so. Science says the world is a certain way, then it is. If women are believed more emotional than men, then they are. If we are creating a product for the good of people, then it is good, and so on.

•Myth four in the White Male System is that everything can be totally objective, rational and logical. There is an assumption that subjectivity, feelings and intuition are suspect. Women, because they are emotional, are irrational and must be watched and evaluated much more closely than men. To be successful in the White Male System, a women can't be seen as illogical or emotionally weak.

Schaef indicates that there is one more myth in the White Male System. This is the belief that it is possible to be God. This myth is the ultimate summary of the other four myths. The white male is all powerful and controlling. The male sees himself as superior to everyone, the one who knows everything, the one who is the primary force for everything in the world, and who is totally rational about reality. The idea of the male as all-powerful God is the driving force of Machine leadership.

For men and women leaders, the Machine allures them to riches, power and prestige. They are at the top of the power pyramid in the culture. They have replaced the priest, the doctor and the political leader. They run our world. From the men who integrate the economy worldwide, down through the multinational presidents and the company CEOs, these individuals are determining what happens in our world and in our lives. But the Machine is eating them up, just as it is consuming us. Inside the Machine's culture these men and women believe they are doing the right thing. Their perceptions tell them that the Machine is the way the world works today. They are being rewarded for hard work and professional expertise. But, like most of us, they are also rationalizing what they are doing and cutting off their basic feelings from their own deep internal suffering and the suffering of others and of the natural world. From our leaders, as well as ourselves, there is a growing despair that we are all victims of this Machine world. As we look for a way out of this dilemma, and the lack of meaningful leadership, let us pause and consider the state of mind, the context that is creating this victim feeling. Let us consider the mental shift we need to make in order to consider other alternatives to the world we find ourselves participating in today.

Changing the Context of Our Minds

*S*ince the fall of the Berlin wall and the crumbling of the Soviet Union, we've held the assumption in the West that capitalism has finally won out in the ideological world struggle. Capitalism, our ideology in the Machine, represents the economic idea that demonstrates the survival of the fittest. Basic to the power of the capitalist idea is the belief that competition — the ability to have winners and losers — is what makes capitalism so successful. Capitalism fits the popularized Darwinian notion of natural selection of the fittest in the economic jungle. Overcoming one's competition, taking the terrain of market share to dominate one's industry, and using all available resources to one's advantage is the practical day-to-day experience of most enterprises that exist in a capitalist system. Struggle, fighting, and death is basic to the functioning of capitalism. In not too subtle ways the advocates of the capitalistic Machine claim that capitalism is similar to how nature works with dominance, power and control as the determining values for survival. Yet, this popularized equating of capitalism with how nature works doesn't hold to our understanding of systems theory or environmental knowledge. Systems and environmental theory both show us that nature is in a dynamic balance of relationships that cooperatively acts in a reciprocal give and take to maximize the survival of all elements in the system. There is no attempt to create winners and losers in nature.

Competition and the Scarcity Assumption

The development of the clockwork, mechanistic view of reality developed in the West over the past 500 years was also melded with the Darwinian evolutionary theory proclaiming that nature's primary "method" was competition for survival. Thomas Hobbes, John Locke and Adam Smith each used this competition idea as the primary cornerstone for building a capitalist theory of economics. This competitive view of how nature and reality worked focused our cultural perception on the notion that economic systems are based on a value of scarcity. Scarcity encourages the idea that I have to take from you before you take from me, or I won't survive. This view fractures nature's fundamental principle of wholeness, interconnectedness, cooperation and sharing. The net result of this idea is a breakdown of trust, community, and mutual support between people as fewer individuals hold more and more of the wealth. Instead of encouragement toward life and creativity, what we get in the capitalist's model of the Machine is a movement toward alienation, separation, and fragmentation of family — along with poverty, homelessness, and all the other social ills we have today. Economic competition, with its winners and losers assumes the belief that there is only so much to go around, and the so-called notion that "I will get mine even if it is at your expense."

Socialism and communism both acknowledged the destructiveness of competition, but still believed in the scarcity idea. Rather than winners and losers, Karl Marx said that the scarcity problem could be solved through a different form of distribution and by way of who controlled the actual means of producing the goods of the society. Both capitalism and socialism/communism focused on hierarchy as the method of controlling the economic functioning in society. In capitalism, control rests with the bankers and financiers who decide what amounts of money will be allocated into specific products, and which people (the market) will pay the most money for those products.

Socialism/communism, as it is practiced, works in a cumbersome ideological bureaucracy that controls the choices over what goods will be produced for the whole society. People as individual consumers (the market) do not decide in these two systems. Rather, "wise" representatives of the people decide what goods and services the people will want. In capitalism there are supposedly choices; in socialism and communism there is less choice over the goods of production. What is important to notice is that in both systems an industrial-technological Machine emerged that defined and used people as parts while convincing citizens that being a part within the Machine, a consuming robot, was good.

The scarcity idea is a critical one for us to consider. Communist ideology said that because of the scarcity of resources, the social system will make sure everyone gets at least something. The fact that it might be neither what you want nor the amount you want is irrelevant. There is, however, only so much to go around, and the State knows what's best for everyone. The group, not the individual, determines and decides the scarcity level in this system. Capitalistic ideology, on the other hand, promotes the idea that not everyone can have the resources; so in capitalism we compete with each other and the best "whomever" or "whatever" will get the most. In short the stronger, more competitive one is the more one gets. If some lose and get nothing, this is also irrelevant — that's simply the way things are. One needs to try harder the next time. The "fittest" will get the "mostest."

Scarcity, however, is not the issue in nature. The message from nature is balance and sustainability. The giving and taking of animal life is reciprocal and balanced according to what a particular biosystem can tolerate. Resources of every kind have their natural limits, but they generally are renewable. This was true of the human animal when we were in our hunter and gather period for many millennia. We proved over thousands of years that a culture of sophisticated art and ritual could live in balance and view itself as part of an entire resource system. Living lightly on and with the land occurred throughout North and South America up until a little over a hundred years ago. White settlers claimed and overtook lands of native peoples here in the 1700s and 1800s because they could not understand how anyone could be stewards and not owners of land. With native tribes living so lightly upon the land without boundaries or markers, white European settlers presumed it was theirs for the taking.

Our own pre-Christian European ancestors, as well as native peoples around the world, knew how much game to take from a territory, how many people a particular watershed could handle, and how to limit their population through contraception. They knew and practiced the principles of balance because the larger forces of nature and the otherworld were a daily part of their lives. Abundance of the natural world, and respect for it, not scarcity, was the guiding perception of our ancestors and of many native peoples today. Even with the problem of world hunger, we have the means of production and the ability to distribute food to those who need it. The problem is not scarcity but reconceiving and redefining our values and priorities about people's lives and the beliefs we hold about our economic systems.

Competition, as the underpinning of capitalism, no longer works. And communism's focus on control of production and distribution of goods has also failed. We are at the end of a voracious 500-year binge on the planet's natural resources. Throughout the globe, our natural resources are disappearing because we've given up our individual and collective responsibility for balance and sustainability. Capitalism lives within the illusion that it has won the economic battle of this century. Communism, having become bankrupt, rushes to embrace the free-market system of capitalism as its salvation.

The struggle between capitalism and communism these past 70 years has created a state of mind, a definition of reality, in which we have come to believe that we are victims of our circumstances. As victims, then, we must compete within the scarcity model. Because of the power of the scarcity belief, fewer and fewer people seem to have the ability to get what they believe they need and want. The belief in scarcity then fosters the competitive-victimizing power of capitalism's or communism's control over us. Most people simply feel too overwhelmed by this power to do anything about it. In view of this situation, is it possible to switch from a competitive/victim view of reality to a cooperative/resource view of life that can permit a different kind of social and economic structure to emerge?

Being a Resource Rather than a Victim

Social systems grow out of ideas, perceptions and beliefs. The deep-seeded idea and belief in our collective unconscious is the notion that problems and circumstances are too big, and too far removed from our individual influence for us to do anything about them. Underneath this deep feeling of victimization is an individual and collective fear. To confront the complexity of our current Machine-world condition doesn't mean we have to surrender to this condition of fear and be destroyed by it. However, our collective psyche, our deeply held fears about the consequences of this Machine world we live in seem to be calling forth a world apocalypse.

But each of us has a personal, internal choice. I can choose either to be a *victim* or a *resource* to the problems we face, or I can choose to be a cause rather than an effect in the overall conditions of the world around me. I can choose to take the position that I am by definition a part of everything, and that I am not only responsible for the conditions of the world, but that I am accountable for creating them. It is easy for me to say I didn't create the nuclear waste, nor inner-city problems, nor the oil spill in Alaska. But if I fundamentally change my mind, if I *choose* to take the position that I am a resource — that I have ideas, capabilities, insights, ways of acting within me — then, I can positively affect both the situation of my personal life and the larger problems in the world around me.

Rather than embracing fear as the context in which we decide and act, we can begin to shift more and more to love and trust as a basic condition for how we live. Rather than choosing separation and exclusion from others, we can move to the choice of openness and connection. These and other value and attitude shifts come from a choice to create a new individual and collective context for acting.

The only way to produce a new set of actions, and to produce new results, is for us to choose a new context in which to think, talk, and behave. For example, your willingness to be open and honest with me sets a different context in how we can relate. Your choice creates a state or condition in which it is easier for me to be more open and honest with you and others. I may take advantage of your honesty, and try to use it against you, but if you choose not to be a victim of my action you can use the so-called negative part of the interaction (my abuse of your honesty) both as a mirror to reflect some learning for you, and as an opportunity to reframe a choice about how you will respond to my action.

We will begin to get different responses in our actions and results, whether the issues are personal or global, as more and more of us change the context (the victim or resource perception/belief pattern) in which these events, problems and conflicts occur. As we will explore in Part III, our ability to think and talk together about new ways to solve the mammoth problems before us is facilitated by first designing and embracing a new container for our beliefs about these issues and our role in solving them. If we continue to try to solve problems from the same negative assumptions about ourselves and the world, our dialogue will be shallow and filled with the dark colors of fear and despair.

But if we enter into a new way of sharing our lives together, new ways of acting will begin to emerge among us. What is deeply needed in our robotlike lives, are the sudden "aha's," the insights, the intuitions and the epiphanies that lead us out of the Machine labyrinth.

Making the choice to change is the genesis of a holy mechanic. The holy mechanic is one who is choosing to live as a resource agent. These choice-making people are already among us, and they are showing us how to rebuild our imaginations so that the novel, unexpected and epiphanal experiences can be realized in our lives and our communities. From within the Machine itself, the holy mechanics are the ones who change and transform it. The openness to change begins the process of creating new space inside our minds so that we can become aware of the unfamiliar and the un-thought. A holy mechanic is nothing more than a rebuilder of her or his own mind. A holy mechanic sees herself, himself, and the world through a different window of perception than those of us who have been conditioned to serve the Machine.

The Epiphanal Community

W hen two or more holy mechanics get together, insights can merge and expand beyond their original conception. When several individuals begin to coalesce around a deeply felt insight an "epiphanal community" emerges. An epiphany is the appearing or manifesting of something that hasn't existed before. Often an epiphany is a sudden recognition, a moment in which the light comes on! An epiphanal community is a group of individuals who have a common insight to manifest or bring into reality; who desire to explore a problem; or, who want to explore a particular solution, or creative activity. Epiphanal communities do not become organizations or institutions. They are more like ad hoc groupings. Through an epiphanal experience a number of individuals are bonded together for a period of time to manifest a particular purpose. When the purpose has appeared and flowered, the structure disappears and the individuals join with new groups to manifest other creative activity.

The idea of epiphanal community first occurred to me in 1980. A group of 12 people were meeting weekly to listen together in silence for inward guidance as to how to respond creatively to world conditions. Someone got the idea in a listening session to bring a larger group of interested people together for a weekend in order to listen together. The group got excited about the possibilities and the creativity that could emerge from such a gathering. Patt and I knew some of the people in the group and we were invited to participate in planning the event.

The idea that emerged and developed in our cooperative planning sessions followed a listening format. We would raise the issues and concerns before us, summarize and state each one clearly, and then sit in a companionable silence in order to listen to our intuition for answers to these questions. It was amazing how similar ideas developed between people as we sat in the silence. From this intuitive silence the sudden "aha's" would synthesize various ideas that seemed, at first, very divergent. The excitement and lightheartedness that emerged from being with a group of people, as ideas naturally and spontaneously unfolded, was an inspiring experience for Patt and me.

The weekend event occurred in the summer of 1980 with 80 people invited by word of mouth to come to a conference center on the California coast for a weekend. There was a general structure to the event, but the primary focus was on the group listening together.

For four years we held this summer gathering, which we called "Confluence in the '80s." The idea of "confluence" was that many streams of events, experiences and people were coming together in the early 1980s. The wealth of ideas and inspiration that came from these four gatherings were a tangible measure of our expanding imagination and our openness in being together.

Ideas flowered into action, commitment and results. For example, one of the first citizen diplomacy groups to the Soviet Union emerged from the first session. Sharon Tennison, the founder, continues to connect people of the former Soviet Union and our country in a variety of ways. A group of women came together from these sessions and launched an inventive conflict-resolution team that continues to work with a variety of organizations. Futurist Willis Harman, as a participant, was later inspired with others to start an organization called the

World Business Academy that challenges the business community in a unique way. Harman urges business leaders to a different level of responsibility when he says, "Business has become in the last century the most powerful institution on the planet. The dominant institution in any society needs to take responsibility for the whole. Every decision that is made, every action taken has to be viewed in the light of, in the context of that kind of responsibility."

These and many other people gained inspiration at these four yearly gatherings as we listened, shared, and created structures to manifest new expressions of realities that might thoughtfully confront the human-robot culture. What is notable is that Patt and I, as well as others, didn't attend all the Confluence gathering over the four years. We felt we had received what we needed in the first two years and went about working out our inspirations. New people came in to participate, and finally after the fourth year everyone knew that the original "aha" had flowered, fulfilled its purpose, and was no longer needed. The yearly weekend structure disappeared, having completed the cycle of energy for those who had received from it.

Epiphanies occur when the sacred comes through our imagination. The inspiration of our imagination connects with the inspiration of the imagination of others. The blocked, depressed states that we find ourselves in, particularly within the Machine's environment, are unlocked by the mutual "aha's" from others. This sudden recognition of what to do releases energy and creativity, and enhances a sense of partnership with others. An epiphanal community may start with only two individuals who feel the connection to a mutual imagination that inspires them. As the vitality and pragmatic expression of their inspiration grows more, people who are ready for an "aha" in their own lives respond and are attracted to the community. People like to play and create with each other. An epiphany is the result of that playing together.

The Breath of Inspiration

An epiphany is an expressive and enacted inspiration. The meaning of the word "inspiration" gives us the clue about its unusual role in our lives. The root meaning of the word "inspiration" is from the Latin, *spirare,* to breathe. To inspire is to breathe into, to stimulate, to motivate. Inspiration has to do with the breathing process, and as such has to do with what gives life and sustains vitality and health in us.

The breath is fundamental to religious and spiritual traditions of both the East and West. In Buddhism there is a basic meditative practice in which one simply watches the breath go in and out of the nostrils. One meditates on the connective point between the inner and outer world as one breathes. Central to this practice is the view that if one watches the breath long enough in a state of quiet and peace, something transformative will happen to the mind that will create clarity. This clarity opens and expands awareness so as to integrate daily experience into a richer and more complete understanding of the events and situations that make up the tapestry of our lives.

In our Western spiritual tradition we have the concept of the Holy Spirit. The concept comes from the Greek word, *pneuma,* which means air, wind, breath. The Holy Spirit is seen in our Christian tradition as the voice, the guide, the comforter for God the Creator. That which comes from God into us is a breathing process. The Holy Spirit inspires. We are breathed upon by the Creator through the agency of Spirit to ignite a power and aliveness in our lives. When Jesus breathed (*rhua*) the Holy Spirit upon the early Christians, it is reported that fire appeared over their heads. This could be interpreted to mean that the ancient knowledge of spiritual, psychic energy (that also runs through each of us) was opened and that unusual powers and knowledge in the otherworld of the sacred moved through these first-century men and women.

Whatever our individual metaphysics, to be breathed upon from the sacred world allows us to breathe out this same power; in so doing we make sacred again the world we live in. Epiphanies are sacred moments of inspiration where the spiritual otherworld and our physical world meet and interweave with sacred energy.

Inspiring Epiphanies

Each of us, in this growing tension and breakdown within the Machine, needs to inspire epiphanies. The question we often face is what can one person do? Buckminster Fuller, the inventor and systems genius, was a person who inspired epiphanies and addressed this question. After being financially broke and broken in spirit because of his apparent personal and professional failures, his question to himself was, "What can one individual do, given the power and control of giant companies, governments and military systems?" After formulating this question for himself he did an unusual thing. He didn't speak a word for three years. He had a wife and child, but he chose not to work. He intuitively knew that if he failed to remain silent and find that unique gift he had to give to the world, he could not live. His simple answer to his question after three years of being silent and listening to himself, was that one person can choose to live and think differently and "take initiatives without anybody's permission." Bucky's 50-year experiment to think and live differently, continually led him to find solutions that connected all systems together.

Early on in his explorations he discovered the laws, principles, and practical inventions that could join people together on what he called, "Spaceship Earth." The fruit of this one man's answer to his own question reveals the tremendous influence of such a common and simple inspiration to choose to live and think differently from the Machine. Because we have been trained in the Machine's culture, our possessiveness often gets in the way of the evolution of an idea, project, or invention. Bucky Fuller had a practical perspective on his epiphanies. He said that whenever someone suggested a refinement on a theory or invention of his, it was time for him to move on to something else. Bucky gave away his inspirations, his epiphanies to others, so that more would come to him. This notion of letting go and giving away our inspirations is basic to receiving more sudden "aha's."

An epiphanal community of two or more people expands the imagination of the culture around them. The more organic, less structured the community is, the more powerful the pace of change. A group of people who are inspired from an imagination that has been illuminated by Nature's presence, and has contact with the Voice of the Sacred within each of them, generates a great deal of power to move through large, rigid organizational structures.

Holy mechanics are arising throughout these structures. These are the people who are experimenting with new insights and "aha's" in practical ways. Within large organizations and small groups I have experimented with new ways to encourage people to let their inspirations blossom into epiphanies. One experiment has been with creating what I call "bandit organizations" within bureaucratic corporate structures. A second technique, one we'll explore later, is the "aha" conversation for people in small groups.

Bandit Organizations

In the literature and folklore of the world, the Robin Hood myth is a story that follows the tradition of the rogue-bandit. The Robin Hood-rogue-bandit gang is generally a group of individuals that lives outside the norms of society and traditionally robs the rich to give to the poor. These individuals have a higher cause and purpose that distinguishes them from ordinary robbers and thieves who rob for their own gain without concern for the welfare of others. The rogue-bandits believe that those in authority are abusing their power so they undertake their hit-and-run adventures for two primary reasons: to bring about change and to champion the common folk they believe they serve. The code of the rogue-bandits is not to kill, but rather to be creative in their choice of targets, and yet, to be defensive and cautious with their weapons. Bandit groups are focused on results, on pragmatically changing conditions and being clear in their basic purpose.

I use the Robin Hood story as an analogy for suggesting how I've seen epiphanal communities confront some of the negative and demeaning conditions most of us have experienced in modern organizations. Robin Hood, bandit-style organizations can emerge epiphanally when the structure and dynamics of large companies and systems are unresponsive and slow to change, facing questions of survival. Bandit organizations follow the pattern of an epiphany. They can emerge, blossom, and flower for a period of time, and then die back and seed the larger organization with the fruits of their ad hoc creation.

Bandit organizations tend to arise as coping strategies within Machine corporations. They serve as an infiltration process to break down old hierarchical structures. Generally this strategy is most effective when the organization is in trouble or in a survival mode. The willingness of senior management to "try something that will work" creates a receptivity that normally is not present when the organization is doing well. The energy for a bandit organization occurs when one or more individuals shift from roles of benign robots (victims) to roles as holy mechanics (resources).

In my own experience the level and size in which the bandit organization can work is varied. A general manager, a division director or even a department manager has used this bandit idea to create an epiphanal community nested within a larger organizational structure. Like rogue-bandits who leave the dominant culture and survive on the fringe, individuals who choose to create a bandit organization within an existing structure must be committed personally to radical change. The most difficult structural change that occurs is the need for managers to let go and give up their traditional power role.

Although there are leaders in the bandit group, their role and function is different than in a hierarchical structure. New norms emerge, and a new way of managing, or providing leadership, also tends to emerge.

Fundamentally, bandit organizations are pragmatic in style. They have a clear purpose that is sharply defined, and they can be started by anyone from the company president on down. One chief executive officer (CEO) I worked with ran a subsidiary company in which he had been forced to reduce his work force from 200 to 25, and to eliminate all products but one. With nothing to lose except his job, he had the idea to organize the remaining 25 people differently. This company was deeply imbedded in a larger seven company system and he had to sell senior management and the board of directors on doing some different things. In a series of meetings with his people, they decided to throw out the old structure and together agreed to "make up a new structure as they went along."

As I followed the development and flowering of this organizational epiphany I observed a number of behaviors:

1. The first thing I noticed about this bandit group was that they were constantly communicating as if "sitting around the campfire everyday" in order to solve problems and inspire each other. I was reminded of the image of the pot-bellied wood stove in the general store where townsfolk would gather to ruminate, argue, and problem-solve. They had an open area in the center of the office where there were tables and chairs and available hot drinks. Often, at the end of the day, the whole company gathered to talk out issues or share problems or successes.

2. The bandit group focused on results by constantly changing the process for how they achieved those results. Members lived day by day in a state of dynamic tension that urged the question, "How can we do this creatively and differently?" This one question seemed to bring to the surface many "aha's" because it challenged, motivated and helped people to be supportive of each other's ideas, notions, and insights.

3. People in the band loaded up their own jobs with more responsibility and accountability than was in their job description. The more accountability they accepted the better job they did. The emphasis on doing good work that is self-satisfying was basic to the bandit organization.

4. People encouraged each other to take personal risks and court mistakes. Robin Hood and his band were opportunistic. They did not sit around camp all day dreaming about brave deeds; they were out doing them, even when their choice of adventures sometimes got them into hot water with the Sheriff of Nottingham and his men.

5. Learning, problem-solving and insight about what the work was teaching them personally was discussed by the group as a fundamental purpose and by-product of why they were working.

6. Conflict was viewed as opportunity for discovery. Bandit organizations seem to recognize that if conflicting issues are swept under the carpet, the band's motivation, agreement and commitment to its purpose and to its mission will decline sharply. There were some long after-hour sessions to work out interpersonal problems between people in the bandit group. This, in turn, would free up more creative problem-solving energy. There seemed to be a direct correlation between the capability of the group to work interpersonal issues and their ability to both individually and collectively work effectively at their tasks.

7. In the bandit organization, work-related training was not perceived as an event to merely attend, but as an opportunity to improve the capability of the band in achieving both individual and collective purposes. Most training that emerged came from each other on an ad hoc demand or immediate need basis.

8. Bandit leaders/mangers, when they were at their best, were flexible to the demands of changing situations, people, and events in the workplace. When power trips were exercised by a leader/manager over an individual member of the group, the energy of the band died. The energy was recovered when

someone in the group recognized the power issue for what it clearly was and challenged the manager. A climate that encouraged a constant development of individual esteem and self-worth is what permitted the bandit group to continue functioning effectively. The primary focus for a leader was to learn how to adapt to the changing needs of people and the dynamic changes of the environment. The image and role that the leader seemed to play was that of a seesaw, attempting to balance between the relational needs of the employees and the environmental demands of the business. The old patterns of business or tasks being more important than the people seemed to sabotage the band's level of trust and its level of productive and creative problem-solving.

9. In giving people more responsibility, bandit managers negotiated the balance between the technical requirements of the job and the individual's competence with the added dimension of including into the discussion the individual's needs and desires.

10. Openness, honesty, and trust created an intimacy between the manager and his or her employees that would shift the bandit organization from an adversarial position between employees and management to one of a cooperative community. In the epiphanal community that emerged, differences of opinion, strategies and decision-making could be worked out with respect and integrity.

11. A fundamental emerging norm that permitted the bandit organization to go through the epiphanal cycle was the total lack of secret information between management and employees. Everyone in the band had access to the current month's financial figures, every member knew what negotiations were going on, and the like. No matter what the person's role, just as with Robin Hood and his gang, there was a sense of ownership and membership in the bandit organization.

These are among the positive elements that I've identified in a successful bandit organization. My observation is that organizations that attempted bandit-style structures failed because the leader was personally not ready for the magnitude of change, or to take a significant professional risk to grow beyond his or her learned leadership and management style. The epiphanal community is doomed once the leader cuts off the free flow of creative energy and contributions of every member in the band and moves back into a dominating role. I was fortunate to be around a few managers in companies who were open to these new possibilities and who were willing to share their positional power and take a chance. Each situation was not without its problems or setbacks, of course, but there was a magical flow of creative energy that allowed the epiphany to increase the faith and confidence of the participants in themselves. The tragedy, unfortunately, is that these kinds of Robin Hood bandit type structures usually don't last long in the Machine's environment. The old hierarchical norms are often too strongly entrenched — and the campfire is soon extinguished.

My role as a consultant to a number of bandit-style organizations has been to provide feedback and help the band work through its own energy blocks so that the natural inspiration and creativity could flow. A further role was to coach the leader of the band on ways to meet the power demands that the larger organization imposed on the bandit team.

Since so many of us work in Machine organizations, I wanted to offer some positive images of epiphanies actually working in difficult environments. Individuals who participated in these bandit organizations experienced some of the holy mechanic in themselves (even though the Machine was trying to confine and stop them). After watching epiphanal type of communities emerge in the bandit organization, I observed members begin to rebuild their own courage and ethical commitment in order to make the decision to leave the unhealthy Machine environment.

"Aha" Conversations

Peter Senge in his book, *The Fifth Discipline: The Art & Practice of the Learning Organization,* inspired me with the work that physicist David Bohm has done with the idea of dialogue. Bohm's concept and mode of practicing dialogue is to create an environment in which a group "becomes open to the flow of a larger intelligence." This notion piqued my interest because it matched a similar experience I had with a group when an epiphany began to grow and flower among us. Senge's discussion of Bohm's work with dialogue is instructive for understanding the dynamics of epiphanies and creating environments that encourage more of them to happen.

Bohm first makes an important clarification between *discussion* and *dialogue.* Discussion has as its purpose the narrowing down of conversation to a decision, a judgment, some action or even a win position. "Percussion" and "concussion" come from the same Latin root as "discussion." There is therefore, in discussion, a give and take and a knocking away of the elements that don't fit the bias that people may be holding until a position or result is arrived at. This process, by its nature, is a convergent mode of thinking. Discussion tends to constrict and tighten conversation. Therefore, it also tends to limit the dynamics of the thinking so that energy is then not free to spread out and be inclusive of differences and anomalies.

Dialogue comes from the Greek, *dialogos: dia* is through, *logos* is meaning or word. Thinking of dialogue as "through meaning," Bohm gives the word "dialogue" the image of a stream passing through a river bank. *Dialogue then, is meaning passing through a group of people.* Dialogue in this sense suggests that meaning doesn't reside in one or more persons individually. Rather, meaning is part of the whole group. It is more than any one single event or person. Meaning will grow and expand as the riverbed that contains the meaning expands. As the individuals who are, collectively, the container of the dialogue open themselves more to wider and deeper interchange with each other, conversational meaning grows. Within, and because of the synergy of the conversation, or dialogue, individual group members will develop understanding and insights that they would never get by thinking alone. Bohm's conclusions express exactly the "aha" experience of an epiphany. "A new kind of mind begins to come into being which is based on the development of a common meaning. . . . People are no longer primarily in opposition, nor can they said to be interacting, rather they are participating in this pool of common meaning, which is capable of constant development and change."

When I have experienced this type of dialogue in a group, the feeling is like being in a pool of water. We are somehow all connected through the medium of shared insights and feelings. What someone starts another finishes. What someone describes and thinks is unimportant to them actually widens awareness for the group. Although the attention, concentration, and intensity within the group is high, when one is in this common pool of meaning there is no frantic rush for members to push out individual thoughts. There is rather a patient soaking in the new awareness or ideas, and there may be long silences in a group of 10 or 15 as everyone contemplates the flow and rhythm of the conversation. This kind of dialogue is quite different from the high intensity interaction of a brainstorming session.

A major objective of the dialogue is to challenge each other in the spirit of positive inquiry in order to help us actually identify our underlying assumptions. Assumptions are the filters for our thoughts. They frame the windows by which we see the world around us. Assumptions and beliefs cause us to filter out both positive and negative information we hold on a subject or issue. A simple illustration: I am a Republican and you are a Democrat. Given our different political positions, it is easy for me to assume that you hold some views different from mine. As you speak, I project my assumptions onto your notions, opinions and ideas. When you talk about welfare programs, for example, I assume that you, as a Democrat, are in favor of them. Even though in your conversation you may be questioning their value, I may not hear this notion and filter it out because I assume you are in favor of welfare programs. Let's say, however, that I would first ask you what your assumptions are about welfare. Then, I tell you what my assumptions are about this subject. If we can then agree that we won't defend either position, but examine other possibilities, we now are in a much larger pool of possible meaning than either set of assumptions permits us to hold. This expansion outside of our strongly held assumptions opens the door for the epiphanal "aha" to happen.

The basic container for establishing a pool of shared meaning among people who want to dialogue has some simple requirements. Peter Senge suggests the following:

1. Suspend assumptions. Consciously talk about the beliefs, theories, ideas that individuals and the group have about the topic. Continue to acknowledge and refer to these assumptions as the group continues to dialogue.

2. Regard everyone in the conversation as a colleague, no matter how strongly held the differences of opinion, status, or position. Make any of these differences part of the conversation. A mutual exploring of ideas, a willingness to be vulnerable and courageous risk-taking is needed for individuals to expand the pool of meaning and create deeper insight and clarity.

3. Develop a spirit of inquiry. Encourage each other to explore the thinking behind each other's views. Ask each other questions such as, "What leads you to say or believe this?" "What makes you ask about this?"

4. Have an agreed upon facilitator whose role is to "hold the container" of the dialogue. Different from Senge's idea, I suggest that the facilitator not be a participant in the content of the dialogue. The facilitator needs to use his or her creative "containing" energy to watch for and acknowledge unspoken assumptions that may be blocking the widening of the group dialogue. The facilitator also encourages and manages participation when needed. And the facilitator can measure how deep the dialogue has gotten by commenting from time to time in a summary fashion.

5. I have added one more step in the dialogue process, that of an inner-listening process. From time to time either the facilitator or a group member can suggest that we temporarily suspend the dialogue and have a Quakerlike silence. The person making the suggestion states the present condition of the conversation as a question or a problem to solve ("what do we . . . how do we" statements) and then asks the group to intuitively listen for the inner voice, the body sensation or the internal image that arises in them around the query. After a period of silence, everyone has a chance to state, if they wish to, what they received. After each person has commented, the conversation continues. I have found that this added step both deepens and widens the conversation into new territory each time it is included in the process. It also begins to sensitize us to the subtleties of our inner knowing, and gives us some comparison and validation as we hear others respond from the collective silence.

What moves Bohm's dialogue more fully into the "aha" of the epiphany is that the dialogue process widens our view and lets the "aha" emerge as a shared experience. But for the epiphany to grow, flower and bear fruit, it needs focused action. It is at this point that the value of *discussion* comes back into play. The dialogue has provided the wide angle, divergent view, and created the conversation of possibilities. Discussion, as a narrowing process, now urges us to consider and make choices from all these possibilities. Within a larger context we can also have "aha" experiences as we begin to bring the possibilities into both pragmatic form and definite action toward some result or end. Even more helpful now in the discussion phase of the "aha" conversation, is the inner-asking process. This is a powerful consensus-building step that asks each member to go into the inner quiet and listen for the steps to be taken, listen for the answer to a problem, or listen for a choice to embrace. There is much power, enthusiasm, and deepening connection with each other as the group continues to explore the larger group mind for the practical decision-making and consensus that creating together requires.

When the "aha" conversation of possibilities and action is used in the context of bandit organizations or with family and friends, some remarkable shifts occur in how individuals choose to operate within the Machine's structure. My observation is that when a group uses conversations of possibilities combined with action steps the members are more confident in themselves to act assertively. They are also more trusting of each other to act on behalf of the group's best interests. They are less antagonistic of the leadership, and they have fewer assumptions about secrets and conspiracies. Members also experience deep ownership and participation in decisions, and offer little resistance and hesitancy to change direction when the group dialogues, listens, and decides together.

Epiphanal Action

The epiphany acts as a resonator to inspire others to spontaneous activity within any system or structure. Epiphanies act like acupuncture points on the body of the planet. One epiphanal action that opens the flow of energy that has been blocked in one place, helps to return health and vitality to other places on the planet as a result of the energy release. Like a spider web, an epiphany in one place reverberates through the whole web of connections. Buckminster Fuller's challenge to us is that we have no alternative but to let inspiration flow through us at this time in our evolution. He says, "Clearly, we are here to use our minds, to be information gatherers in the local universe. . . . Either you're going to go along with your mind and the truth, or you're going to yield to fear and custom and conditioned reflexes."

Fuller points here to both the human robot and the holy mechanic. If we are to be the holy mechanic we must let our minds and the truth of the universe move through us. Then we automatically become problem-solvers. The interesting point, however, is that we don't solve the problem. When we are in the mindset of the holy mechanic, the problem gets solved through us. Our challenge is to surrender to the "aha's" and, yet to be fully cognizant, critical and impassioned by the conditions around us.

The Loving Resistance Fighter

One major condition we need to seriously dialogue about as a people is the assumption that technology will in the end save us. To open a broad-based cultural dialogue about the value of technology and its proper role in our life is a significant and important conversation to have at this time. We who live in this Machine must challenge both the technological assumption that its discoveries and inventions are always good for us, as well as pursue an on-going discussion that questions whether we should continue to use many of our current technologies or not. Somehow we assume that if we have the technology we *must* use it. Our task is to have a public dialogue that challenges the technology of the Machine while not resisting the potential creativity within it. The burden is on the side of the technologist to prove to society that a particular technology provides added value to our lives and culture. And it should always be our right as a people to say "No!" and not use a technology.

Neil Postman, the author of *Technopoly: The Surrender of Culture to Technology*, gives a brilliant critique of how technology has changed our culture. He, like Jerry Mander, describes the tyranny of those in control of technologies to impose them upon us without our permission. He argues convincingly that new technologies change everything, and that they mount total war on old ones. For example, he says human verbal interaction will be gone in the schooling process within 50 years because of computers and TV. Is it in the best interest of the members of our society to limit the interaction and human communication in learning by substituting machines to teach our children? This notion of substituting technology for teaching cultural structure is what Postman calls technopoly. Technopoly "is a system in which technology of every kind is cheerfully granted sovereignty over social institutions and national life, and becomes self-justifying, self-perpetuating, and omnipresent." Technopoly is the handmaiden of the Machine. It is the fantasy that keeps the Machine ever growing, and which, in its frenzy and greed, will disregard the cry from the environment, from the people and from all creatures of nature to stop, to reconsider or to consider other alternatives.

Postman, after taking us through the affects of technopoly on such things as family, religion, the arts, history, politics and privacy, concludes with some creative ideas about what we can personally do. He says for us to be "loving resistance fighters." By this he means, "A resistance fighter understands that technology must never be accepted as part of the natural order of things, that every technology — from an IQ test to an automobile to a television set to a computer — is a product of a particular economic and political context and carries with it a program, an agenda, and a philosophy that may or may not be life-enhancing and that therefore require scrutiny, criticism, and control. In short, a technological resistance fighter maintains an epistemological and psychic distance from any technology, so that it always appears somewhat strange, never inevitable, never natural." Clearly, this illustrates what the Australian aboriginal has learned from the Dreamtime about being cautious of any man-made tool or system that changes the land. And it illustrates what modern environmental theorists describe as introducing elements that upset the balance of any ecosystem.

To awaken from the Machine trance is to question authority. This awakening urges us to continue to be cautious, skeptical, and inquisitive. It urges us to change our minds and alter our perceptions of how we see the world around us. It urges us to challenge each other's assumptions and beliefs in the way we conduct our lives, raise our children and interact at our work. It urges us to be loving resistance fighters against the

Machine wherever we are. The response to one of Buckminster Fuller's questions to himself offers one of the loving resistant fighter's mantras. He asked, "What can one individual do, given the power and control of giant companies, governments and military systems?" His response: *"Take initiatives without anybody's permission."* And I would add, let these initiatives come from that ancient Voice that we all have access to deep within us.

What To Do as the Machine Breaks Down

*T*he world's clock is about to strike the hour of the Machine's judgment. To be participants, resource agents and not victims to the growing destructiveness of planet Earth, we must choose to awaken and become holy mechanics to ourselves and to each other. To awaken means to shift in awareness and to change fundamentally within ourselves.

My call is for each of us to be willing to turn our psychic backs on this Machine's corporation-economy and its culture. By this I am not suggesting that we totally stop watching TV or stop consuming meaningless goods (although that will probably be the end result). Rather, I believe we must change our view of ourselves, and alter our relationship to the earth and to each other. This means changing our minds, our perceptions, and our vision of what life is. It means living and behaving differently, making different choices, spending our time in different ways. And it means looking at the world through a different window than the one we have looked through in the past. Our response to what is happening in the world need not be some fearful reaction or angry rejection, but rather a response that is hopeful and more honestly committed to change because some other imagination and sacred voice within calls us in a different way. As we feel this inner pull, this call toward some unnamable change, we must ground ourselves in the serious and realistic challenges we face in the world today.

How Possible Is the Breakdown?

The Futurist, Robert Gilman, in his article, "No Simple Answers," gives a sobering evaluation of the probable collapse of our future. The focus of his discussion is a computer model developed by three systems scientists and computer modelers: Donella Meadows, Dennis Meadows and Jørgen Randers. Their study, "The Limits to Growth," that appeared 20 years ago, was updated this last year in the book, *Beyond the Limits: Confronting Global Collapse, Envisioning a Sustainable Future.* Their model tracks non-renewable resources, industrial output per capita, food per capita, population and pollution from 1900 into the 21st century. The pattern of rise and fall of all five curves represent a cycle in which non-renewable resources are seen to be declining rapidly through the year 2000 to near exhaustion by the year 2100.

Using current worldwide patterns of these five variables, Gilman shows from the model how resources will become harder to extract in the next 50 years because of the drain on capital and the energy needed to translate them into products. The result is that the economy will no longer be able to provide agricultural, industrial, nor consumer goods and services. In Gilman's words, "The economy thus spirals down, pulling down agriculture, and health care with it, yet still gobbling up lots of non-renewable resources along the way. Death rates rise dramatically through hunger and disease, desperate humans ravage what is left of the world's ecosystems and the foreseeable future is uniformly bleak." This, indeed, is not a pretty picture.

Gilman then tests the model with different scenarios by changing the variables in the model. He concludes with the same result. The only difference is that the collapse gets delayed, at most, by 20 or 30 years. He points out, however, that the resulting outcomes are understated as to dire consequences, because the model doesn't take into account war, violence, or the breakdown of society as we begin to move into both the severe depletion of resources and the rise of population. Given this apocalyptic portrait of our future what does Gilman propose? "What can we do to avoid such a fate? We have to change our behavior." Gilman then takes each of the five variables in the model and makes some radical suggestions for each concerning how he believes we will need to "behave" in order to have any meaningful future. Among the most radical of these new behaviors is for individuals choosing not to have children, to stop the exploding population, limiting the world's average industrial output per capita to a maximum of about 80 percent of current Western standards, stopping our use of non-renewable resources like oil, and stopping the damage of land by discontinuing use of chemical and agribusiness methods.

Gilman and other notable thinkers such as Ivan Illich, Jacques Ellul and Lewis Mumford have long argued that a Machine culture, one based on an ever-expanding technological mania that uses up non-renewable resources, becomes extremely dangerous to all species on the planet, including itself. The Machine has a built-in self-destruct mechanism. Like E.M. Forster's short story, "The Machine Stops," the nature of the technological Machine is the tendency to destroy both itself and its human participants. "To change our behavior" as Gilman urges is our necessary task as the Machine faces increasing breakdown.

But to know what behavior to change we must first acknowledge the magnitude of the present situation. To awaken our souls, we must know what has happened while we have slept, robotlike, inside the Machine.

The State of the World

Every year the World Watch Institute issues a report called, "State of the World." The 1992 report covers in depth such topics as biological diversity, nuclear waste, women's reproductive health, shaping cities, livestock economics, jobs in industrial countries, and environmental governance. The 1992 report represented a kind of a watershed of whether any real progress toward a sustainable society was being made. On the positive side, institute president Lester Brown said that the 1992 report was now being published in 27 languages and that sustainable ideas were spreading around the world. Another positive was the willingness of the world community to talk about and propose some solutions to our global dilemma. One of the most significant events in 1992, he believed, was the United Nations Conference on Environment and Development in Rio de Janeiro. Ten thousand official delegates attended the conference, including numerous heads of state, and 20,000 concerned citizens participated in a parallel Global Forum. The primary question confronted was what direction should the nations of the world would take environmentally as the entire global village goes through convulsive changes — there was much talk but little action. Hopefully, however, we can look back on the Rio conference as the turning point for world governance on environmental and social issues.

Although concepts and talk are hopeful, there is a negative side to the 1990s scenario: *Things are getting worse.* In Brown's words, ". . . overall, global environmental trends are not reassuring. The health of the planet has deteriorated dangerously during the 20 years since Stockholm" (the last U.N. meeting on the environment). From this 251-page report here is a sampling of Brown's and other World Watcher concerns.

First . . . a few of the environmental trends:
- Some 140 plant and animal species are condemned to extinction *each day*. This totals some 51,100 a year.

- Two-thirds of the world's 150 primate species are at the edge of extinction. Some 100 species may die in the next few years — everything from rhinos to dolphins.
- Heat-trapping carbon dioxide (from cars and coal burning) is 26 percent higher than 100 years ago, and is climbing.
- All forests around the world are being destroyed at a rate of 17 million hectares a year. One hectare equals a little more than one acre. This total equals an area the size of the state of Washington. Tropical forests are now half their original size and increasing their loss annually.
- Current world population is 5.4 billion. Population will double to 11 billion sometime in the next century. World population is growing by 92 million (the population of Mexico) yearly, and by 88 million in developing countries.
- There are 1.2 billion people in the world who have no access to safe drinking water.
- Carbon dioxide reached 354 parts per million in 1990, and global average temperatures were the highest of the past century. There are 540 million automobiles on the world's roads. In Bangkok one million residents were treated for respiratory problems in 1990 due to carbon dioxide from automobiles.
- We now use one-quarter of all plant life for food. By the time the population doubles during the next century there will be no plant life available for wild animals.

Second . . . economic and societal trends:
- One in three children worldwide are undernourished.

- One billion adults cannot read or write; 100 million children are not in school.
- Over 85 percent of the world's income goes to 23 percent of the people, mainly in the white Western countries. One billion people survive on less than $1 per day. There are 202 billionaires and some three million millionaires worldwide.
- Currently 413 commercial nuclear reactors produce 5 percent of the worlds energy and have now created some 84,000 tons of nuclear waste. Within eight years we will have 190,000 tons of nuclear waste, and by the middle of next century 450,000 tons of irradiated fuel waste. This radioactive material is threatening to human, plant, and animal life and remains lethal for 240,000 to 710,000 years. A single deep geological burial site for 96,000 tons of this waste today costs $36 billion to build. No dump site will be ready until the year 2020. Seventeen countries are building these sites. Due to earthquakes and volcanic eruptions these nuclear waste sites will be a constant toxic threat to humankind.
- $170 billion were spent in Third World countries for military hardware. Incomes in 40 Third World countries fell this past year as much as 29 percent, and will continue to fall yearly. Of the 4.7 billion people increase that will be added to the world by 2050, 90 percent will be in the Third World.
- Some 630 million hungry people are unable to buy food. World grain production has dropped since 1984. Animals and birds grown for meat-eating production is at 15 billion a year. The rich countries produce 61

percent of the world's meat. The United States is the number one meat eating country in the world at 112 kilograms per person. India is the lowest meat eating country at 2 kilograms per person — 38 percent of the world's grain production feeds these animals — 70 percent of grain in the United States is grown to feed animals for meat consumption. The destruction of rainforests throughout the world is primarily for the purpose of increasing grain production and to pasture animals for meat production. Overgrazing is forcing more and more forest destruction in order to provide new pasture land. The overgrazing of meat-producing animals has turned to desert 73 percent of the world's dry range land. In the United States alone, 50 percent of range land is severely degraded.

- Half of the world's 2.6 billion women are now between 15 to 49 year of age. In this age group, 20-45 percent of all deaths are due to pregnancy-related causes in developing countries, compared to only one percent in the developed countries. Worldwide, 250 million infections are sexually transmitted to women each year. Over 2.4 million Africans have the AIDS virus. The conservative estimate is that 8 million people worldwide have AIDS with 3 million being women of childbearing age. It is estimated that more than 600,000 women will contract AIDS in 1992.
- Five manufacturing industries in the United States — metals, paper, oil refining, chemicals, as well as stone, clay, and glass — use 21 percent of the energy consumed in the U.S.

economy, and provide only 3 percent of the jobs. They are the biggest polluters accounting for 80-85 percent of toxic releases from the manufacturing sector.

Even with this small sampling of environmental, economic, and social conditions, the numbers and issues are overwhelming. In fairness to the report, there were some bright spots such as the reduction of oil usage in the developing countries along with an interest in exploring alternative energy sources. This was offset, however, with the fact that oil consumption is actually increasing in Third World countries. Lester Brown, in the concluding chapter of the report, raises the question of whether the changes needed to meet this wide range of issues can come at a worldwide level. For the change to come, he argues, it must be basic and fundamental. "Muddling through will not work. Either we turn things around quickly or the self-reinforcing internal dynamic of the deterioration-and-decline scenario will take over. The policy decisions we make in the years immediately ahead will determine whether our children live in a world of development or decline. There is no precedent for the change in prospect."

To build a sustainable future, he argues, will mean changing the global economic Machine, solving population increases, as well as changing values, behaviors and lifestyles. "This," he says, "adds up to a revolution." This environmental revolution, however, cannot take 10,000 years to occur like the agricultural revolution, or the Industrial Revolution that took 200 years. For civilization to survive, the environmental revolution has only a few decades in which to happen. As Brown reviews the possibilities he looks long and hard at corporations and businesses. Although pointing out some of the environmental efforts companies have already made, he notes that these efforts are usually from younger and smaller firms, not the old-line Fortune 500 type industries who are continuing to operate in the old hierarchical patterns. To phase out fossil fuel, shift our food habits, alter our throw-away consumption mentality and shift to a sustainable economy is a change of enormous magnitude.

Yes, the obvious question emerges: "What can I do?" Individual actions like recycling, pressure on government and corporations, organized boycotts and the like is Brown's standard fare. But in the overwhelming magnitude of the changes that are needed, is there hope that we can make a difference beyond lifestyle changes? Brown frames this question in its starkest terms. "The issue is not our survival as a species, but rather the survival of civilization as we know it. Individually and collectively we have to decide whether we are prepared to make the efforts needed to reverse the trends . . . Unless *more of society mobilizes* [my emphasis] in support of the Environmental Revolution, it will not succeed."

From Fear to Hope

Because I am not a nihilist, I do affirm the concern that Lester Brown and the "State of the World" report gives to us about the staggering situation we indeed face in the world today. But the questions surface: Do we want the kind of Machine civilization that we've created? Or do we want to make some other choices? Will the conditions we've created force choices on us that we don't want to make? Brown and others who pose possible answers suggest that psychological internal solutions will be as important as practical concrete ones. This Environmental Revolution is, "in the most fundamental sense a social revolution: the product of changing values, of seeing ourselves again as a part of nature rather than apart from nature, of recognizing our dependence on the Earth's natural systems and resources and on the goods and services they provide." When one looks at the sample of alarming statistics and devastating trends from the "State of the World" report, the uncomfortable conclusion looms: Destructive conditions flow from the Machine in developed countries that have used the rest of the world as a resource colony. If we in Western countries can begin to find ways to stop the pillaging of Third World country resources, practical shifts can happen. Here, for example, is one epiphanal "aha" from a dialogue between Terence McKenna and a small workshop group at Esalen Institute.

Terence pointed out that one middle-class American child consumes natural resources equivalent to 200 children in developing countries. This comes in the form of baby foods, car seats, Nike shoes, clothing, toys, roller skates, Walkman radios, and so on. We point to Africa, India or China as the problem of over population, and that these countries are the cause for the population problem. But in terms of real impact on environmental problems, reducing the number of children in the United States to one child per family would have dramatic effect on world resource depletion. As strange as this idea sounds, middle-class women and men, who represent the top 5 percent in consumption of the majority of the world's resources, would be more easily convinced to make this population reduction compared to trying to convince farmers in India to change their cultural and survival pattern of having large families. Someone in the group pointed out that women in the United States would have direct control over this issue. Regardless of what the male-dominated power structure is doing about these issues, women could have a direct impact on world population by choosing to have only one child. If as few as 15 percent of middle-class women decided to have only one child, by 2020 there would be a dramatic reduction in resource consumption from the United States. The problem of large families in India may not be solved, but real resource reduction could be affected by actions here in the United States.

With others coming together and expanding on this "aha," an epiphanal community of action could begin to form that moves this idea from possibility to action. This idea, like many others we need to entertain, demands that we challenge in a spirit of mutual inquiry our fundamental assumptions and beliefs about current problems. If we will seriously engage in "aha" conversations, these simple ideas, that at first may sound heretical, will begin to be discussed and acted upon more and more among us.

At the Threshold of Changing State

Teilhard de Chardin, the Jesuit priest and paleontologist, argued that evolution moved forward in two streams. One was complexity; the other was consciousness. In evolution, complexity and consciousness move the developing pattern of a species to a critical threshold point where it radically changes and becomes something else. He called this threshold a change-of-state condition.

Change of state for any species, he said, was that point where the entire species faces an evolutionary jump toward a radical and unpredictable next step in its evolution. Either the entire species moves across the chasm and jumps together, or the species flames out and dies trying to change. The most critical condition for change-of-state to happen is that environmental conditions must be present that could actually cause the extinction of the entire species. The threat is not illusionary, it is real. What is also critical for this change is that the complexity of the organism and its surrounding environment must be able to interact so that it accelerates what de Chardin calls the consciousness of the species upward in the evolutionary process. This upward movement of the curve of consciousness toward what he calls the Omega Point is away from the downward pull of complexity and destruction. In his view, this movement inward toward consciousness, rather than toward the outer focus on complexity, is a race for survival. The complexity and pressure of extinction intensifies the emphasis on consciousness to spread through the species. As increased specialization and complexity begins to kill the organism, then consciousness, the soul, that is embedded in the complexity of matter begins to be released and externalized to move the species to its natural next step. The question we face for our time is whether the pressure of consciousness will be released widely enough in our human species before the complexity of the Machine takes us down.

If the Machine's culture is truly beginning to break down, perhaps our evolutionary step is really a returning to the archaic, to that which is called the primitive within us. Returning to this primitive (or original) part of ourselves would be a step into a knowledge and experience that has been hidden deep within us, a spiritual energy that has been waiting to be released at this time. The indigenous peoples of the planet may be the guardians, the holders and the releasers of this inward flow of connection to the consciousness of the species. To destroy the indigenous peoples with the Machine's all-consuming complexity would be to destroy the access to the potential knowledge that could awaken our awareness for radical change in behavior.

Messages from Planet Earth

A major physical impact on our living conditions in the near term may come through environmental and weather changes. Because of the ozone threat and other ecological triggers like droughts, floods and freezes, our food and living conditions will become an increasing concern. Volcanoes, earthquakes, hurricanes, and typhoons may prove to be such massive calamities that we will exhaust the resources or capability to deal with them. One or two more major volcanic eruptions that send ash into the upper atmosphere and change weather patterns may have disastrous effects on world food supplies. The volcanic eruption of Mount Penatuba in the Philippines in 1991 put the largest amount of ash into the atmosphere of any volcano this century. It has affected weather conditions and crop production around the globe. Scientists believe even larger volcanic eruptions may take place in the next few years.

Scientists who study the issues of global warming predict that by the year 2040 an increase of global temperature by one degree (which current studies point to as beginning to occur) will do serious damage both to our economy and environment. For example, the major bread-basket region of the United States, the plains states, would become a dust bowl. California, our major producer of fruits and vegetables, continues to have extreme water and drought problems; this poses a threat to supplies of these fresh foods. Scientists warn that the growing threat of global warming happen so rapidly that U.S. forests will be unable to adapt to the temperature change and will die. Forests in California, eastern Oregon, and Washington are now dying because of the extended six year drought. Even more immediate is the concern about the ozone layer depletion.

Startling evidence surfaced at the end of 1991 showing 40 percent ozone depletion, instead of the assumed 5 to 10 percent depletion of ozone worldwide. The ozone hole in the Antarctic is now as large as North America. It is an elliptical hole that covers nine billion square miles.

Although scientists are alarmed, our world governments engage in trivial political in-fighting setting up a long-term timetable to stop the production of ozone destroying chemicals rather than taking collective action to fully ban those chemicals now that they are destroying the planetary shield. It is difficult to predict the global and personal implications this ozone depletion will have on all of us. We know, however, that skin cancer and damage to plants and animals have already resulted from ozone depletion.

Since 1988 skin cancer has increased in Tasmania by 80 percent (the populated area that has been closest to the Antarctic ozone hole). In October of 1992, The Argentine weather service reported that the edge of the hole had shifted for the first time over a populated area, the island of Tierra del Fuego, off the southern tip of South America, between Argentina and Chile. About 50,000 people live on the Argentine side of the island. A major concern reported by the weather service was that the hole was 80 percent thinner than it usually is at this time of the year. The ozone filters ultraviolet rays, and without this filter these rays can cause cancer and eye diseases in humans and animals as well as cause damage to agricultural corps. Increasingly high levels of ultraviolet radiation due to ozone depletion will also destroy algae and microorganisms in the ocean that are critical to the overall world food chain.

The impact of the Machine culture on the natural environment may offer signs that the "spirits" of the world are becoming increasingly intolerant. Archaic cultures and native peoples understood natural cataclysmic events as communication from deep within the earth. They listened and responded by purifying themselves in sacred ceremonies and by making fundamental changes in their lives and in the use of the earth's resources. The challenge to ourselves and within our communities of families and friends is a willingness to listen, notice, and respond to the earth as it warns us of the probable collapse of the 500-year-old Machine culture.

Our stance, however, is not to cheer for the world to collapse. Rather, our position must be to actively recover that "holy" part of ourselves and be conscious mechanics fixing the negative effects of this machinelike world. The conscious-complexity curve that Teilhard de Chardin described is accelerating. The second law of thermodynamics states that with each increasing change in the complexity pattern, more energy is needed to make changes. The increasing complexity of the machine world is using up everything on the planet. As the complexity curve is forced downward from the continued resource depletion, the conscious curve, according to de Chardin, is forced upward. The Attractor outside of time, the Omega point, pulls consciousness from within us as intensely as machine complexity grows. The demand and commitment, however, from each of us will be intensified. Each of us will need to find deeper reserves of insight and a willingness to act differently in order to respond to the critical years ahead. Literally, we are being forced by the pressure of events to engage our collective consciousness to figure out creative and different ways to change, alter, and repair what we humans have done to this planet so that we can take our next step of evolution.

The "End of the World"

In Western tradition and history we've relegated the Otherworld to the Goddess or God, Holy One, Oversoul, Mystery, Creator or Great Spirit. We've given it many names. This Force, by whatever name, has been experienced as both inside and outside the movement of time and history. This Force, outside of time as we know it, is accelerating present events toward some type of conclusion. The Force that moves outside of time Terance McKenna calls the Hyper-Dimensional Object or Transcendental Beingness. It is this Hyper-Dimensional Object, McKenna suggests, that is generating an "archaic revival" of the plant-based, feminine-partnership model of living. This renewing force is creating a growing counterweight to the Machine society. Like an attractor beam at the end of time, this Transcendental Object is pulling us forward toward itself at an ever accelerating, faster pace. This Attractor is like a magnet at the end of a funnel pulling historical time toward it. McKenna argues that this theory accounts both for the "end of the world" beliefs that pervade human experience and our rapid decent as a species into an increasing complexity-consciousness struggle that Teilhard de Chardin theorized.

Archaic cultures like the Mayan, the Hopi, the Navajo, the Egyptian, the Vedic, the Australian aborigine, the Bantu of Africa, and many others have had sophisticated "clocks" that give a time sequence related to an eschatological, or end-time view. Our own Western religions of Judaism, Islam, and Christianity in particular, focus on an end-time scenario. Throughout the psychic history of our species there has been this pull toward an end point. And it has been interpreted in many ways. Some have held it as the Judgment Day where the good are rewarded and taken to another realm, as in Christianity and Islam. Others have viewed this end point as a cataclysm that will result in a golden age, as in Hindu philosophy. The Mayans saw it as the point when time ends. Many groups have set dates for when these end times would happen, such as when Jesus would return, or when California would fall into the Pacific. Most of us remain skeptical of these finite dates. The Mayans, however, seemed to be the most involved and the most accurate in predicting time-based events down to the day they were to occur.

When the codex of Mayan glyphs were finally understood, researchers were amazed at the sophisticated astronomical and mathematical system that the Mayans had created. Of great interest to our notion of end times is the point when the Mayan calendar ends. The Mayans set the end of history to be December 21, 2012.

Our fascination with a doomsday is rooted in a fundamental desire to have the unexpected, and the unpredictable happen to us. There is some kind of twisted suicidal feeling in us where we hope for disaster to upset the mundane of daily routine. However, beyond this unconscious urge we need to be careful not to misjudge the very real signals and "signs" of structural breakdown that are all around us. Current economic, social and political conditions in addition to the signals of nature itself give warnings that need to be attended to and seriously considered. To remain with minds closed, in a state of denial, and pretend that the Machine is healthy may cause us to miss the warnings and fail to listen to ourselves and to the deep inner voice of Gaia — our planet. Yet, in the remaining years of the 1990s, as we approach the year 2000, there will be opportunities to change the way we live, change how we work, and change how we can be more creative in our lives. The following two sections on "The Economy" and the section on "Don't Face Change Alone" gives an appraisal of these conditions and specific examples of how various groups are responding to this end time.

The Economy

Beyond the environmental breakdowns, due to our megatechnology, what are the probable, practical and near-term signals to this change-of-state condition that is approaching? With the inability of the technological Machine to function economically and effectively, its breakdown in the short term, will probably happen in several ways:

The first possibility is that there will be a breaking down of the Machine's corporation-economy itself. The so-called economic recession of the 1990s is a different animal than has been experienced before. Bulls and bears may give way to sacrificial lambs. The United States is the key player in the worldwide economic web. With our huge five-fold debt — in the government, the banks, insurance companies, the large corporations and with consumers — the Machine is clearly unhealthy. For example, U.S. consumers, including you and I, had in 1990 a collective personal debt of $735 billion. Through credit-card use and personal loans this debt grows every year. As a nation we have the lowest personal savings average of any of the First World countries. Japanese citizens have the highest savings rate per person in all industrialized countries.

The projected 1992 national deficit as calculated by the Congressional Budget Office will be a record $362 billion. The Budget Office projects that by 2002, that year's deficit will be $423 billion. With all the compounding of interest our total national debt will probably be $6 trillion dollars in the year 2000. Given the poor record of the government to accurately predict the deficit increases, H. Ross Perot, the maverick businessman and presidential candidate, gives a much bleaker view for the year 2000. At a National Press Club speech in March of 1992 he said, "We're spending our children's money. Never forget it. It'll be a $12 trillion debt by the year 2000. Let me just put it to you in plain terms. Do you realize that at $12 trillion, you could buy a $120,000 house for every family in this country? We can't afford a $12 trillion debt because the interest alone on a $12 trillion debt would be approximately $1 trillion a year. And guess what the gross receipts in our country are right now. One trillion dollars a year. You'd just be spending it all on interest. It won't work."

We will have to borrow money from foreign governments simply to finance the interest payments. The question is, given the worldwide economic web, will those governments have money to loan us? Probably not. Already we see the change in Japan's financial support of us. Because of changing economic conditions in Japan, Japanese investors have, during 1991-1992, pulled back to their country between $30 and $40 billion dollars in investments from the United States. The Japanese had invested heavily in our bond market and Treasury bills, the financial instruments that are used to finance our deficit.

From 1985 through 1990, Japan pumped $596.2 billion in investments that helped finance the U.S. deficit, corporate takeovers, construction of automobile plants and other investments. However, statistics are now showing that the Japanese are not investing in the United States, but in their own country and following better interest rates to Europe. Rather than money flowing into the United States through these direct investments in government securities, businesses and real estate, the Japanese are pulling away from us. The Japanese are not only *not* buying our financial instruments or investing in property or businesses, but investors within the United States and from other parts of the world are finding that Japanese investments are much more attractive than in our country. The result is that even more available capital is moving from the United States towards "Japan Inc." How does all of this impact us in the near term?

Traditionally, housing construction and real estate leads the economy out of a recession. Lower interest rates permit people both to refinance and buy new houses. The ripple effect through the economy tends to generate general consumer confidence to return to buying. Economists and the media reported increases in housing starts and sales in early 1992, but then housing starts declined by the spring. Administration economists still prophesied hope for the future to help in the Bush re-election prospects, and the media played up the positive side. The general confidence generated by the mass media that the recession was coming to an end made things appear better than they really were. However, one financially knowledgeable friend suggests that we watch what could likely happen in early 1993. After the 1992 election, he argues, the country could experience an inflationary depression. (The word depression would not be used.) He asserts that this could happen because the Federal Reserve would print money to offset the inability of the government or private industry to feed real money into the economy. This means, that businesses wouldn't be investing capital in any significant amounts into new plants and the like. As seen since early 1991, major Fortune 500 companies have been cutting personnel and overhead, buying down their debt, and taking as much profit as possible.

An inflationary economy means that the cash we hold becomes increasingly worthless. A society as deep in debt as ours, will find at some point that cash will be devalued. When this happens it simply will cost more to pay for groceries, cars, and houses. People could lose houses and cars as the value of the dollar gets less and less. People with cash in banks, money-market funds, and stocks would find savings and retirement funds will become less and less valuable.

Second, our Machine economy is linked worldwide. Germany, in taking on the massive $1 trillion turnaround of East Germany, does not have the capital to fuel Europe as it once had. Japan's economy has sputtered with a worldwide lack of consumer buying and its own financial weakness by capitalizing the building of factories throughout the world and making some bad investments. The breakup of the Soviet Union and Eastern Europe, with their own deep economic problems, acts as another drag on available world capital. And the Third World cries out for more capital investment. What we could expect is a domino effect to a worldwide economic downturn. As one country or sector of the world gets into financial trouble, it will affect the rest of the world. What effects one part of this gigantic web, all the rest of the web also experiences. If we are indeed at the brink of an economic change, the strong message is to prepare to personally get out of debt.

Don't Face the Change Alone

The third message is that it is hard to be in tight economic straits alone. We need to find a community of people we can align with for practical, emotional, and spiritual support. Urban environments will be far more difficult to live in during difficult times. Tension, fear, anger and depression will be high. Crime and violence will probably increase as well. The L.A. riots in 1992 added a shock wave of fear through the nation. The increase in gun sales purchased by people who had never owned guns rose dramatically after the riots. Listening intuitively and engaging in dialogue with others in order to determine viable alternatives to "guns for safety and security" will probably be a critical challenge for us in the near term.

Families in more rural environments tend to do better during severe economic changes. The fact is that those who live in rural areas of the former Soviet Union are doing better with basic food needs than are families in Moscow or St. Petersburg during this difficult time. But most of us in the U.S. live in or near cities. If a hard rain is comin' we need to be as wise as the animals to prepare.

Strategies such as paying off as much as we can of our personal debt, talking with friends, thinking through what to do to help support each other *if* a major shift happens in the economy, can help us refocus our priorities and values. Putting up supplies of foodstuffs may be a useful precaution as well. We can actively begin to talk about how to disconnect from the Machine and make other choices in our lives. The value of crisis or impending crisis is that we can decide to move out of a victim role and begin to determine how we want to live differently. For some of us the choice may be to get out of large urban areas. Or, we may make a deeper recommitment to the place where we are currently living. A recommitment to our community will help to guide us into new forms of actions that can both heal and resolve the rising tensions.

Our challenge then for the near future is to engage in communal rather than private social and economic activities.

The following are several examples of alternative approaches to the Machine world that can provide some pathways through the short-term challenge of breakdown. Each of these examples focuses on cooperation, on a redefinition of how money and economics can work, and how, through social structures, we can reclaim our relationships and connectiveness to each other and the Sacred. As examples, I am also hopeful that these stories can stimulate our imaginations to conceive even more novel approaches to the changes that will need to be made as we move through the 1990s toward the turn of the century.

Co-housing

Co-housing projects have gained popularity in recent years in Scandinavian countries, particularly in Denmark, and are beginning to gain a toe-hold in the United States as well. Co-housing creates mini self-contained communities that use environmentally sound technologies along with principles of privacy, family integrity, and communal interaction. Co-housing combines private ownership of one's own dwelling with the sharing of common grounds, shared governance for decision-making, a commons area for social interaction, coupled with an economy of savings with shared laundry, shared child care and shared gardens. The ownership process is similar to that used with condominiums, except the intention and purpose is to create a community of involvement and interaction, rather than a living situation of separation and privacy that is so common today. The focus on ecological building, energy-saving systems, resource conservation, community interaction, and self-sustainability sets co-housing apart from simple condominium living. The Danish co-housing model has a particular design to facilitate the community aspect of living. The common building is the largest in the complex and serves as a combination common area, kitchen, and recreation room for the people living in the complex. Usually a co-housing complex will have about 30 units to house families and single people. Garages and parking are not connected to the living complex, but kept away from the grounds in order to create a pedestrian-only environment. The village idea of the co-housing project is its strong appeal, because it creates in the structure and in the way buildings are laid out a more economical, integrated, and neighborly form of living

Mondragon Cooperatives

Along with the European influence of co-housing is the Mondragon type of economic system that originated in the Mondragon region of Basque Spain. This is a thriving economic region where the people of several towns totally finance, own and maintain everything from the banks to the research facilities. It is what Terry Mollner of The Trusteeship Institute, calls the Third Way Economics.

In a forthcoming book about Third Way Economics, Mollner describes an economic model that is based on cooperation rather than on competition. Capitalism and socialism, Mollner argues, is based on a compromise that tries to resolve the economic assumption that there is competition in society for a limited amount of wealth. This assumption creates poverty in capitalist countries and less than material prosperity for the majority of people in socialist countries. Third Way Economics does not rest on the compromise of competing forces. The cooperative assumption, Mollner asserts, is the view that all parts of an economic system (people, natural resources, goods, services, etc.) are connected. This cooperative assumption is supported by systems and environmental theories that demonstrate that an action by one part of the system has a direct effect on all other parts of the system. Rather than making capital-development issues and social responsibility competitors, Third Way Economics makes them partners. The notion is to have capitalism use wealth to create more wealth for the good of everyone in the society. Third Way economics is a servant to the individual within the context of community and societal decision-making. Mollner points to communities that have been testing out this cooperative, socially responsible economic model.

The most notable of these communities is the Mondragon cooperative in the Basque region of northern Spain, the Central Union in Poland, and Japan's formal government/business working relationship. Although Japan represents the cooperative element in creating both individual and societal capital, the Mondragon cooperatives and Central Union go far beyond Japan's form of cooperation. These two examples are what Mollner calls nations within nations. These associations represent a large group of people who are freely joining together not only to create a new economic system, but to re-establish the balance and perspective of where and how economic structures should play out in a different kind of social system.

Central Union in Poland has over 500,000 members. Mondragon is over 23,000 worker-owners of over 200 enterprises that manufacture such things as clothing, electronic equipment and appliances. The Mondragon cooperatives have their own schools, farms, banks, research facilities, and an organization to help start new businesses. These businesses are selling over $3 billion a year in goods and services. They sell their products throughout Spain and other parts of the world. The Bank of the People's Labor, which is run by the cooperative, has over 20 branches throughout the Basque region.

Significantly, the cooperative has redefined money as an accounting and exchange system rather than a commodity. In this sense money is viewed as part of an infinite supply rather than a limited one as in the capitalist or socialist systems. The loan policy of the bank is unusual in that the riskier the loan, the lower the interest rate. In over 35 years of making loans without collateral to new and existing businesses, there have been few defaults. This system of loans works because money is used as a form of cooperation and to help build relationship; this idea is to help each group of people who want to start a new business to be fully successful.

Everyone in the cooperative owns and has responsibility for the success of everyone else's business. There are no divisions between workers or owners in a business. Everyone is an owner, with the structure of management and decision-making being delegated to a specific group who are held accountable and helped by the owner-worker committee of the enterprise. The whole Mondragon association of owner-worker enterprises, governing organizations, medical facilities and banks has a long-range research institute that looks at the social and environmental needs of all the people living in and around the Village of Mondragon. This institute also recommends what enterprises are needed, initiates new ideas suggested by a group of individuals who want to start something new, and provides training, financial and personnel support to establish the new venture.

Mondragon has a unique integration of hierarchical management structure within a context of democratic decision-making, by all worker-owners. Each enterprise has an interconnected system of democratic representation and accountability for the business and the social needs of all the worker-owners. These representatives interview and hire either from within the enterprise or from outside a management team that manages day-to-day operations. Decision-making, not ultimate power, rests in the management hierarchy. Power is distributed equally through each person who works in the venture, and each is accountable for the successful results of all aspects of the Mondragon community, not just their own individual enterprise. Over the more than 35 years that the cooperative has functioned no worker-owner has been laid off. In difficult national economic times in Spain the Mondragon cooperative has continued to flourish and prosper. Money is infinite rather than limited in Mondragon's system, so monetary wealth becomes a relative measure of the people's imagination of how they will cooperatively help and support each other and the surrounding communities they live within.

The schools, the network of 200 food stores, the banks, and different enterprises are in nearly every Basque town and village. Although this idea was started in the 1940s in the village of Mondragon by Father Don José Maria

Arizmendiarrietta, a Catholic priest, the association is rooted both in local places (villages and towns) and in a non-geographical idea that imagines relationship and cooperation as the fundamental values of social and economic life.

LETS Economics

Another system that attempts to reimagine how economics can work differently brings together the notion of goods exchange, or barter, and a redefinition of money or unit exchange. This idea is known as LETS, a process based on a new form of economic barter that re-establishes relationship as the primary factor in any economic transaction.

LETS stands for *Local Employment Trading System*. LETS was originated in Canada by Michael Linton in 1982. LETS has now spread to numerous other communities throughout the world. The idea migrated to Australia with LETS groups forming in every major city and throughout many rural areas. In Australia the LETS name has been changed to *Local Energy Transfer System*.

The LETS idea is to move the economic interchange back to a relationship level, rather than an abstract impersonal exchange. First, this is done by having people engage in direct economic negotiations about the value of goods and services. Second, it begins to remove individuals in a community from dependence on the external national economy, particularly the government currency exchange, or money. What LETS does is create its own currency or unit of exchange. It does this in two ways. First, two lists are created: one listing people and the services and goods they have to offer and one listing what people in the LETSystem want. The second part of the LETSystem is usually a small office to service a central recording system operated manually, or by a computer, that people can call into in order to record either a credit or debit on a transaction that is made with someone for goods or services. The LETSystem derives from the observation that the real wealth of a group of people comes from the goods, services, and skills of its people rather than from the amount of money that the group has available to them. In this sense, personal or community wealth and status is not linked to employment and the money gained from it, or from the larger financial control of the corporation-economy. The flexibility of the LETSystem enables members to integrate the local national currency with the LETS units as a fully negotiable collective fund for obtaining any particular good or service. For example, if you have an auto repair shop, and I come to you to have my car fixed, we would negotiate the LETS units for your labor to repair my car. But because you have to buy parts with dollars you would negotiate the parts value with me. In the barter you would disclose your need to charge 2 percent more in order to cover costs of picking up the parts and stocking them. The point is that in the relationship of exchange all information is open, honest, and is operated on the basis of trust and fairness with each other.

Where the LETSystem has grown, as in Australia, goods and services range from car repair to building houses, from grocery store goods to income-tax service. In a LETSystem it has been determined that from 30 to 300 participants make the best size of working organization. In Australia different LETSystem groups trade with each other, bartering goods and services that each group can offer the other. LETSystem groups have confronted such problems as federal income tax on the barter, and negative debit balances run up by people using the system. But in all cases where problems have occurred, the value of relationship in the system has enabled the local or regional LETSystem group(s) to work out the difficulties.

Hearthstone Village

It is not just what we do to survive economically, but also how we live together in our communities that is becoming increasingly important to us. Most of us who live in urban and suburban areas have little contact or relationship with our immediate neighbors. Many of us feel threatened and insecure as we walk our streets. We feel isolated and in many ways alienated from the geography we call home. We often don't know the names of the people who live in the houses or apartments on either side of us. We might feel uncomfortable going to a neighbor for help. And we may not feel confident that when our children are playing outside that other adults in the neighborhood have a personal concern and relationship in terms of the safety and well-being of all the children as a collective group of playmates.

One example of a neighborhood that attempted to recover community in a self-conscious manner is Hearthstone Village, a group of more than 50 people in the Baker Road area of Shutesbury, Massachusetts. Intentionally the people in the households along Baker Road decided to cooperate as friends in many ways traditional to small communities that existed 50 or more years ago. They extended a commitment to help each other with building projects and child care. And they made a commitment among themselves that they would confront any kind of personal or collective crisis along their road with mutual support and help.

The community of Hearthstone Village is named after the highest hill in the area, which is also the site of an old Native American ceremonial long house. Members of Hearthstone Village see themselves as a kind of membership into a tribe of friendship. Membership is by self-selection; there are individuals and families along the road who don't identify themselves as part of Hearthstone. However, these people are always invited to participate in anything the Village does.

Governance (how things are decided and get done) within this community of friendship is determined by what they call "eldering." "Eldering" is the willingness by someone along the road to take the initiative to create an activity, offer leadership and encourage others to join in the activity. One person, for example, "eldered" a newsletter for the Village. Another set up a land trust to purchase a house to be used by members of the village for guests or temporary housing. One person saw the need for office equipment and set up the purchase of a copying machine, computer and fax machine for the common use of the village. A community garden was set up with families in the village paying the full-time gardener a monthly stipend to provide them with fresh vegetables and fruits year round. Another person started a system called a Rota for people who choose to eat together, with dinner preparation rotating among the households who participate. A bulk-food buying system, along with periodic meetings, parties and community rituals are other examples of "eldering" initiatives.

The efforts of such community models as Hearthstone Village can offer us ways to reclaim our own neighborhoods as a container for our daily lives. Specifically, self-conscious neighboring can benefit our children and our growing concern for personal safety and security. To establish a self-conscious community of friends in a neighborhood permits our children to grow up with an extended group of friendly folks of all ages. In Hearthstone Village children feel free to go in and out of many of the Village homes. Then, too, children have the chance to have friendships on a day-to-day basis with adults other than their parents and teachers. This neighborhood-village model can provide the opportunities for varied relationships and also can create a healthy atmosphere in which children can grow emotionally secure and confident, having been supported by many adults. This also provides elders in the community the opportunity to regain positive relationships with youth. Elders can give balance, insight, and wisdom to the growth of youngsters. Elders can act as a check on parent's frustration and as a source of refuge and comfort for children when they are in conflict with their parents. It is known that some of our child abuse is directly related to the fact that often both parents and children have no safety container or emotional-release system to help with the difficult emotions and tensions that arise in parenting. Other supportive members of the neighborhood-village can provide this important safety-value function.

In a self-conscious neighborhood like Hearthstone Village, friends of all households are well known in the community. Strangers are immediately noticed and offered assistance. Because of this continual awareness and mutual responsibility for noticing and monitoring who is in the neighborhood, people in the village feel safe and more secure.

We need to reclaim our neighborhoods, whether they are in the city, suburbs or rural areas — for both psychological and practical reasons. In addition to our work environment, the geographic location of our home is that specific place in our lives where we can have the most direct influence for positive change.

These and other alternative community housing and economic systems are being explored by many people around the world as positive and workable ways to separate from the Machine. To create any reasonable and sustainable future separate from the Machine's economy, especially if national economies become more difficult to manage, and actually collapse, we need to learn to take care of ourselves and our families within some healthy and productive form of intentional community setting.

PART III

RECLAIMING OUR SOULS

Everything I've put you through, each of the things I've shown you was only a device to convince you that there's more to us than meets the eye. . . . We begin then to *see* — that is, to perceive — something else; not as imagination, but as real and concrete. And then we begin to know without having to use words. And what any of us does with that increased perception, with that silent knowledge, depends on our own temperament.

JUAN MATUS TO CARLOS CASTANEDA
IN THE BOOK
THE POWER OF SILENCE

Introduction

*I*n this dark portrait of the world we are living in; I have asserted that within our Western historical tradition over the past 500 years we've negatively changed our relationship to each other and to the earth in robotic fashion. The current manifestation of this tradition is the drive to create a monolithic machinelike culture that is based exclusively on materialism. Both from our history and our present consumer mania we are losing the fundamental sacredness about how we — humans, plants, animals, the earth itself — live together. I am neither a romantic about regaining some lost primeval past nor am I overly optimistic about changing the dominance of a machine culture in the near future. What I am clear about is that individually and collectively we must learn to regain the ability to live from the *inside out*. We must relearn to access a place of inner guidance and direction within us that is connected to a personal experience with the sacredness of another reality, one that focuses itself through nature.

The battleground for changing the impact of the Machine in our lives is found in our imagination; it is here that we can first become holy mechanics. We need to conceive and image something beyond the Machine. Our machinelike culture lacks either the suppleness or the wholeness to meet our human and spiritual needs. The mechanistic ideas of the clock along with the notions of the body and universe behaving like a machine are metaphors that have caused us a great disservice. It is now time to fix the clock by repairing our robotlike selves, by tapping into our unconscious and imagining ourselves as holy mechanics. It is time to cast off the role of being human robots.

As we begin this section on Reclaiming Our Souls, I offer four calls: first, *to face fully the destructive results of what generations of our ancestors have done to the earth,* and face the fact that all of us today are participating in that destruction by being part of this Machine world.

Second, that *we must go back to go forward.* We must go back to reclaim a fundamental connection that we as modern individuals have lost. This means going back to Paleolithic times. In these ancient times, some 15,000 years ago, our ancestors were physically and intellectually like us today, but they were still deeply connected with the Sacred Other as it was mediated through nature. Paleolithic human experience still exists today on planet Earth in indigenous, native and aboriginal peoples. I am not urging that we "go native," but rather that we listen to, learn from, and understand the messages and teachings the natives peoples are willing to give to us.

Third, that *we must learn to initiate again in our time what I call elder-leaders.* In our materialistic, youth-oriented culture we have abandoned the natural wisdom and natural human transition of individuals as they grow older. Our ancestors held some important wisdom about leadership, about the elders, and how best the community can be served by elder wisdom. We must rediscover and initiate a new form of leadership in our world today.

And fourth, *we must find the way out of a machine world we've created — to change from human robots into sacred mechanics.* We accomplish this through deepening our capacity to imagine. The doorway of the Sacred is in the imagination. Again, indigenous people know this, and they have much to teach us as we recover this gateway and reservoir of power within our hearts and mind.

Along the way, in our discussion, some practical suggestions will be offered — ways that I and others have found useful as we continue to explore this return to the Sacred.

Rejecting the Machine:
A Return to the Sacred

*M*any of us discovered in the 1960s that we weren't
alone. During the period from 1964 to 1974 a
generation of individuals awoke and many arrived at similar
viewpoints, experiences and feelings about themselves and
about how to live. The music, the happenings, the communes,
the political actions against racism and war arose out of these
inner experiences. These artifacts of the sub-culture articulated
what we were feeling. The music, the long hair and the
psychedelics initiated and communicated an interior set of
perceptions and values about reality. These external
manifestations gave context and shape to our inner life. We
could see the contrast between two worlds. We were strangers
in a strange land. We wanted a new world, and we shoved it
into the Machine's face, but it frightened our parents and the
power structure. We lived out our expressions of creativity,
freedom and our deviation from the American norms of
sexuality and gender identification. We idealized Thoreau's
Walden Pond and made Ghandi and civil disobedience our
spiritual/political credo. When the principles of the feminine
with its feelings for nature started to emerge into cultural
awareness, it further scared the patriarchal power structure.

As we grew in numbers, however, we did not know how
to sustain the growth and experience of our vision of the "new

world" culturally. Because we did not have well-defined structures and forms of our own with which to have cultural impact, we used the current forms like the Peace Corps, or radical politics, or spiritual disciplines from the East, or new psychological modalities. We poured our energies into these forms believing and hoping that they could be used to change society and have an impact on the world's problems. But the Machine stole this youthful energy and absorbed the "movement" into a fad. The Machine created movies, TV sitcoms, psychedelic clothes, and natural-food stores.

Not all of us in that period, in our late teens and twenties, took the leap and tried to live a different lifestyle. But a great majority in that generation were infected with a different feeling and viewpoint. I talk with executives today who were "straight arrow" individuals during this period. They were in the military, never took psychedelics and hated the hippies, but they talk about something that happened to them during that chaotic, mind-opening time which shaped their present view of the world. They have a hard time articulating the feeling, but it is a desire to create a different kind of world than the one we have now. They are as yet not clear how to bring this feeling into either their personal or professional lives, but the earnestness of the conversation indicates that they, too, were infected by something in their youth that presses upon them today.

Those who did jump in to a vision of a new world, however, went through a change in self-consciousness. As we grew older, we drifted away from each other and from our new-found inner vision. We tried to live our dream by going back to the country or dedicating ourselves to teaching or simply taking responsibility for raising a family. But the years swept us up into the rapidly growing Machine culture. With a strong work ethic and a creativity that wouldn't die in us, we kept looking for interesting pathways into the New World. We've lent our skills and talents to the Machine, while not fully being comfortable in it. Now with our children mostly grown the old feelings of a different kind of life returns to haunt us. Is it time to uncover the awareness we hid away, and perhaps discover even more deeply the pool of ancient knowing we began to understand at that time? Is it time to reject the Machine and replace it with new models? And more importantly, is it possible to do so in time?

The Luddite Tradition

It is my belief that positive societal environments for learning, for growth, or for change in the individual and the community are being killed by the post-industrial-information-economic Machine. *I believe that we as a species took a wrong turn with industrialization.* Mechanization and moving from the land to industrial cities intensified the destruction of family, community, and earth-based spiritual traditions. The imagination of steam energy and mass production led independent farmers and craftsman to leave a way of life that still had balance and some connection to the land and the Otherworld. This experience was co-opted for the slavery of wage earning.

People who take a position against technology and its fruits are labeled "Luddites." The name comes from a cottage-worker's movement in England between 1811 and 1816. The goal of the movement was to stop factory industrialization. The name Luddites came from Ned Lud, an alleged imbecile who had broken two stocking frames when he participated in one of the rampages of destroying machines in a factory. As independent cottage-workers rebelled at a technology that took away their livelihood and traditions they were labeled Luddites — imbeciles in technology. But, over the years, anyone who took an opposing position to challenge and question technology, and not worship it as humankind's savior, was labeled a Luddite.

My call to reject the unconscious acceptance of Machine culture is a Luddite position. Many of these authors I've cited hold a similar Luddite position. The individuals and groups in the 1960s and 1970s who attempted to establish an ecological perspective, were Luddites. Individuals like E.F. Schumacher who advocated "small is beautiful;" and conservationists like David Brower, who pleaded for nature preservation; and advocates of recycling and appropriate technology, all fall into the Luddite tradition. The radicalness of Earth First! to stop all timber cutting of old-growth forests is an extreme Luddite position. The challenge to agribusiness' chemically produced food verses the appeal for a return to organic chemical-free food is a strong Luddite position. Many groups and foundations that emerged out of the 1960s that support a sustainable future, like the WorldWatch Institute, attack the corporate-economy technological Machine. A strong Luddite tradition is seen in the Amish of Ohio, who for religious reasons reject technology in their lives in order to preserve a simpler way of living. In particular, they practice a more humane way of farming that is more productive and profitable than the agribusiness factory farms around them.

To resist progress and growth means one risks being labeled a Luddite. But being a modern-day Luddite is deeper than just resisting technology and industrialization. To be a Luddite means that one believes that we, as members of Western culture, made a mistake and that we are paying the consequences personally, socially, environmentally and spiritually for the direction we are taking. But I think we made the wrong turn long before the industrial Machine started. We took the first wrong turn at the fork in the road some 5,000 years ago when patriarchal society destroyed the partnership, plant-based, feminine-oriented cultures of that time.

Remembering Where We Made Wrong Turns

Riane Eisler, in *The Chalice and the Blade*, lays out a strong historical argument for the "wrong turn" position. The "blade," Eisler argues, has been the symbol of male patriarchal dominance and control for the past 5,000 years. But the blade with its war and violence, and the male dominance of society, has not been the only pattern for human beings to embrace and perpetuate. Going back to prehistorical data, Eisler, demonstrates that there was a different cultural structure that supported the feminine, earth-based values symbolized by a vessel metaphor, the chalice. As she asserts, from anthropological evidence during the Neolithic era some 5,000-10,000 years ago, "the view of power as the *feminine* power to nurture and give, was undoubtedly not always adhered to, for these were societies of real flesh-and-blood people, not make-believe utopia. But it was still the normative ideal, the model to be emulated by both women and men." She goes on to describe that these societies were not arranged hierarchically either on a matriarchal or a patriarchal pattern where either one or the other sex dominated. Rather she says our ancestors had a different form of human organization, "a partnership society in which neither half of humanity is ranked over the other and diversity is not equated with inferiority or superiority." Her work explores the changes from the chalice to the blade and opens us to the conditions by which we can and *must* return to a partnership mode of societal organization.

Following Eisler's argument, what we can see in the Machine today is the natural extension of the blade metaphor — a male-dominated, patriarchal value system. In spite of the domination of this value system, however, some older archaic cultures outside the influence of the Machine have survived in their primitive forms. Most of the Native American cultures of both northern and southern hemispheres embodied partnership values up until their eradication 100 years ago. Small groups in Central and South America, as well as in Oceania and Asia, have kept these plant-based, feminine-oriented ideas and practices functioning, that is, until our current practice of destroying the world's rainforests gained alarming momentum worldwide.

Critical to the gradual loss of these cooperative-based cultures over the past 5,000 years, and an accelerated loss to us today, is the destruction of a meaningful connection to the sacred. What gave balance and meaning to the plant-based, feminine-partnership cultures, was the belief in a reality of the sacred in all parts of their lives and the way that the sacred infused and reflected all things in the world around them.

Modern educational and scientific culture has dismissed as naive this long period of humankind's experience with the sacred as simply some form of animism or pantheism — spirit and nature worship. Our scientific "priests" have disregarded any truth or reality that there may be non-human forms that co-exist on this planet with us. Or that we need to respect and learn the modes of personal interaction with them. In Western patriarchal societies, I believe the emphasis on a masculine God that lives outside this world underlies the rationale that turns animals, plants, water, and the Earth herself into inanimate objects to be manipulated and used for man's purposes. To view these objects as kin, as having a familial connection with them, as indigenous people do even today, is a difficult perception for us to hold because our masculine-God myth in the book of Genesis tells us to "rule over all things."

In the *Living Bible* translation of the Old Testament, chapter one of Genesis tells how God creates *man,* and then instructs him to "Multiply and fill the earth and *subdue it;* you are masters of the fish and birds and all the animals. And look! I have given you the seed-bearing plants throughout the earth, and all the fruit trees for your food." This story is quite different from the creation stories found in Native American tribes, or the Upanishads of India, or in the Popol Vuh, the sacred book of the Mayans in Guatemala. In these stories man does not subdue and have dominion over the earth and its being. A Mother/Father Creator teaches the children of the earth to regard the animals and birds, and even the rocks, as brothers and sisters. In these stories the Great Spirit infuses everything with knowledge so that all of created life becomes teachers to humans. In the Haida creation story of British Columbia, for example, Raven is the creator of the world. In this story humans came out of a clam shell at the coaching of Raven. Catherine Feher in her book, *Ravensong,* tells this story. In the last part of the story the relationship between the Raven spirit and humans is portrayed clearly. "Raven played with the First people for a long time; he taught them many things . . . Raven taught them to cure sickness with herbs and songs and magic. . . . They (the Haida) know that Raven is the Creator of the World, they know they go through many cycles. They know that the time of Human Beings may not last forever but that Raven the Transformer, Raven the Bringer of Light, is one who is, was and always will be." Knowing that "humans may not last forever" teaches the Haida to be humble, open and respectful toward all living things. I believe that if we continue to play out the Biblical injunction to subdue the earth, humans may indeed not last much longer.

The Transition:
Living from the Inside Out

*D*avid Riesman, Nathan Glazer and Reuel Denny in their work, *The Lonely Crowd* (1950), relate a study of the American character in transition. Their study marked, parallel with the steep rise of the corporate-economy Machine, the movement of society from what they termed "inner-directed" to "other-directed." This transition, they wrote, is a "shift from an age of production to an age of consumption." (This idea of an age of production follows my historical recounting in the chapter on the "Rise of the Machine World.") Their notion of a production age grows over the last 450 years, in Europe and America. In Riesman's analysis these are marked by people internalizing early in life a common set of beliefs and goals that guide their outer choices and decisions as members of a society. This internalization of common beliefs and goals formed the inner-directed personality. The American dream that dominated our societal consciousness until the 1960s represents this common belief and goal for American culture, and ultimately represents the fulfillment of the age of production. In fulfilling the American dream, inner-directed Americans transformed the production age into the consumption age.

The consumption age that has increasingly dominated us for the last 50 years is the culmination of norms and values that have been growing in Western culture for 500 years. In the view of the writers of the *Lonely Crowd,* the consumption age represents the desire to be seen and approved of for our outward appearances and accomplishments. In Andy Warhol's description of pop culture, he claims that Americans want to be seen on national television for 15 minutes at least once in their lives. Being popular, in the spotlight, and having star status is the strong drive of the other-directed personality, and fuels the consumption environment.

When we are externally oriented, with little inner centering and grounding within ourselves, then there is insufficient space to contact an inner world of wisdom. When our guidance comes from the conscious and unconscious external clues of people and the environment around us, with its amplified hype of media sound bytes and glittering images, there is no interior framework from which to be silent, to feel, to hear and to see the Mystery of life. With the absence of some form of inner maps or guides from our culture, a return to the Sacred becomes, at first, a difficult task.

Between Two Worlds

We who were in our twenties during the 1960s are a transition group in our culture. We have some of the old myth of the past 450 years in us, and we've also been influenced deeply by the new myth of the Machine. We are both inner- and other-directed. Our younger brothers and sisters and our children didn't experience an unconscious inner drive that was supported by a culture of shared common beliefs and dreams; becoming instead, hypnotized by the materialistic images of products from the Machine to be merely consumers. This conditioning away from our inner world begins the day we are born. It happens for most primarily through the messages and experiences of intense and prolonged television viewing. Equally, the supporting structures of family and school encourage a consumption culture.

Most of us in this transition generation who are today in our late forties to early sixties have fallen under the Machine's hypnotic spell as well. If we've struggled with the Machine to resist the hypnosis through some kind of spiritual or artistic discipline or by some kind of commitment and connection to the natural world, we still find a part of ourselves in contact with an inner life. But given the growing pressures from the Machine, how do we reclaim more of our inner world? Snared as we are as human robots, how do we turn toward something more aboriginal — meaning something more innate, approaching life with the newness of a "beginner's" mind? Because of our historic and planetary dilemma, as well as the daily pressure to cope with our personal lives, we are at the crossroads in which we have no alternative but to live and act from the inside out. The quality of our circumstances is so critical that only a *leap back* to something primary and innate in human experience can give us direction and guidance for the labyrinth we must move through, and ultimately, discover in our ancient inner world a means to make a *leap forward* into a new direction.

Living from the Inside Out

The ability to go forward and embrace some other type of world culture depends on re-exploring and remapping the archaic topography of our imagination. Access to the terrain of sacred imagination, the primary source for our ancestors more than 15,000 years ago, was in the collective form of their artistic images. In these images were brought together ritual, art, and a clear relationship to otherworld beings and forces. For example, our ancestors left us images that are reflected today in the bark paintings of Australian aborigines and in the ivory animal carvings of Alaskan natives. These contemporary images of a spiritual view of life can also be found in ancient artifacts: the 20,000-year-old goddess figures that have been found all across Europe and Asia; the 16,000-year-old cache of ritual animals, figures and necklaces found near Lake Baikal in Siberia; and the majestic Paleolithic cave painting in Lascaux, France. Stone and bone carvings that were used in burial ceremonies and worship of the cave bear have been found throughout the world. All of these artifacts testify to the sacred imagination of our ancestors. Joseph Campbell, in reviewing the mixture of the artistic and religious expression in our forebears says, "Neither in body nor in mind do we inhabit the world of those hunting races of the Paleolithic millennia, to whose lives and life ways we nevertheless owe the very forms of our bodies and structures of our minds." The ways of our ancient ancestors are inside our bodies and minds. We must begin to re-explore and remap our inner world in order to reclaim these old pathways and memories.

To remember our ancient memories and live from the inside does not mean acting from the cues of other people. Rather, this means we must find pathways inside ourselves that lead us to a clear awareness of how we are to act, practically, in today's circumstances. Through listening and seeing from inside ourselves we restructure our daily pattern of activity, alter our relationships with each other, reconfigure the form of work and creativity that is balanced and healthy for us, and build the kind of physical environment and community life that will give us a new perspective on the natural world. The reclaiming of our archaic traditions offers us the opportunity to do this.

Just as our Western ancestors at the beginning of the Renaissance went back to the Greeks and Romans to get inspiration and direction for the forward movement of their culture as it emerged from the Dark Ages, so we must go back even further, to the Paleolithic period, to rediscover the principles and values that will engage and allow us to move out of our own dark ages of Machine culture. Terence McKenna calls this struggle of reclamation the "archaic revival."

The first consideration in rejecting the Machine and making the leap toward the sacred is to determine where this archaic revival shows itself in our current circumstances. We must also determine where we personally orient ourselves to this archaic period and how we practically proceed. My belief is that we need to first reconsider what began in the 1960s as the starting point for the release of a new imagination and the beginning of the return to Paleolithic times, to the archaic . . . and to the sacred.

Reconsidering the Sacred

*E*veryday we are taught through glitzy consumer messages that the world is nothing more than a non-living object that we have neither relationship to nor need to respect nor honor. Consumer message-makers reflect the attitude built into our mythological history. One of the primary myths is building towers to heaven rather than honoring the spirits in the trees and the animals that live next to us. The tragedy of erecting monuments on earth to the heavens is that all towers of Babel seem to end in self-destruction. Yet, as giant phallic symbols, these towers symbolize the aspirations and deep longings of a patriarchal society.

The aspirations of groups to create an architecture into the heavens often reveal what is considered sacred in a society. Joseph Campbell pointed out that one can trace the evolution of a people by the dominant buildings they erect. He points out that before the Renaissance the church spire ascending to heaven was the dominant structure in a town. Following the Renaissance to the Industrial Revolution, government structures took over the center position — the town hall with the clock tower, the mechanical clock that regulated people's lives. From the Industrial Revolution to the present, commercial buildings dominate the skylines of our cities — punctuated by insurance and banking high-rises. Today we have raised up as sacred the god Mammon and placed him in a mahogany paneled office on the top floor of the tallest bank building downtown. What is absent in this scene is not the church or city hall, for we can see them down the street. What is lost is our psychic, interior skyline. For most individuals in this culture, the phallic, male-dominated skyline has cut off from inside of us the most natural images of all: sky, clouds, trees, mountains — places in nature where one can be connected to the otherworld wisdom of spiritual reality, the sacred.

In a culture that has disregarded, or at best trivialized the idea of the sacred in daily life, we need to reconfirm the vitality of sacredness in our individual and community experience. The Latin root of the word "sacred" comes from *sanus,* meaning *sane,* and from the German *saos,* meaning *safe*. It is curious that Webster defines sacred as something "that is not to be profaned, violated or made common; and is to be set apart as hallowed or holy." When something is sacred, it is acknowledged with respect and even reverence. And it is sacred because at the root of experience this sacred thing has sanity and safety. To consider the earth and nature as sacred reflects the same sanity, safety, or sacredness within us. As robots in the Machine we have lost the sacredness — the respect, reverence, and sanity for our own lives and for the planet. We have lost the sane place, the holy and safe place inside us. The invasion of the Machine culture into our inner core is toxic, and we project this same toxic condition back to the earth. *To begin to regain sacredness is a dramatic decision to reject the toxic conditions out of our psyches,* to reject what has profaned both us and our world. To regain sacredness is to regain the holy, sane place within each of us.

The Absence of the Sacred

Some would argue that to reject the Machine culture would be rejecting the belief that science and technology, with all its gadgets, makes life "better" for us. All cultures have some form of technology — fire-making devices, stone-chipping tools, basket weaving, etc. The question is not one of having technology or not, the question is what technological choices do we make and what importance do we place on the value and purpose of technology in society.

When people draw our attention to the negative side of technology we tend to rationalize that it is simply the "price of progress." But on the Machine's own terms, is it really progress? For example, the policy to explore the last Alaskan wilderness for oil fails to acknowledge that when discovered, this oil would provide as little as two year's supply for the worldwide oil demand. Would not the same investment in other, more renewable energy sources make more economic sense?

We, as human robots in the Machine, have lost a feeling of sacredness when we shrug our shoulders and say that these kinds of problems are "the price of modern life." Yet, those of us in Europe, the United States, and Japan are but a tiny fraction of the world's population, and we, by our choices and through our leaders are making critical decisions for the future of this planet. We, the 5 percent of the world's total population, reap the benefits of science and technology's "comforts and progress." We are also taking the majority of the world's natural resources to accomplish this so-called progress.

Jerry Mander in his work *In The Absence of the Sacred (The Failure of Technology & the Survival of the Indian Nations)*, insists that we in the West have all but lost the connection to nature and the spiritual world. We have lost this sacred connection because we are not challenging the fundamental assumptions of our technology. In fact, he says, we have a taboo against questioning whether a particular technology might not be good for us. We have a blind faith in technology, and we are all too willing to believe the promises for safeguards as well as the fundamental argument that one can't stop the application of new discoveries.

Thirteen years ago Mander wrote *Four Arguments for the Elimination of Television*. In that book he argued not about the content of television, or how to appropriately use it. Mander presented reasons why television is harmful and why it should be eliminated. Mander then goes beyond the impact of television on our psyche and culture in his next work, *In the Absence of the Sacred*, to examine how the technological Machine (what he calls megatechnology) uses television as a training tool to interconnect with "a single technical-economic web encircling the planet." The Fall 1991 issue of *Whole Earth Review,* noted that Mander is "attempting to prove that the toxic side of technology is intimately connected to the structure of the corporation and the fate of indigenous people worldwide." His critique of technology is disturbing because he calls into question the methods of corporation-economy leaders to manipulate us into supporting and accepting technology that is not healthy. But even more damning is our unwillingness as members of society not to question, challenge and engage in public debate with the science and technology establishment concerning the kinds of products we believe are healthy or unhealthy, beneficial or not beneficial to the planet.

The hope that Mander provides is his research into the response of indigenous peoples around the world to the Machine culture. It is from the indigenous, "primitive," archaic peoples of the world, Mander argues, that we have the most to learn about the connection between this physical world and the otherworld of spiritual power and healing — the world of the sacred. He notes that just as many of us yearn for the spiritual values of this ancient way of life, we also seem to be bent on systematically destroying it in these peoples. What do we fear so profoundly that we are willing to participate in our own destruction? Do we fear the sacred? Do we fear losing power, influence, and profits?

This "absence of the sacred" in our lives, this loss of safety and sanity in our world, is contrasted to the traditional, indigenous peoples who continue to resist the power of the Machine's invasion into their lives. These people do not have the comfortable and progressive life we have. They are often illiterate, live often in conditions of abject poverty, and they struggle with poor health and often with alcoholism. Why would we choose to idealize or romanticize these native peoples as examples for a sacred, holy or superior life? "Shouldn't we bring them into our Western value system," we ask, "so they will have a better life than what they have now?" In various parts of the world, however, these people with their ancient knowing, have tried to say no to this idea. When our own Native Americans said no, white settlers and government Cavalries killed them, took their land, and forced the remaining survivors on long marches, such as the Trail of Tears, to concentration camps called reservations. The superiority and arrogance of our own white ancestors rested, even in this condition of semi-slavery, in our not allowing native peoples to practice their earth-based spiritual traditions or to retain their own languages and customs. This is both past and present history. Two recent Supreme Court rulings threaten the rights of Native Americans to continue to practice their religion because it would upset corporation-economy objectives to gain control of land and mineral rights both on reservations and public lands where native peoples practice their religion. I'm not suggesting that Indian powwows or weekend shamanism workshops will recapture the sacred for us. Something more radical, more at the root of our dilemma must take place in order for us to find our way back to ourselves. Traditional native peoples seem to point to the path of the sacred that can lead us back.

The Voice for Sacredness in the World

Primitive peoples around the world have been dying for hundreds of years because they want to live differently from the Western standard. Because of the increasing demand for precious minerals, oil, timber, and other natural resources, transnational companies around the world, as well as the military units that support them in the taking of these natural resources, have rejected the desire and wish of the indigenous people to be left alone. They want to be left alone and in place in their unaltered natural environments because they know something that we have forgotten. In the centuries of working to survive with their stories and myths about the earth, with their rituals and experiences of honoring the natural world, with their understanding and respect for the interplay of nature with human beings, they provide a continuity and wisdom about how to co-exist with all living things in a sacred way.

The Penan people of the Borneo rainforest are one of the few remaining hunter-gatherer peoples left on the earth. They number some 7,600 and are spread across Malaysia and Indonesia in small isolated groups. The principle value of their culture is sharing, generosity, and a belief that the land is sacred. In *Penan: Voice for the Borneo Rainforest,* by ethnologist Wade Davis, the Penan speak for themselves. One Penan elder explains, "The land is sacred; it belongs to the countless numbers who are dead, the few who are living, and the multitude of those yet to be born. How can the government say that all untitled land 'belongs to itself,' when there had been people using the land even before the government existed?" The Penan have been driven out of their homelands by the Malaysian government in order to log the rainforest, and they have been sent to live in government resettlement camps. The government wants the Penan to become part of mainstream Malaysian society. The minister of environment and tourism, who owns and regulates logging rights in the lands that have been with the Penan for thousands of years says, "We don't want them running around like animals. They have to settle down; otherwise, they have no rights." And this has often meant, for indigenous people, that they will be destroyed. The fact is that by taking them from their lands both they and their scared way of life are being eliminated.

In five Western states we find a deep cultural clash and disregard for the Native American view of sacredness. In the 1990s, Indians who want to practice their tradition-based religion are experiencing the power of Machine values.

At Enola Hill, in Oregon, a third of the sacred mountain there has been marked for logging. This sacred site has been used for over 11,000 years by several tribes in the Mount Hood area. In the summer of 1990 staff of the Mt. Hood National Forest Service secretly put Enola timber out for bid in an attempt to undermine an administrative appeal to stop the proposed logging there. This attempted action was discovered, however, and the Cascade Geographic Society filed a lawsuit. The result of the lawsuit forced the Forest Service to conduct an ethnographic study to prove or disprove that Enola was a sacred mountain to the Indians for cultural and religious significance and use. The anthropologist who was hired by the U.S. Forest Service submitted a report that Forest Service personnel were disappointed with. In his findings the anthropologist affirmed Enola as sacred and eligible for the National Register. Although the report supported the claims of many Indian Nations of the region, the agency sent the report back to the anthropologist instructing him to modify it. Unlike a similar situation on Mt. Shasta, California, where another anthropologist was asked to modify a report and refused, the Enola researcher did as he was instructed. As Michael Jones, head of the Cascade Geographic Society, said in response to current Forest Service actions, "If the agency can log Enola, then they can cut timber anywhere they desire. If this happens there will be no such thing as 'sacred land' — just destroyed natural areas that they will eventually turn into monoculture tree farms."

What is occurring in Oregon is also happening in Montana where Blackfeet traditionalists are fighting against plans for exploratory oil and gas drilling on sacred lands that Blackfeet communities have used for thousands of years. In Wyoming, Indians are fighting the government over the ancient Medicine Wheel in the Bighorn National Forest. Traditional Indians are struggling with the Forest Service to protect this ancient sacred rock site from future logging, grazing and tourist development, as well as trying to have exclusive right to use the sacred site for religious ceremonies 12 days each year.

In Arizona, Apache Indians are fighting the University of Arizona and the Roman Catholic Church to prevent construction of an observatory on Mount Graham in the Coronado National Forest. This has been a sacred ceremonial site used by Apaches for generations.

In Northern California, on Mount Shasta, Wintu Indians are working to get the Forest Service to reopen the review process in order to protect a sacred spring that will be included in a new ski development in the area.

In the Four Corners area of Arizona, New Mexico, Colorado and Utah, Native Americans are trying to stop strip mining. The U.S. government has created a land conflict between Navajo and Hopi in order to get certain land for mining that traditionalists of both tribes have fought against for years.

At no time since the late 1800s has there been such a concentrated effort to disregard Native American religious rights. But sacred land is an inconvenience for the economic minded National Forest managers who help corporations to develop timber, mineral and recreational rights as the first priority for "public" land use. These are the lands, however, that once were home to millions of indigenous native peoples. Indigenous and native peoples still go into the wild places to seek guidance and direction for personal decisions, as well as to gain the understanding that brings meaning and purpose to their lives. To them nature is a beloved relative. The stone people, the four-leggeds, the creepy-crawlers, the plant people and the bird people are as important as one's own children to native people. Native American people take seriously their relationship to the environment, and see these "relatives" as teachers for them.

Well before the Pilgrims landed at Plymouth native people had sophisticated governance structures to help keep their relationships with each other and nature in balance. Benjamin Franklin and other founding fathers of our constitution visited and talked with various Native American tribes. Many of the structural and democratic principles that were adopted into our form of government came from native peoples, particularly of the Iroquois confederacy.

The Iroquois confederacy existed 200 years before white people came to this continent. This confederacy consisted of five distinct tribal groups in the eastern woodlands: the Senecas, the Onondagas, the Cayuga, the Mohawk and the Oneida. In their councils, these Native Americans made decisions viewed in the light of seven future generations of consequences. They agreed on hunting territories so that not too much game would be taken, the locations of new villages, and the settling of inter-tribal disputes so that tribes wouldn't go to war with each other. It is also noteworthy that the women were responsible for choosing and removing the chiefs. The women would initiate action if the male leaders of the various tribes, and the council, failed to perform on behalf of the good of all the people. (It is noteworthy that the influence of women on male leaders was left out of our constitution.)

In the cosmology of the 700 distinct native language groups on the American continent was the common theme of the sacredness of the earth and the responsibility of the two-legged people to respect and honor the land. Gratefulness and appreciation for the world was at the heart of this sacredness. The Seneca thanksgiving speech is still given to this day after every tribal ceremony, except at the ceremony for the dead. This address gives the basic cosmology of the Seneca people, naming and giving thanks for all things. The speech embodies and recounts the equality of all things living together, and the purposes of the Spirit Creator for its gifts. People, water, plants, stones, animals, wind, thunder, moon, sun, stars, and the spirit beings that come in dreams, are part of this remembering and weaving together of all life. Each living being of the world is honored in thanksgiving. It is difficult, if not impossible, for machinelike corporations to convince native peoples that the land, the whole of the world, is not sacred. As the traditional Hopis say, "The land is the people."

Mander states the dilemma strongly when he says, "Since the beginnings of the technological juggernaut, the only consistent opposition has come from land-based native peoples. Rooted in an alternative view of the planet, Indians, islanders, and peoples of the North remain our most clear-minded critics. They are also our most direct victims. That technological society should ignore and suppress native voices is understandable, since to heed them would suggest *we must fundamentally change our way of life*. Instead, we say *they* must change. They decline to do so."

What would it mean for us to *fundamentally change our way of life?* What would it mean to reject the Machine we live in? To refuse to be robotlike cogs in the Machine? Is the only escape from the Machine to fall into a giant apocalypse of nuclear destruction, or to suffer an economic collapse that comes from natural resource depletion, or to experience over-population pressures and ozone and global warming catastrophes? Most of us can comprehend the problems inherent in all the above issues, but most of us find them too large to grapple with in our daily lives. Simply coping with our own tensions and problems is struggle enough.

In returning to the sacred, I am not calling for us to idealize indigenous peoples. I am suggesting that these ancient peoples still embody a sacred viewpoint that lies deep within our own memories. Our construction of reality, because we are raised in the Machine's value system, is different from aboriginal and native peoples. As much as drumming and rattles appeal to some deep psychic root in our consciousness, the reality is that we make up our world differently than they do. We live inside our heads with an ego that talks to us all the time. Indigenous people hear the otherworld voices of spirits and ancestors. Actually it is easier for them to be swept up into our Machine world of television, VCRs and Coca Cola than it is for us to move into the spiritual strangeness and physical inconvenience of their world. Part of the problem of "going native" for either an anthropologist or any one of us, is that we find it difficult to change our interior world. It is just as difficult for indigenous peoples to give up their perception that the earth is sacred.

Part of being "hippie" in the 1960s was the idealized state where we threw off our clothes and returned to nature. Nudity, "free sex," and the communal life was part of this return-to-nature feeling. It didn't stick as a lifestyle for middle-class kids and young adults then, and it won't lead us out of our present abyss. But those feelings about wanting to return to nature and rejecting the so-called American dream" is part of what we are recovering in ourselves today. At that time, as now, we were breaking through some of our fundamental belief patterns about our culture.

Something initiated us into another set of beliefs, another set of perceptions, emotions and behaviors. We were baptized into some Spirit, and no matter where our lives have taken us since, that Spirit is still in us and has, in fact, been passed on to our children. It is my belief that this Spirit is the core of the Sacred, of the sane place inside of us that we want to recover. For our children as well as for us, a new initiation into the Sacred is now needed. Elders among native peoples around the world still know the secret of this Sacred initiation. The need in our culture is to recover respect and honor for our older men and women and to give back to them the role of elder-leader. We need to reclaim the tradition of affirming the role of elder as initiator of young men and women into a balanced and healthy relationship to the earth. And we need to rediscover the ancient tradition of initiating our elders into the powers of the otherworld. By learning to initiate elder-leaders, we will once again be capable of reinstating the sacred as a powerful and healing force within our own culture.

A Call for Elder-leaders

*T*he role of the elder woman and man traditionally has been that of a person with authority and dignity within the community who carries the values, traditions, and experiential wisdom of the people. Elders can help balance, heal and restore the constant strain of interaction between people, environmental conditions and the relationship to the spiritual world. Being in a different stage of life, elders are slower to action, more cautious in their decisions, and, most importantly, are more willing to take the longer view on issues. They have fewer pressures generally and no deadlines to meet. In the life of the community, elders can act as a balance to the impetuousness, heat and quickness of youth. But true elders do not squash and control the energy and dynamics of youth. The elder's role is to channel, focus, bless and encourage youthful energy toward constructive and creative ends in society. There is a direct link between elders and youth. If the elders are doing their job appropriately, youth move into adulthood contributing to the community. From the elders they can learn how to temper their youthful fire. Elders, give guidance through adulthood and help to sustain a balanced life of economic fulfillment, artistic and creative expression along with spiritual and political governance within the community.

With the growth of the Machine over the past 100 years, elder leadership has waned and all but been destroyed in Western culture. Rather than given dignity and authority, our elders are often separated from families and put into retirement compounds. Rather than observing youngsters in their communities and helping to guide, initiate and mentor them, our elders often sit and watch the problems of youth played out on *Days of Our Lives* or other soap operas and sitcoms. Until 75 to 100 years ago there was no retirement for older people. Their role was to focus on the children, share their wisdom and insight and prepare for their own crossing through the portals of death. It was acknowledged by society that as older people they were at a different stage of activity and purpose in their lives, but clearly there was a role for them.

Our current idea of retirement is associated with the release from the daily job as if it were a prison. Retirement is the release from the isolation, alienation and fragmentation of a life compartmentalized between work and what we call our "real" life of family or hobbies or recreation. Retirement means we can have our own lives back once again. Retirement means we no longer have a boss telling us what to do. The problem is, that by the time we reach retirement age, we have been so conditioned by our jobs and hypnotic consumption that we don't know how to reclaim our lives for ourselves. We replace the time we spent at our jobs with more of the consumption and recreation pattern rather than learning to grow and change into a different role as a responsible elder in the community.

Within the fragmentation that occurs between work obligations and personal fulfillment, we have lost a sense of individual and collective purpose and direction. Our formal education hasn't taught us about the stages of life and initiations that humans need to go through. And our parents and grandparents were removed far enough from this knowledge themselves that they couldn't articulate it to us. Without this elder wisdom, community and society no longer provides us with the wider vision and context in which to develop and grow as a human being. Without this context we are cast into life alone without an operating manual that can show us the connection between the beginning of life and its end.

Out of our loss of a meaningful sacred connection to life, we became frightened of death. We lost the sense of the stage in human development that death plays in each of our lives. As a result we have lost meaningful rituals for those who die. Our only alternative for those who are dying is to try to keep them medically alive, often, far beyond the wishes of the ill person and the family members.

We are taught to fear aging and death so we create a cultural facade and pretend that we never get old. Our facade is eternal youthfulness. Beauty is defined as a certain age, a certain physical look, a certain style of living. The propaganda of the Machine reinforces the fear of death with new products. To preserve youth we create the need for "things" from hair dye to facelifts to tummy tucks. In the disconnection from both the sacred and the purposefulness of old age, our older leaders learned to copy the media hype — the youthful patterns. Our older leaders are dieting, jogging, often wearing the most youthful fashions; many participate in seniors-level marathons and so on. In the most basic way those who should be our elder-leaders are unwilling to accept their natural stage in life; they use their energy in trying to look and be younger. Our cultural taboo of growing old is robbing us of the human resource that is most needed at this time.

My call is for us to recover elder-leadership in a youth-dominated culture. Young people often turn toward novelty, and challenge the structure and dynamics of current values and traditions. With this natural challenge, society needs to have a big enough container so that the living essence of those values and traditions aren't destroyed. Because young people lack groundedness as they work and play and experiment, elder-leaders can provide the context, the experimental ground, the depth of perspective, and the boundaries that help not only young people but the culture itself to stay healthy and in balance.

The indigenous people of the planet still know the principles of elder-leadership, the initiation process into this stage of life, the perspective of how it functions, and the tools that are needed by elders to foster the capacities of leadership within themselves. From indigenous peoples we can observe the practical results of thousands of years of elders being the carriers of the sacred for their communities. This knowledge can give us insights and understandings that can help to reclaim the souls of the millions of older women and men who have not been initiated into the next-to-final stage of their life's journey. This knowledge can help them restore the dignity and honor that their life experience deserves.

The Elder Stage of Life

To those of us in our late forties and early fifties, this "spirit," this imprint of the sacred in our lives has been an unconscious beacon. It has been pulling us toward something. In our twenties we broke free from our families and from unconscious societal conditioning. In our thirties we explored our strengths and capabilities. In our forties we tried to create something new in the world. But now that we are in our fifties, we need to take the responsibility to give shape and direction to our culture.

Carl Jung in his classic essay, "The Stages of Life," submits this question of culture to us. He asks, "Could by any chance culture be the meaning and purpose of the second half of life?" He goes on to observe that old people in tribal cultures were always the guardians of the mysteries and laws of the people. He then says, "How does the matter stand with us? Where is the wisdom of our old people, where are their precious secrets and their visions? For the most part our old people try to compete with the young." Jung then tells us that the confusion and fear about old age and the "cult of youth" occurs because the only purpose that is taught older people is to keep expanding what they did through the first half of their lives:

making money, increasing position in society, and continuing to expand personal prestige. "The afternoon of human life must also have a significance of its own and cannot be merely a pitiful appendage of life's morning." The reason for this failure, Jung says, of having few wise elders is that we now "have no schools for 40-year-olds. That is not quite true. Our religions were always such schools in the past, but how many people regard them as such today."

Many of the older cultures gave men and women a second initiation around the age of 50. Even today there are still indigenous peoples who initiate people at different periods in a person's life. The Dagara people in West Africa initiate boys and girls between 13 and 17 with rites of adulthood. This initiation gives them direct connection to the sacredness of the otherworld of the ancestors and a larger spiritual reality. The rites also gave them a deep respect and clear knowledge of the cosmology of their tribe.

Initiation with the Dagara of West Africa

Malidoma Somé, who wrote the preface for this book, went through the last officially sanctioned initiation as a Dagara in his African village at the of age of 22. In a forthcoming book about his life, Malidoma describes in detail the six weeks in the African bush that stripped him of dependency on parents and Western cultural experience, and the process that gave him direct and conscious connection to the world of spirit with his ancestors. Through the guidance of several elders, Malidoma and 63 other boys, between the ages of 13 and 17, were taught to see, hear and physically go into other-dimensional experiences. Malidoma's tradition teaches that initiation can only occur in nature. The trees, the plants, the rocks, the animals and the land itself that are the teacher-initiator. The elders simply work in harmony with the natural world to open the door into other dimensions.

Malidoma was taken away from his family by the Jesuits at the age of five years, and not permitted to return home until he was 22 years old. At that time he was thrown out of the Jesuit seminary. He no longer knew his own language or customs. Malidoma walked 150 miles to get to his village, and for six months the elders discussed what to do with him. The elders finally concluded that their only hope for Malidoma's sanity and health would be to initiate the young man in the traditional manner. In the Dagara initiation one either dies or returns alive and changed after six weeks in the bush. After returning home to himself and his people through this initiation, the elders then instructed Malidoma to go back to the Western world. The elders told him his purpose for returning was threefold: to remind Western people about the sacredness of this world; to enlighten and teach Westerners about the sacred world of the ancestors; and, to urge Westerners to help the Dagara people find a way to preserve the traditional and spiritual life that is rapidly being destroyed by consumerism, materialism and the disappearance of both natural resources and animal species.

In the 12 years following his initiation in the African bush, Malidoma, returned to school where he completed a master's degree at the national University in Burkina Faso, a master's and a doctorate from the Sorbonne in Paris, and another master's and doctorate from Brandeis University in New York state. But for all this Western education, Malidoma asserts that it was his six weeks of non-Western education, that of being initiated into the realities of the Otherworld by the Ancestors in the African bush that taught him real knowledge. Malidoma is a bridge between two worlds of information and knowledge. He carries two separate worlds within himself: the Western world of the highly educated and the Otherworld of knowledge and wisdom that comes through the doorway of Nature.

Malidoma recognizes that Westerners can't be initiated as he and his wife, Sobonfu, were initiated in Africa. But he says that we must be *responsible* to ourselves and to this Western world in a different way than we have been up to now. He says, "To be responsible is to *remember*. In Africa, initiation is a process of recalling and reactivating lost memories. The first step in the process of initiation is knowing and managing knowledge. The result of initiation is to make oneself the primary project of one's life."

Malidoma's call to the human robot in us is make a commitment to gain knowledge by remembering. Within us are 40,000 to 60,000 years of memories about how to live in relationship to nature, to spiritual reality, and to each other. The indigenous, native peoples of the planet still hold some of this knowledge. Their ultimate value to our time is to help us remember the pathway between this world and the world of spirit around us. Indigenous people tell us we still have the doorway of remembrance — Nature. We need to learn how to use nature's doorway again before we destroy every living thing on the pathway to its entrance.

Initiation Is Remembering

Malidoma, in responding to the question of how we can be initiated into remembering, acknowledges that we need elders who have themselves remembered. Remembering means having gained knowledge and wisdom, and having been given techniques from the otherworld in how to initiate young people into the sacredness of this world. Many of the older cultures gave men and women a second initiation around the age of 50 to do this.

The initiation of men and women around 50 years of age in Malidoma's village gives them direct knowledge and communication between the world of spirits and the physical world. In this initiation they are given the knowledge and power of the *primary* language. This is the language of the spiritual world that can create unexpected events in the physical world. Basic to being given the primary language is the understanding of how to initiate boys into manhood and girls into womanhood; how to keep balance and harmony between the natural world and the unseen world; and, how to resolve emotional and physical sickness through ritual and ceremony. The initiated men and women have their own family and day-to-day living responsibilities, but they also do physical and spiritual healing and survival work together as critical situations occur in the village. But most of their days are spent talking together, doing artistic and ritual work together, singing and playing together, and as a sacred obligation holding together a sense of responsibility for their community and people.

It is this communal initiation that we have missed as women and men moving into our fifties and sixties. This is an initiation in which we come to know the language and roadmaps of moving between the otherworld of animistic and spiritual complexity and this physical one. Some of us have had spontaneous experiences of the otherworld and feel connected to it. But we don't seem to have a common experience or language in order for us to work together in channeling the power of the non-material world into this one. We seem to do well at diagnosing problems here, but we don't seem to know how to get power from "over there." We are beginning to experiment with ritual, but outside of traditional Native American experience in this country we have little context, experience or understanding of the procedures and dynamics of particular sacred rituals for specific situations.

Most of all, we lack a personal and shared connection to the otherworld on a daily basis. Our dominated Machine-driven lives give us little time to do the real work of meditation, healing, ritual, and little time alone to listen and hear the Voice of the Other in us.

Myth, Ritual and Power

Mircea Eliade, the great mythologist, believed that myth, ritual and power were linked together. In fact, all ancient cultures have known for thousands of years that power was an interaction between the seen and unseen. Power came from outside the material world, and myth (the cultural story that links the Spirit world to this one) provided the understanding of the power. Myth gave the boundaries, conditions and approaches to the power. Ritual was a technique for using and determining how the power could be used. Ritual protected us from the power. Ritual proscribed the conduit through which power could be channeled safely.

Rediscovering the relationship between myth, ritual and power may be one of the paths back to our ancient roots. The lessons of history and current anthropological research indicate that peoples worked with this power in communities. *To revive our mythic roots, to restore vital and living ritual and become conscious and respectful so that we can interact with the power and force of Nature — of some Force beyond rational definition — this is the fundamental change we must make.*

What frightens and even depresses us at times is this seeming inability to make this kind of fundamental change because of the magnitude and overpowering quality of Machine life. Time and time again we see what happens to men and women who buy power and influence with money — they ultimately fail and cut away part of their soul. Given this dark power and its hold on us, I am convinced that we cannot change our lives alone. We need others to help create environments of learning and growth that will allow and urge us to change. Most of all we need environments that encourage and nurture the sacred in us. We need environments that connect us daily to the ancient and musical rhythms of the natural world. We need our work and activity connected to our innate creativity, not just to our economic survival. We need to regain a myth — a story — that can channel the power of our lives at this time.

Ancient societies even today in Africa, Australia, the South Pacific, and South America spend an average of just three days a week providing for food and shelter. Members spend the rest of the time participating in creative arts, sacred ritual, festivals and human interaction. In contrast, we in the so-called advanced civilized cultures, have made economic survival our all-consuming activity. And we've created not only work communities but a consumptive culture that separates us into cells of private pain, fear and meaninglessness. We spend more and more time at work activities that remove us farther and farther from each other and from the sacred dimensions of nature.

Jerry Mander states strongly that the ability to make this personal and cultural change is rooted in how well we protect, or fail to protect, these indigenous peoples who carry the sacred remembering. These endangered peoples possess values that we need to have as guides through this critical contemporary period. "In the later stages of an epic worldwide struggle," he says, "the forces of Western economic development are assaulting the remaining native peoples of the planet, whose presence obstructs their progress. . . . Upon the ultimate outcome of this battle will depend whether a living alternative world view, rooted in an ancient connection with the Earth, can continue to express what is insane and suicidal about the Western technological project." Yet, even with the dark and voracious mouth of the Machine eating us up, we can answer a call: Men and women who are moving into the second half of their lives, need now to share the wisdom and gifts from what they've learned in order to bring balance and harmony back to their communities.

Agnes Vanderburg is a 79-year-old Flathead Indian tribal leader. In the journal *Parabola,* an entire issue was devoted to the theme of "The Old Ones" and Agnes was asked to share her gifts of wisdom as an elder-leader. She describes how she attempts to teach the young people the old ways. For one thing she is concerned about the influence of TV on young people. "They even show on TV how to steal a car, how to break into a house . . . that's what I don't like. That's where they learn all these bad things." In the article Agnes goes on to describe her work teaching young adults their native language, how to dry meat, and how to take care of their bodies. "The way the old people was, they never had no doctors . . . They knew what the roots and plants were for. Now there's all sorts of sickness, heart attacks, cancer, all that stuff; we've got the medicine for 'em, if they'd just leave these drugs and pills and shots; that's no good for your body. I start showing them all our medicine." Agnes mourns the loss of community and tradition, and says that her purpose is to teach people to remember the old ways. And to us who need to be reminded of our duty and role as we get older, Agnes says, "Tell 'em what you know of the old ways. A lot of 'em don't care, but some of them do. . . . *What little you know, tell 'em* [my emphasis]. You feel good afterward; you get everything right for yourself. And some of them will listen."

Initiating Elder-leaders

John W. Gardner, in his book *No Easy Victories,* says, "Leaders have a significant role in creating the state of mind that is the society. They can serve as symbols of the moral unity of the society. They can express the values that hold the society together. Most important, they can conceive and articulate goals that lift people out of their petty preoccupations, carrying them above the conflicts that tear a society apart, and unite them in pursuit of objectives worthy of their best efforts." Without a new leadership, without healthy, mature elders to help raise up new images at the center of our world community, we will continue to live in a narrow economic definition of reality that excludes, or minimizes the importance of an inner spiritual world. Without new forms of leadership there may well be no elders to teach the rituals and the various stages of life, none to teach how to be truly human, none to bring us into contact and balance with the natural world, and none to show us the inner guide that can help us redefine a new world. Without this kind of elder leadership in our families and communities, we will increasingly drift away from life's deepest knowing, life's greatest joys, and lose ourselves in the Machine.

Yes, it is true that our initiation as elders will not be easy. In a youth culture we have regulated older people to the role of useless parts. Our culture no longer values older people like Agnes Vanderburg, and most people who have aged have, themselves, not learned how to tap the sources of wisdom that come through consistent contact with the natural world. Many older people are caught in the pseudo-life of television soaps and sitcoms, and therefore, they tend to only reinforce the Machine's values in younger people when they interact with them. We who are in our fifties and sixties must learn to reclaim the role of elder in our culture. One of the first steps of initiation is learning to be quiet, and in turning off the media and entertainment input. We need to spend as much time as we can in natural settings and listen to what nature will teach us. Slowing down, being quiet, and listening are, in my view, the first initiation steps to becoming an elder-leader. In these ways we can begin to rediscover the old and new ways that can return health to our communities.

Old and New Forms of Leadership

It is with these critical issues in mind, and with the awareness that we come together within *the crisis of the crossroads*, that we must examine the potentials for a more healthy pattern of elder-leadership in our world and communities. The crisis of the crossroads has been with us as long as we've been on the planet. But the resolution of our Machine's cultural crisis may determine our most basic survival as a species. *Leadership from those of us in our fifties and sixties must take both old and new forms if we are to get through our current crisis.* We have some work to do individually and collectively:

• We must return to the past of our distant ancestors and find the images of the ancient power that comes from outside and beyond the material world.

- We must understand anew the value and power of myths and how they create boundaries for the choices we make in the world.

- As elder-leaders we must discover the potent use of ritual that creates a conduit through which power for healing can be safely channeled.

- We must also explore the forward flow of today's circumstances to find the elder-leader pattern that best works for us now.

Somehow we can all feel that our political and economic leadership, and often our spiritual leadership, is bankrupt. The Machine sucks up our leaders and warps their capacity to be responsible to members of society, or to the natural world. We, who would be initiated into an elder-leader role, walk this same fine line as we try to distance ourselves from the Machine's values, beliefs and perceptions. Our saving and protecting power in this crisis of leadership, however, is in the natural world and it's access to the world of the Sacred. The world of the Sacred is fundamentally more powerful to help us than the Machine.

There is an old African ritual designed to meet such crises. The ritual calls for two groups lined up opposite each other, giving a call-and-response chant back and forth. This particular chant is used when the problems in the village are very great and the people have no answers about what to do. In this chant they call to the gods to come to the crossroads to help them, protect them and guide them in a safe direction. During the ritual the people sing loud and strong as they move in line toward those opposite them; they also make exaggerated body and hand movements to demonstrate their serious intent and resolve in calling the gods to help them. Through this generating of physical, emotional and spiritual intensity a clarity, direction and new way is revealed to the community.

In small and large groups and with great intensity, we must call forth together for a new direction and leadership. Our challenge is to find the way to reinitiate our elders so that healing and help can come to our wounded brothers and sisters and to our wounded communities. This call and challenge is to each of us individually who have arrived at this elder-leader stage of life.

Our Essential Uniqueness

*T*he challenge for me, personally, as an oiler of the Machine is to release my grip on the oilcan and store it on the shelf. I see both the outer events of the Machine collapsing and my own inner voice calling to me. But the question for many of us is "How do I survive?" How do I "live in the world of the Machine and not be of it?" How do I redefine my life and move from dominator values to partnership, nature-based values of living? These questions point to two possibilities: feeling the pull of the Oversoul toward something in the future we can't rationally describe, and an urge, that natural impulse in all of us, to express ourselves creatively and uniquely. How do women and men in the midst of this change-of-state condition take the natural next step of growth in their lives?

Choosing to take this fork in the road implies taking on a different kind of leadership role as well as being more receptive to an untapped part of our lives. An idea from Robert Bly offers one challenge, the notion of choosing the "one precious thing" in our lives. There comes a point for each of us where out of the myriad of interests and capabilities we narrow our focus and commit ourselves to one thing, one issue, one idea, one vocation. It is often difficult to awaken our unique creativity when scrambling to maintain our work as well as being absorbed in hours of reading, or listening and watching television, films, videos, radio and the like. To nurture our creative potential will require a reordering of our time, priorities and commitments.

When I hear people talk about what they creatively want to do, our discussion usually centers on choosing one thing over another. And the choices often are based on decisions about "what do I want to do when I grow up?" These women and men say for example, "I want to make money as a writer, or a full-time artist, or I want to study some healing technique and open a practice." *Choosing*, in our culture, implies an ego-centered decision. "I choose" implies I am in control of what is going on in my life.

I want to suggest another possibility about choosing. It is not so much that I choose. Rather, it is that I commit to something that is presented to me — that is choosing *me*. I believe, as we move into our fifties, the personal attraction from the Oversoul pulls at us. It *chooses us* for some focused kind of activity that is uniquely suitable to each of us. This appears to be the experience that indigenous people also go through with their initiations in their early fifties. The challenge of the initiation from the otherworld is not personal but communal. The question is not what issues or things will I choose as priorities, but, rather, will I get quiet, listen, and make a commitment to what is obviously being made apparent in me and to me? And, further, will I choose the quality of expression in my life that will most help in the balancing and healing of my community?

Finding Our Iron

Heeding the call and making this choice and commitment is what Robert Bly calls letting go of the copper and becoming iron. By allowing ourselves to remain copper we continue to be conductors of everyone else's feelings, wants and needs. For example, I have used my copper for many years by being the mediator, the diplomat who smoothes the way and takes care of everyone else's needs. Everyone else's energy and feelings moved through my copper personality: I was a strong conductor of other's energy rather than clearly expressing my own energy and creativity. Iron, on the other hand, grounds and holds the power and energy in itself rather than immediately conducting it away from the source. I've slowly learned to promote myself for other opportunities beyond teaching or working with organizations. I find it easier to say no to those projects that won't help me learn something new, or that won't contribute to some healthy change in people. The time has come for us to find and heed our inner iron, to ground our own energy in the place where we can live and create.

For me the critical shift came when I started a new company with two other men. We named the company, Ontara, which in Sanskrit means "to take the next step in balance." Our company vision was to help organizations take their natural next step of growth in balance. This company was going to be my "last" major effort before retiring. However, this endeavor was the threshold for my next step of growth, finding both my iron and beginning to be called to my uniqueness. This challenge and shift toward letting the attraction and energy from the Oversoul choose me, came first from the experience of going out of balance in my personal life. This then led to my having to make a difficult professional choice.

Because of the market opportunities, Ontara grew very quickly. We added people, took on new office space, and dramatically increased our demand for monthly cash flow. As with many fast growing companies we got caught in a cash-flow problem. We were 60 days out on our receivables, but needed to pay salaries and bills every month. Our operating capital was being eaten up, and we were facing all the classic start-up dilemmas. At this point our unique vision and organizational structure risked being forced into a frantic survival mode. Although I reduced my consulting load in order to focus on running the company, when the financial pressure on the company grew, I put myself back into full gear as a consultant (notice the Machine language). In order to keep the company going, I committed to 20 calendar days a month consulting, and bringing in business for the other consultants as well as. Although I succeeded, I did so at a price to my body and soul, and to my relationship with my wife.

Consultants normally try to schedule 12 billable days a month. The other eight days of the month are for preparation, marketing, selling and doing the necessary administration of running a business. At 20 billable consulting days, and also participating in running the company, I worked nights and weekends. I kept this frantic schedule going for four months. And to complicate life even further, I lived in the mountains three-and-one-half hours from the office, so I was on the road constantly. The final stress included my wife's health — Patt was very ill with a serious physical and psychological condition, Chronic Fatigue Immune Deficiency Syndrome.

Several things happened to me during those busy months. The first was an intangible. I learned, somehow, in the commitment to keep the company going how to create money. Like most people, I had a basic anxiety about maintaining an income, and fear of not having enough money. In this experience the copper part of me concerning money changed to iron. I made some kind of connection deep inside about how to manifest money. Work, or sources of income, as they are needed, simply come to me now. I no longer feel that deep unconscious fear about surviving.

As long as we are in a place of fear about where the money will come, it is difficult to focus energy on living out our unique creativity. Others have asked what I did to make the change inside. The best way I can describe it is that when I gave myself totally to something larger, more transpersonal than myself — the survival of a vision and 13 other colleagues — the fear disappeared about personal survival and having enough money. I believe the universal truth is this: When we focus on a purpose larger than ourselves and not on the fear, we can tap the creative, generative force available to all of us for manifesting our hopes, dreams and aspirations.

The second thing that happened was quite a shock — I had to face the fact that I was as crazy, stressed out, and totally immersed in the business as any of the executives that I had been coaching in my consulting. My body was exhausted and my soul was empty. One night, late into the fourth month, while driving the three-and-one-half hours to our home in the mountains, I realized suddenly that I could feel nothing inside. I was an empty vessel. I could find no place of contact with my soul or that spiritual part of me. I had a frightening thought. In trying to save the business, had I sold my soul to the devil? I arrived home deeply shaken. Patt greeted me at the door saying, "I can't live this kind of life any longer. You are never home, and when you are, you always have a phone in your ear. I talk to you and you don't answer me. Either this changes or I am leaving."

For the next five days we argued and struggled with our relationship and my commitment to the company. Within a month I resigned from Ontara. Although I had been playing the role of Superman in those four months, my body, mind and soul were way out of balance; something deep inside was dying . After I gave up Ontara, I began a two-and-one-half year analysis with a therapist that helped me break open some of the fundamental blocks in my life. During these transition years, the initiation and hearing of the inner call from the universe to my unique contribution on the planet began to happen. It was a painful and dark night for my soul. In releasing old negative energy I faced a life-threatening disease and a loss of outer purpose in my life. Afterwards, when I went back to a private consulting practice, I did so on entirely different terms than from the frantic way I had worked before.

In his work, *Iron John*, Robert Bly states that "the passion in our nature urges a human being to choose 'the one precious thing,' and urges him to pay for it through poverty, conflict, deprivation, labor, and the endurance of anger from rejected divinities. It is the warrior [in a person] that enables the human being to decide to become a musician only, or a poet only, or a doctor only, or a hermit only, or a painter only. It is the lover in a man or woman who loves the one precious thing, and tells him what it is; but it is the warrior in Rembrandt or Mirabai who agrees to endure the suffering the choice entails." It seems that it is in the act of discovering and paying the price to commit to one thing, to our uniqueness, that we begin to exercise the iron of our lives, and move through this special and intense part of our initiation.

The Male-mother and the Crone

This discovering the "one precious thing" of uniqueness in one's life is not a random happening. In the classic process of initiation there are several stages. The first stage is the bonding and separation from the mother. The second stage is bonding with the father and separation from the father. Bly notes at this stage that "we often postpone the father bonding until we are 50 or so, and then separation still has to be done."

At the age of 47, while still in analysis, I went through an experience where I came to appreciate and love my father and accept who and what he was. I let go of my anger for his abandoning me, and for devoting all his energy in building and running his business. My own experience with starting Ontara showed me that I was playing out the same dynamics and the same workaholism as my father had done years before. Through the therapeutic work, I healed both my own hurt and his hurt. This enabled me to let my father go in peace, rather than reject him. In this experience I could get free of many unconscious, pleasing patterns that I had adopted around getting approval from him. I noticed also that many women and men friends and acquaintances said they shared similar struggles and insights about their own mothers and fathers at this mid-life age.

The third stage of initiation is the one that particularly interests me at this time. It is the arrival of what Bly calls the male-mother, or a nurturing, wise guide for a man. And, for a woman, it is what the Jungian analyst and teacher, Marion

Woodman, in her work, *The Pregnant Virgin,* calls the Black Madonna, Sophia, or Crone — the deep-soul teacher of wisdom. These guides help us build a bridge to our own essence or to our essential uniqueness. This male-mother or Sophia can be in this world or in the eternal one. But their work is to bring to us what Bly calls a "horse of power," an internalized creativity that carries us forward in our life. The horse of power reconnects us with some creativity that may have frightened us when we were younger.

I had several encounters in my late twenties and early thirties with otherworld spirits and energies that seemed as though they might be life threatening if I pursued them. My interest in these encounters has driven me to the threshold of needing some guide either in this world or in the other who can help me through the fear. As I talk with others, I hear the same desire in them as well.

Woman's Sacredness and Her Body

Women seem closer to this threshold of the otherworld and often find it easier to go through this doorway of fear because of their stronger connection with the physical body. Marion Woodman in another of her works, *Addiction to Perfection,* says, "The natural feminine way to feminine maturity is through the body." She goes on to describe that the ancient initiation of women was through the process of getting women into deeper contact with their body wisdom. From this body wisdom, women seem to more easily connect to earth rhythms, and have through the millennia literally claimed the earth as their mother. In the goddess tradition, the initiation called for breaking away from the personal mother in order to connect deeply to the Mother Earth. But Woodman laments what is true for both women and men. "In our society, however, we have no rites and there are few older women who can initiate us into our own femininity. Most men and women, are unconsciously identified with the masculine principle (the conscious value system of our mothers), with little or no consciousness of our own feminine instincts." Woodman says that the Black Madonna plays an important initiation role for women in this time. While the White Madonna is the pure virgin, the Black Madonna plays out what the Hindus called Kali. Kali is the devouring and destructive energy that cuts deeply into the core psyche of a person. The Black Madonna takes a woman deep into earthy experiences, into sensuality, and into the fecundity of life. This initiation destroys the pretense of how women are supposed to perceive and behave in the White Male System. It gives the knowledge and wisdom of healing and the nurturing and creating of community. Either from this world or from the other world, women, perhaps even more than men, are feeling the call for this wisdom and power to return to them and to the earth. Women are coming together in small circles to explore their unique gifts in order to take this wisdom and power into to their communities.

Crying Out for Our Gift

There is a tradition with Native American Indians of crying or lamenting for a vision. Black Elk recounts the traditional manner that a Lakota Sioux woman or man would seek direction, guidance, and vision. Of importance to the Sioux and to most other tribes, was the seeking of the vision not just for oneself but for the tribal community.

As Black Elk describes the process, a woman or man would feel a strange urge, or an anxiousness, or a concern about someone or something. Recognizing this inner condition as a message, the individual would then go to a holy person in the tribe for help in preparing for a quest that would provide answers. The holy person helps prepare the individual to accomplish three steps in the process: (1) go through a purification in a sweat lodge or Inipi; (2) take part in a ritual smoking of the sacred pipe; and (3) prepare a sacred site for the lamenting ritual. Several others help the lamenter ready the ritual site and then lead the person, naked, to this place for a three- to four-day fast and crying. The site would either be in a high mountain area for men or in a low valley for women. Throughout these three or four days, the person cries and prays to the Great Spirit, Wakan-Tanka, to give a vision that will guide them, and that will help give strength and health to themselves and to their people.

Over and over the man or women prays and cries, "O Great Spirit, be merciful to me that my people may live!" During the days and nights the person is confined inside a four pointed area with a center pole representing the Great Spirit. The holy person instructs the lamenter to watch the weather, notice the birds and animals, note their dreams, and to be attentive to any strange occurrences. After the four days helpers return to the lamenter and lead him or her back to the community where the visions and experiences are first shared and then interpreted by the elders. This crying and humbling in one's nakedness, to seek guidance from the Spirit, reduces control of ego. In a time of isolation outdoors a person is sensitized and opened to a much greater range of feelings and perceptions; at the same time the lamenter knows that others are supporting him or her as they go through the physical, mental, and spiritual ordeal. Everyone knows the lamenter is doing the quest not just for himself or herself, but to benefit the community as well.

Women and men at mid-life in their fifties and sixties need to call out to reconnect to some deeper essential and creative part of themselves. We need to seek a focus that permits us to contribute to the world around us, in our circle of influence, in ways that genuinely can help bring hope and renewal to our communities. I believe many of us are longing, crying out, for true elders in our communities who can help guide us through these difficult and dangerous waters of the psyche and soul, and help initiate us into mid-life. Many of us may have to go into some form of seclusion to cry out to be initiated and to be given our unique gift for our sake and the sake of our community and world. However, to seek this initiation may be dangerous.

It is potentially dangerous because the creative "gold," our fundamental gift, emerges at this stage of initiation between the ages of 50 to 55, if the interior bridges between our heart and our soul have been properly built in us. The emergence of this gift in us can threaten others by its power and beauty. It is a dangerous time, Bly says, because this gift can open us to our grandeur, and what he calls our "mirrored greatness." I call this our *essential uniqueness*. This uniqueness begins to emerge, I believe, out of our contact with the otherworld. This powerful uniqueness is what mid-life women and men seek. They want to display and honor this power of the otherworld reflecting through them.

The traditional and ancient pattern of the Dagara people of Western Africa, for example, calls for women and men to display the healing power of the ancestral world through themselves. This display of power in themselves is honored and respected by the tribal community. Malidoma, the man who now bridges two worlds, describes being in his grandfather's healing hut late one night. Grandfather was staring into a bowl of water that he used as a psychic viewing mirror to watch the cattle at night. One night Malidoma watched his grandfather take a small arrow and send it out a hole in the side of the hut. The next morning grandfather told the younger men of the village that he had seen a lion stalking the herd and that he had sent an arrow to kill the lion. Later in the morning the men brought the dead lion back to the village, affirming that it was found dead in the place that grandfather said it would be. Malidoma also describes his grandmother, who was crippled, changing herself into a dog that would carry her out to the fields to tend children while their mothers worked the fields. In Malidoma's village the initiated elders had these strange powers, which they claim comes from the Otherworld. This power was used for the practical help of the village. To our Western minds these are indeed "high tales."

But perhaps we live in a larger, more mysterious world than we can imagine.

Elder Initiators

The warning that Bly gives for our culture is that this need for "mirrored greatness," this taking on the role of creator and healer, and the desire to be affirmed by others for doing it, may be dismissed and crushed by others in our society as being too grandiose.

In a culture that values neither old people nor a person being too different from the norm, individuals who display the strength and genuineness of themselves are often discounted, "killed off" by put-down, rejection, cynicism and scorn. This can be so crippling that they are then sucked into the group mind of the larger culture — a kind of losing of one's soul in the societal abyss. More than ever we need to support and affirm each other in the task of being initiated into our unique capabilities. Many executives that I've worked with long for this affirmation of "mirrored greatness" from their colleagues and those who work for them. But the lack of a strong connection between an awareness and development of an inner life and their outer circumstances of maintaining power and prestige, drives them into self-protective strategies of rage and abuse toward people around them. They become destroyers rather than healers. They act out the role of tyrant over others, demanding that others acknowledge their position of power as a substitute for the true greatness that actually is there, ready to radiate from their inner core.

Many of us who need the initiating must come together, ask, and call out for help. Our challenge is that we need to regain the pathway into the otherworld. The only way to regain the sacred pathway is to ask for help from that world. As Jesus said, "We have not, because we asked not." In the cultural twilight before the darkness it is time for us to ask together.

Bly has become a guide for many men in our country, as has the Jungian psychologist Marion Woodman become a mentor for women. They and other older men and women teachers have begun to encourage the notion of wisdom-elders in our society. But Bly, Woodman and other spiritual elders of prominence can't be the only kind of mentors that many of us need in order to learn to cross to the other shore of initiation into our essential uniqueness. We need also to have some kind of direct, personal connection with something or someone that initiates us into our role of being "connectors" between this world and the spiritual world of creative power and life.

If we choose the "one precious thing" (this essential uniqueness) or are chosen by it, something will happen to us. A mentor, an elder, a wise person will come to help connect this creative essence of ourselves to the Otherworld. It will then awaken our psyche's inner "king" or "queen." If we move from attitudes and behaviors that are adolescent, based on survival, to something that is mature, strong, natural, and powerful in us, we become the servant king and queen for our communities. To make the choice of the "one precious thing" is critical. But, again, the question is how do we begin to know what that "one precious thing" is?

How can we discover what we love well enough that we want to defend it? But even with a feeling of love and defending, something often stops us from being focused and taking action.

Elder-leaders Who Wake Us From the Trance

Part of the problem of consciously knowing that we've been chosen by our uniqueness is that we've learned to put ourselves into a trance. Further back at some point in our lives, we said no to this precious thing, and we hypnotized ourselves into believing we couldn't do this thing and be this person. A therapist friend suggested that the longer I remain in the trance, the farther away I am from the truth of me. Or, the longer I am "asleep" the farther away I am from the choice toward that one thing I long to awaken in me. In effect I remain in denial about my true calling. Watching daily for what entrances us and then acting to awaken from our sleep will get us closer to the "one precious thing." Sometimes the hypnotic trance that engulfs us is obvious. I can awaken and decide to break the habit of watching television soaps, sitcoms, football games and commercials. I can learn to acknowledge and accept what people tell me about my hypnotic behaviors. But more subtle are the interior trances of denial, depression, guilt, anger or fear. For this we probably need help from spiritual and psychological counselors who are able to guide us through our protective trance defenses. Our challenge is to begin focusing on that one important thing that calls to us, that notion or idea that awakens us to the bridge between learned perceptions of cultural reality and the natural world. And we also need the elders to help us awaken from the personal and cultural trance of the Machine.

The Russian mystic and teacher, G.I. Gurdjieff, was this kind of elder-leader. Trained in the Sufi mystery schools of central Eurasia, he focused much of his teaching around what he called the "false personality" which keeps us in a trance and causes us great suffering. Basic to the waking up process of Gurdjieff's work was overcoming the personal and cultural hypnosis by using attention exercises. These were both physical and mental exercises which he described as self-remembering and self-observation methods that would break up the false personality (or ego), and allow a person to open up and notice their essential uniqueness. Leading thinkers and creative people in the early part of this century found a strong initiation of body, mind and spirit in what Gurdjieff taught. As in most good initiation processes, Gurdjieff's work with people was non-verbal and focused on body learning. This kinesthetic aspect of our nature is then awakened in our connection with the natural world and helps us remember the old ways.

The biggest gift available, the one to help us awaken from our hypnotic trance is the natural world. Taking every opportunity to roam and walk among the trees and rivers, animals and mountains, deserts and flowers will permit the cultural shroud to drop away from our hearts and minds. Indigenous people say that no person can initiate another. Only by being in nature can one learn to connect with the healing power of the otherworld. Nature is our ultimate teacher, our healer, our doorway beyond the robotlike existence created by the Machine culture.

The Sound of Our Soul

When I first heard the sound, I was sitting and facing south toward Flat Top Mountain 50 miles away. I was in retreat in the high hermitage on the Lama Foundation Community property in the mountains of northern New Mexico.

I had joined the community after living for nine months in the Findhorn Community in northern Scotland. Findhorn was an extroverted, service-oriented community of 300 people. The Lama community was small, introverted, closed to outsiders, and focused on personal inward growth. Besides the community buildings, meditation halls and resident cabins, there were two hermitages. One was called the "low hermitage," a cave built in a narrow ravine a brisk walk from the main part of the community. The "high hermitage" was 1,000 feet farther up the mountain from the community buildings and was hidden by the pine forest. Twice a year community residents chose one of the two hermitages for a one to two week silent retreat.

The high hermitage was a small one room cabin perched at the 8,000-foot level on the side of Wheeler Mountain. On a rocky bluff above the cabin I could see some hundred miles up and down the Sangre de Cristo (the Blood of Christ) mountain range, and another hundred miles to the west into the Rio Grande Basin. This was my spring retreat and for four of the days in this high wild place I had done a series of spiritual practices to quiet my mind. In the afternoons I would sit on the bluff above the cabin until the sun set.

It was now the fifth day, and I had been sitting for several hours in the sun above the cabin listening to the wind flood through the trees, and then spill over me as it rushed down the mountainside. I fell into daydreams of ocean waves crashing over me and of women in grass skirts slowly twisting, turning, and making gentle swishing sounds. From time to time the air was punctuated with the caw of a raven or a whistle of a hawk swooping down across the near ridge. I seemed to move in and out of trance listening to the external sounds, and then drifting with the images and sounds that seemed to flow slowly through my inner terrain.

At first I thought an airplane was flying over head when the sound became distinct for me. I looked up and around but the sky was completely clear and clean of anything moving through it. The sound seemed to get louder, and then when I focused on it, it would recede quietly back into the tapestry of the natural sounds. When I couldn't hear the sound, I told myself I had been mentally drifting, and settled back into my reverie. In a short while the sound came again, louder and stronger.

The sound was like a great hum. It was a physical and audible vibration that seemed to move the air around me. The sound penetrated my body and filled my abdomen with a warmth that radiated through me. The conversation in my head stopped and a joy opened within me that I had not known for years. I felt comforted and succored by the sound. After awhile I noticed that the great hum seemed external, arising from the earth where I was sitting. I lay down, curled in a fetal position and received this great vibrating sound like an infant at the breast of its Mother. More than any other time in my life I felt completely at home and unconditionally accepted in this world.

I lay in the sun on the earth, cradled in the sound, for a long time. When I walked back to the cabin the great humming sound was still with me. If I tried to analyze it, or to consciously think about it in any way, the sound would begin to fade out. If I simply noticed it, and allowed it to be in the background of my thoughts or actions, then it remained as a constant companion. The vibrating sound continued to envelop me for the remaining days at the hermitage; I felt held within it as though in some great sacred container. Within this container, my inner world of imagination seemed to flower and open in remarkable ways.

Many times since my retreat at the high hermitage, when I've been in other high, wild places this great vibrating sound will return. After three or four days in higher altitudes, my body, soul, mind and spirit open enough that I can hear what I have come to call for myself the sound of Mother Earth, the comforting vibration of Existence. As weird or strange as things have gotten sometimes when I've been alone in the wilderness, I have never felt frightened when I've been in contact with this universal sound. It is different from the music I described in the first chapter; the music hasn't reoccurred, but this deep vibrating hum has returned every time I go into wild places.

Others have reported hearing this sound. They recount the same experience I've had of deep comfort, centeredness of mind and body, and an extraordinary opening of the imagination in which something sacred seems to be taught to them. It is interesting to note that scientists have recorded a vibrational pattern from the earth that is the same cycle per second as our heart's pumping action, and the same vibration pattern as the monotone of the drum beat used by native people in their ceremonies. Native peoples say that the sound of a drum is the heart beat of Mother Earth reminding us of her presence.

Deep within each of us is the eternal pattern of sacred sound. It is the Logos, the Voice, the Other. In some hidden corner of our soul this sound calls to each of us. It is calling us to something larger and fuller than ourselves. It gives us the sound of our uniqueness. This sound opens the doorway to our imagination so that we can heal and reclaim our souls. It is the sound that comes from ancient human experience and takes us forward into an unfolding future. Its gentle sound is the ground and bedrock of our daily lives. It is the beacon that calls us home, back to ourselves and to our human family. This sound is the echo of the transcendent within our practical daily lives. It is what calls us to be holy and whole once again. It is the universal source that has called us through history and which will take us beyond the dilemma we face today.

The World of Imagination

*F*rom the basic and fundamental teachings of indigenous peoples around the world, we learn that nature opens us to see and hear differently. With the constant input of television, radio, newspapers, books, and films we are hyper-stimulated with myriad sounds and images. The sounds and images in nature and within the nature of our own bodies, however, are much softer, quieter, and more subtle than the multifaceted sounds of the Machine.

Vision and sound, light and vibration: These are the contrasting elements of creation. Both electrify the world of imagination. Both help us experience the ancient tradition of being in balance with existence. Ancient tradition often begins with sound, with the "word," with a strong interior voice that can give guidance and direction to the individual.

Up until about A.D. 100, peoples of the Hellenistic world heard what they called the Logos. This was a voice that directly communicated inside their heads and would answer when they asked it questions. Julian Jaynes, in his book, *The Origin of Consciousness in the Breakdown of the Bicameral Mind,* argues that it was the connection with this Other Voice that individually and collectively guided people. After a many-thousand-year connection with this Other reality within the human psyche, a breakdown and a separation came from the

Voice. The Voice, somehow, in Jaynes' view, became integrated into what we today call our ego. This is the voice that constantly talks inside our heads. The guiding Other Voice that was once connected to the natural world in our past history has been reduced to a conversation of non-stop internal trivia. Our challenge in opening to a new imagination is to re-establish our connection to this Voice within. Most techniques of meditation help to quiet the trivial ego voice so that one can reconnect to the Voice of the Logos. In Greek, Logos means the "Sacred Sound" (the Word), or in the West African Dagara tradition it would be called the "primary language." Working with unusual sounds, mantras or chants, have been used by many spiritual and religious traditions throughout the world to regain access to the sacred sound of the Logos.

Although the Machine is coercive and powerful in our lives, each of us can reclaim our imagination and our access to some original pattern of sound (the Voice or Logos) and light (pictures and images of the Otherworld). Beyond the classic spiritual traditions of mediation and chanting, experiencing the direct connection to this primary sound comes to us from the natural world. All of us need to be encouraged to go into some natural setting at least once each day. For us to make the simple effort to walk, and sit, and be attentive to the natural world for a period of time everyday is a revolutionary act. It is revolutionary because most people don't intentionally seek to re-establish a relationship with nature by sitting in a quiet garden or woodland; or finding the hidden places in a park or forest to observe and be with animals; or, voice gratitude to the sun and the rain for their gifts to all humankind.

And even stronger intention for us in attempting to reconnect to the Logos is to spend an extended period by oneself in a wild area of nature. Moving from our urban or rural environments and making the commitment to go on a pilgrimage into wilderness country once or twice a year would be considered a radical and subversive act against the Machine's hypnotic power over us. But wild animals, deep valleys, high peaks and rushing streams evoke the sacred within us. These natural entities and wild places open a door to the Otherworld. Our inner world becomes imagined in a new way as the sacred reaches through our natural surroundings and radiates new images of potentiality within us.

After a week alone in the mountains, I notice that I began to hear and see differently. I begin to think different kinds of thoughts and I begin to hum and sing strange non-English songs. Rhythm patterns and sounds will slip out of my mouth unexpectedly. I begin to play and experiment with a wide vocal range. Suddenly these sounds will erupt into a wonderful resonating within my body, creating warmth and then causing chills up and down my spine. When I am with others in the wilderness, the natural impulse is to collectively chant and sing and experiment with these ancient sounds.

Through chanting and singing together comes power and healing. In North American native tradition a woman or man is given, from the Otherworld, a power song to help with courage and strength when she or he goes on a vision quest. In this tradition, when one dreams, one is often given healing chants for oneself and others. The *curanderos,* the healers in South American native tradition, sing their Icaros. Icaros, from the Otherworld, are songs that will heal people. It is believed that the song speaks to both the body and the soul of the ill person.

An Eskimo shaman, Uvavnuk, describes her initiation into the mystery of the healing song. Knud Rasmussen, the early 20th century Danish anthropologist, recounts Uvavnuk's story of becoming a shaman. One night, when she went outside her house into a dark Alaskan evening to relieve herself, a ball of light appeared in the sky and fell directly on her. She reported that the fire entered her body and all her organs began to glow. Stumbling back into her house she began to sing. As she sang, she and everyone else in the house became consumed by indescribable feelings of joy. All the people were unburdened from the troubles of their minds through the song. They lifted their arms to the sky and were released from distrust, hatred and fear. The song that Uvavnuk sang seemed to blow negative forces away from everyone. After this initiation, whenever Uvavnuk sang the song, people were healed from both their physical and mental troubles.

Vibration is a mystery. The gift of sound gives us strength and heals us.

When it comes to seeing the world, Aldous Huxley theorized that we each register a minute quantity of the total amount of information that is constantly flooding our receptors. He said that each of us has a reducing valve that cuts out or filters the vast number of perceptions that are coming to us from the universe around us. Our potential, he wrote in his book, *Doors of Perception,* was to learn to open up the reducing valve of consciousness and see this world and the Otherworld in a new way. We would learn, he said, that the door between the two worlds was just a thought away.

The use of fasting, long periods in isolation, plant hallucinogens, and trance dancing have all been standard methods used by indigenous people to purge themselves of day-to-day experiences in order to open the door and see into the Otherworld. Traditional spiritual disciplines from around the world have used the staring at pictures and images as a means of opening another door to seeing. The Yantra in the Tibetan Buddhist religion is a large complex painting that incorporates designs and specific images to evoke interior pictures in the meditator. The same methods are open to us today because they are the universal doors that have been used by all peoples throughout history. We can choose to use these classic methods, or invent new ones depending on our particular likes and our basic disposition. Yet, to touch and see the magical in the world around us is as simple as concentrating on what our pre-Christian European ancestors called the *wyrd.*

The Wyrd

The concept of the *wyrd* was a pre-Christian European understanding of a comprehensive knowledge about how things related to each other. It is what today we might call a metaphysical systems theory. Experiencing the *wyrd* for this shamanic culture was seeing how the flight of a raven down a stream was connected to the birth of a baby in the cabin over the hill; and how the birth was connected to the deer being chased by the wolf; and how the wolf standing over the fallen deer was connected to a ship crossing the sea. The *wyrd* was the ability to see, feel, and sense the non-rational connections that make up the intricate web of all things. For our early European ancestors, the *wyrd* meant that when one part of the web experience was touched by something, everything was affected by it. Watching, feeling, hearing the interrelationships to the natural world provided both information and knowledge for daily life, and the connection of these events to the development of some larger pattern.

The fractal nature of modern chaos theory posits the same notions. Continuous random drops of paint on a turning wheel will, over time, show a pattern. Each fractal drop of paint adds to the emerging, and predictable, mathematical patterns. The *wyrd* was a breaking of the narrow-band focus of eyes and ears and mind. The connective jumps were not cause and effect that moved in a sequential order. Rather, they were sideways leaps that were akin to flying, and jumps of imagining that provided practical information and insight.

Brian Bates, in his work, *The Way of the Wyrd,* describes the potential of the *wyrd* operating in us today. The *wyrd*, he says, is "a way of being which transcends our conventional notions of free will and determinism. . . . Following from the concept of *wyrd* was a vision of the universe, from the gods to the underworld, as being connected by an enormous all-reaching system of fibers rather like a three-dimensional spider web. Everything was connected by strands of fiber to the all-encompassing web. Any event, anywhere, resulted in reverberations and repercussions throughout the web. . . . The web of fibers of the Anglo-Saxon sorcerer offers an ecological model which encompasses individual life events as well as general physical and biological phenomena, non-material as well as material events, and challenges the very cause and effect chains upon which our ecological theories depend."

Dreamtime

Australian aboriginal Dreamtime is similar to the Wyrd. In the Dreamtime all things exist in a spatial relationship within each other. Our conscious waking world is seen as the dream the Ancestors are having as they "sleep." And what we call our unconscious and inner imagination is the waking world of the Ancestors. In the aboriginal view, our perceived, sequential and time-bound consciousness of people, events, animals, weather, rocks, land configurations, and so on, exist in relationship to the unconscious field of feelings, sensations, images, and intuitions within a person. For the aboriginal neither the conscious nor unconscious world is an illusion. Both worlds are wedded and constitute the whole of reality. It is the task of humans to learn how to move between the two worlds; aboriginal initiations and rituals are constructed to provide this learning.

For the aboriginal, the physical earth is the topography of the unconscious. Hills and valleys, deserts and lakes are imprints of the otherworld of the Ancestors. The land is the body of the Ancestors that created us as part of their dream. But all aspects of the physical world are viewed as the psychic contents of human beings. Each world interpenetrates the other. To the aboriginal the Dreamtime is the symbolic space where physical and psychic space, conscious and unconscious experience meet to constitute a total reality of balance, information and meaning for a person and community. Song, as in so many of the indigenous traditions, plays a critical role in the aboriginal moving through this combined topography of this world and the other.

   Singing the songlines becomes a physical and psychic map for moving great distances through the physical territory where the aborigine lives. No one person or tribe knows all the thousands of songlines that can move one all over Australia and Tasmania. Aborigines are constantly learning new songlines. Adults sing the songlines to their children as they walk, and when different groups get together they trade songlines with one another. The songlines are sung as one is moving across the physical terrain. As they walk, the singing and naming of the hill or ravine is not just a description of physical features of the land, it is a depiction of mythic events related to the Ancestors at work in the physical world. If one aborigine is describing to another aborigine how to find a particular sacred site or even a water hole, the individual will first give a common location point such as a significant tree, and then begin to sing the song map to the other, combining fragments of terrain topography with mythical story. These songlines have been passed down for thousands of years, and in the traditional setting become the sacred memory of living in Dreamtime.

   The songlines are probably the oldest geomancy tradition on the planet. The Chinese developed a highly sophisticated art of geomancy, and we have much written from them about its use. The basis of geomancy is the use of ley lines, or magnetic lines that run across the surface of the planet. Biological studies show that various animals and birds use these magnetic lines for migration routes. Studies of homing pigeons, for example, have found that there is a tiny structure in their brain that is supersensitive to the earth's magnetic flow and this magnetic information is received through feathers and nerves. It has been found that feathers contain a protein that is highly magnetically sensitive. Recent research by geobiologist, Joseph Kirschvink of Cal Tech, has found tiny magnetic particles in human brains similar to those found in animals. These magnetic particles are a mineral known as lodestone. Although the Cal Tech scientists "don't know what the magnets do," one biologist at Princeton University, James Gould, suggested that these magnetic particles are "very suggestive that it is playing an orientational role" in humans just as in animals. We, like the animals, have magnets in us that may sensitize and orient us to the magnet ley lines of the earth. The sensitivity of the aborigines to follow the songlines may be their capability to utilize the magnet particles in their brains to detect the magnetic ley lines in the terrain they are singing themselves through.

In geomancy theory, where two or more magnetic lines cross, that intersection is a power point, an intensified magnetic field that can often produce strange phenomena. Any person that spends a period of time in wilderness areas can began to feel ley lines and power points. Traditionally these power points, located in specific places on the planet, have been sacred sites for indigenous peoples since ancient times.

The songlines always have some sacred site that one is sung toward or guided to on the journey. At these sacred sites the ceremonies and rituals of singing and dreaming (of sound and vision) are enacted. Common to these ceremonies is the use of blood taken from each other, or from animals, to create symbolic patterns on the body; bird feathers are often adhered to one's body as well. In less secret ceremonies red ochre is used to represent blood. Both blood and ochre contain iron molecules; aborigines believe that rubbing these substances on the body will make them more sensitive to connecting with the Dreamtime world. The iron molecules may, along with the tiny magnets in the cells of the brain, increase one's sensitivity to the magnetic field of a particular power point. This deep interrelationship between physical body, place, and ritual at a power point is a catalyzing agency for transporting and connecting the aboriginal to the Otherworld of the Dreamtime. They have been taught, from the Ancestors, a knowledge that many indigenous people around the world claim to know, and that we in the modern world are only beginning to perceive as possible again.

Together, the physical journey, the singing to remember the Otherworld in this one, and the rituals at powerful magnetic earth sites constitute the reality of Dreamtime. The *wyrd,* in the same way projects the psychic contents of humankind onto the world in an intricate connecting web through mountains and deep forests, rivers and streams, birds and animals. Being conscious of these larger interconnecting patterns tends to be counter to the tradition of Western science and technology to tear things apart and analyze the pieces to discover their basic reality. Ecology, environmental studies and systems theory have been the break and shift away from Francis Bacon's injunction to early science that if "land is left to nature it is a waste and benefits man a not." In our collective history since ancient times, however, the tradition of sound and light created a magical world that was much larger and more mysterious than one could imagine. Its doorway today is still the natural world. It is the door that all of us are invited to re-enter.

Pilot Rutters

Breaking the rational, machinelike pattern, and learning to enter this world of the imagination, of the Dreamtime or the *wyrd,* offers the opportunity to experience the magical quality of our daily life. Doing this will propel us into a world of different beliefs, attitudes and behaviors. Central to this difference will be our encounter with the Sacred. The magical world of sound and sight that nature opens to us is the archaic and primary pathway to the Sacred. For many, however, it is a pathway of uncharted waters. As more of us launch forward as explorers into this Sacred topography, we need to make charts for those coming behind us.

In the old sailing days, before there were maps, the navigator of a ship used a pilot's rutter to guide his ship in uncharted fresh waters. The rutter was the written description that told of reefs and harbors and indicated where to put in for water. In short, the rutter was the guide compiled from all the previous experiences of a pilot or pilots in those particular waters. In time these various individual pilot rutters were put together and made into maps.

Today our explorations are not into the high seas but into the realm of the Sacred Mystery beyond our current conception of reality. Our explorations into the Sacred may be private adventures of the heart and mind, or explorations into metaphysical and psychic dimensions. For some it may be intense work on the psychological and physical changes of the body and personality. And for others it may be the attempt to work with energy and spiritual dynamics of groups of people. For all of us, it will mean coming to the edge of death, experiencing rebirth, and charting the forces of physical transformation. In whatever form we explore, individually or collectively, hearing the Voice of the Sacred will be the uniting gift to humankind. Each of us needs to formulate her or his pilot rutter — the record of inner and outer explorations into other places. Coming together in circles and communities of explorers, we can create clearer maps into the topography of ancient memories. These pilot rutters will be vital for the deepening knowledge of the *wyrd* and the larger pattern we all are connected to.

A unique illustration of a pilot rutter comes from a woman friend, J'aime Schelz. It is an example of both the journey of exploration and the deepening of personal, and then shared understanding with others. Sharing her pilot rutter has provoked me to explore into some of the deeper waters of my own experience.

While in bed one night, before going to sleep, J'aime felt some part of herself slip out of her physical body. She was able to look down at herself on the bed as she hovered over her body. She had known other out-of-the-body experiences, but this one was to prove different and unique for her.

J'aime was conscious for a period of time of herself both being in her bed awake and above herself looking down. From her bedroom she slowly began to experience herself shift into another space where a lake came into view. At the water's edge she felt compelled to walk into the lake until she was entirely immersed beneath the water. While she was within the lake her spatial orientation shifted again. She was then in a misty place. This space had no physical dimension to it. There was another shift, and she found herself in a beautiful walled garden with people sitting and walking in relaxed concentration. The contact point, while she moved through these interconnecting experiences, was a column of translucent light that gave off different frequencies of sound. Whenever J'aime entered the column, the intensity of the light and the vibration of the sound would rise or lower in frequency. Different frequencies of sound would create different light intensities. The interaction between the sound and the light she believes created the range of different realities she entered into. The higher the sound and light rose in pitch and intensity, the more insubstantial was the world she would step into when she emerged from the column.

Returning to the waters of the lake, J'aime began to walk back to the shore. As her eyes came up out of the water she had a moment of seeing the distant horizon and simultaneously, a sudden image of her room. Then she was aware of being in her body and lying in bed.

In reflecting on her experience J'aime shared that sound created the form, and light gave the form substance. Her mind, she felt, became the blueprint that configured the sound and gave the pattern for the light to fill up. "Thoughts," she said, "have sounds." Thinking (vibrations) evokes and attracts to it a particular quality of light. As she emerged each time from the vibrating column of light and sound, the new realities presented to her were shaped by the sound her body, her being had been resonating to while in the column. The light, the visually apparent reality, occurred because of the particular range of sound she was experiencing. Her experience was showing her, she believed, that light surrenders (moves into harmony) with sound.

Reciprocally, sound is a manifold for light. Together, something is manifested and created as a result of the interplay. J'aime realized from her out-of-the-body experience, that physical reality was a fragile thing. By changing first the blueprint — the way we think or perceive with language — we begin to change how sounds are constructed. By changing the construct — the vibration of tone and pitch — we alter the visual image of what we see — the light that gets attracted to the sound.

J'aime's experience helped me understand some of my explorations with sound and light, and what I've studied of other people's work with them. All ancient traditions used chanting, singing and toning for healing and changing the emotional and physical condition of people. Even today we know the stirring impact of sound and music on our mental states. What if we knew the secrets of creating sound patterns that opened doors to worlds that exist simultaneously to this one? This is what indigenous peoples claim, even today, that their elders and shamans are able to do. Malidoma has suggested that knowing the power of certain sounds is the key to the reality of the world we in the West have called magical.

As J'aime shared her pilot rutter experience it caused me to question her closely, to then share my own stories of exploration, and also to be more conscious of the subtle changes of perception I've had before going to sleep. Her rutter gave me insights that I am still exploring and thinking about for myself. One clear awareness has been the importance of making conscious sounds that change the way I feel and see things. Joining with others to experiment with chanting sounds is a good way to experience the effect of sound on the images that are evoked within us, and its influence on our reality.

"Imaginal" Cells

All of us experience doubts as we begin to earnestly journey into the "imaginal" world. This world has been called fantasy and unreality. But wise teachers, poets, visionaries and dreamers tell us that this world of imagination is rooted and grounded in the great teacher of Nature. The message that comes over and over through Nature is that life works a transforming miracle, like the caterpillar changing inside the chrysalis into the butterfly. I believe that for all its harm, there is a *something* in this Machine world that *is emerging*, like the butterfly. This emergence is the collective soul of all living things on the planet. Holding this vision of emergence will lead us into one of the doors of a new imaging.

The particular metaphor of my vision is the monarch butterfly. The mystery of the caterpillar becoming the monarch butterfly is parallel to the mystery of humankind emerging from the chrysalis into some other creature. Understanding this metamorphosis provides a strong basis for our living in the world of imagination. As the caterpillar creates a cocoon around itself, it enters into a process of transitional reorganization. A breakdown of the caterpillar's cells begins to occur. In this stage a living jellylike mass develops, called the pupa. In this pupa stage metamorphosis is carried out through the appearance of a network of "imaginal" cells. Scientists term these cells "imaginal" because each individual "imaginal" cell carries within it the total transformation and image of the soon-to-be butterfly. The actual transformation of the jellylike pupa occurs from these cells. Through some mysterious and subtle coordination among the "imaginal" members, the identity and physiological functions of the new organism, the butterfly, proceeds and radiates from each "imaginal" cell, rather than from some central focal point. From the spreading islands of these divergent points of life, the butterfly literally creates itself in its own image through these myriad small pieces. Imaginal cells are like a holographic picture fitting itself back together after being broken apart. Any single piece of a holographic picture will carry the complete and original image.

Each one of us is carrying within us the original picture, the image of a new something-to-be. We need no superior leader, no hierarchical structure to guide us. Each of us at some level is radiating this new form. Our challenge is to go into our personal initiatory death, similar to the pupa, jellylike mass, so that rebirth can take place. The more we share our rutters of exploration into these deep-soul places, the easier we will

imagine what we are becoming. The German poet Rainer
Maria Rilke offered many rutters into these sacred lands of the
imagination to help us get through the pupa stage. In a section
of one poem . . .

> *It's possible I am pushing through solid rock*
> *in flintlike layers, as the ore lies, alone;*
> *I am such a long way in I see no way through,*
> *and no space: everything is close to my face,*
> *and everything close to my face is stone.*
>
> *I don't have much knowledge yet in grief—*
> *so this massive darkness makes me small.*
> *You be the master: make yourself fierce, break in:*
> *then your great transforming will happen to me,*
> *and my great grief cry will happen to you.*

I believe that Rilke encourages us to go into the grief of
our Machine culture and its ravaging of the sacred and the
natural world. Then he gives us the hope that as *you* break
through the stony rock of the Machine, a great transformation
will happen to *me*. The promised image is that together we
will all transform each other.

It is interesting to note that the monarch butterfly is
nicknamed "storm king" because monarchs are the most active
before a storm. Monarchs usually emerge from their cocoons
just prior to thundershowers. The first sound they hear is likely
the rumble of thunder. They are literally born of the storm.
Scientists have observed that the monarch rides at the edges of
the storm's winds like a surfer rides the waves of the ocean.
The monarch also sets out on a three- to four-thousand-mile
journey at the time of the autumnal equinox in order to gather
some 40 million strong in two five-acre plots of earth, one
located in Northern California and the other in Northern
Mexico.

We, like the monarchs, seem to be gathering together and
readying ourselves to journey toward some destination as the

storms generated by the Machine culture begins to batter and rail at us and planet earth. Many of us see its lightening and hear its thunder. All of us must continue this unimaginable journey through the 1990s. But the emerging monarch, like us, has never before been to its destination. All of us hold some unspeakable image of the destination. And we have a sense of the route.

Reawakening Our Souls

*T*o reclaim our souls we must make some new choices. These choices are dependent on claiming and experiencing two beliefs: The first belief is that you and I have an inner source from which to meet all the situations life will present to us. I have called this the resource-state, the Logos, the connection to the Otherworld. Along with this resource state belief emerges another belief — that each situation we find ourselves in is a learning opportunity for our growth and change. However difficult our conditions or circumstances, whatever the challenges or disasters, these situations are providing the means to expand awareness, consciousness and perception.

Living our lives in the context of these two beliefs will permit us to be positive contributors in the years of cataclysmic change that lie before us. I've described the possible breakdown of the Machine and the negative effects it has over our lives. The type of day-to-day choices we make will influence the quality of decisions for our families and the world, and the level of responsibility we are willing to take to be a positive force for change.

The Native American tribes made decisions based on the effect those decisions would have on the following seven generations. To begin to think about choices and actions we take that will effect the next 175 years, changes dramatically the context for our accountability and the accepting of responsibility for our actions. Decisions in the light of 175 years quickly forces us to think in terms of systemswide decisions. It forces us to think through the implications of our actions out to the third and fourth level of consequence. Our "consume today, throw-away, don't think about tomorrow" attitude is a narrow bandwidth focus that we are being forced to rethink, reimagine, and give up. If I choose to be a resource to myself and life around me, there is no other alternative than to consider the implications of my actions both now and out into the future. But, again, we need each other in order to help us collectively grow a context, a container by which we can understand the implications of our choices and our actions. We need to learn to give clear and consistent feedback to each other, to help each other continually "true up" against those fundamental values of love, honesty, respect, caring, and learning that are deep within all of us.

To awaken from the long robotlike nightmare and to see ourselves and the Machine culture differently is to change fundamental belief patterns in us that determine how we perceive and behave. Although I might not fully understand or even accept that I am accountable and responsible for all that is going on in the world at this time, I can make the choice to begin to live the notion that we are all creators of our cultural norms and traditions. To make a decision, a mental switch that we choose to be in cooperation, in relationship, and community with all people, animals, plants and the Earth itself, is the personal starting point that returns each of us to genuine power and the positive possibility that we can imagine a new way to live together. This personal and community power can enable us to recreate the world as a more balanced and sacred place to live.

Our challenge is to inspire each other to make this choice to be the source of effecting the world around us. This personal choice will bridge the gulf of differences between us, permit epiphanies and new ideas to spread among us. And through the choice to cooperate and connect, rather than compete and separate, we will recover the mystery that nature keeps calling us back to. Rather than experiencing nature as something separate from us, we, like our ancestors, will reclaim a conscious awareness of being woven back into the matrix, into the interconnecting web, and know again that *we are nature* like all other living things.

A Turn on the Spiral

Awakening from the human-robot trance is possible. The physical, real-world stakes, as Lester Brown and others have urged are very high if we fail to change. But as I've argued, the Attractor, the Transcendental Object that is pulling at us from the non-tangible world is not only accelerating the pace of the Machine, it is also accelerating and intensifying the pace of change in us individually. The "consciousness curve" of Teilhard de Chardin is accelerating in us as a species as the risk for survival gets greater.

Within Hindu cosmology the evolution of life in the universe is viewed as a series of four long turning cycles. This tradition says, that in this time, we are approaching the end of the Kali Yuga — the dark cycle of destruction that leads to death and rebirth. In some strange way this apocalyptic future may be the doorway for us. In one way or another we are coming to the end of the mechanistic model that was given to us by Francis Bacon and Isaac Newton and the other founders of our present "civilized" world reality. The fearful concern is that the Machine may be coming to a stop as in Forster's story and that everything on the planet may die. Can we escape all of this horrific pain? Is it possible to make the turn? No, not a turn to go back, nor a turn around and a retreat, but rather a turn upward on the spiral toward something else. Toward some other imagination.

Turn we will, according to the Hindus, the Buddhists, the Christians and even the neo-evolutionists. But for us today, the challenge is to accomplish this turning so that we recover what is the best, the most useful, the most sacred for us as we go on into the next cycle of humankind's growth and learning. For the Hindu the cycle that turns after the Kali Yuga is the Krta Yuga. Krta means "well done" or the "best" and represents the fundamental quality of self-discipline. Our obvious need, in order to return to balance on the earth, is self-discipline in its many forms. But for now we are deeply in the Kali Yuga cycle of an ever devouring Machine, and the interesting affirmation for people who live in this age according to Hindu myth is to learn *generosity*. For all our affluence and wealth we must turn and discover a new place of generosity within ourselves as individuals and communities. Generosity comes from the Latin word *generosus* meaning of good and noble birth. Our turn on the spiral of change will be to touch again the noble part of our human genesis. There is at our core a willingness to share, to be unselfish and bountiful. For those of us that have been among indigenous people, that core of generosity is still present and alive in them.

The Teaching of Indigenous Peoples

The cynic in all of us says that it is romantic and impossible to return to a non-Machine world. The assumption we hold is that there is no return to a sacred way of living as indigenous people describe the sacred. Or, even more directly to the point, we find it difficult to imagine that most of us would want to give up our daily life of comfort or luxuries. We all know, without recounting the "State of the World" statistics, that our wealth and privilege is the minority position on the planet. We have this position in the face of poverty, disease, and hunger that are on the increase worldwide. Yet, for all its negatives the Machine has been good to those of us who are the middle- and upper-class members of this society. What will move us to a sacred way of living besides the growing breakdown of the Machine?

Our strongest examples of the people who attempt to resist the Machine are those who seemingly would most benefit in their daily lives from it. These indigenous, traditional peoples, however, not only live in the physical world, but also in the world of imagination — an inner world, that is related to nature. When one studies the cosmology of the Australian aboriginal culture, or the Dagara in Africa, or the Hopi in our Southwest, one finds not ignorant people, but individuals who are making a conscious clear choice about how they want to live, based on thousands of years of historical experience. Like the Australian aborigines, many of these peoples consciously reject written language, domestication of animals, and embrace a subsistent way of life.

Robert Lawlor, who has gathered together one of the most complete descriptions of aboriginal ways, as an outsider, points to the purpose of aboriginal life. In his work, *Voices of the First Day,* he describes that the basic value of aboriginal life for over 60,000 years has been to preserve the earth, as much as possible, in its initial purity. The Dreamtime teaching expressly told them not to subjugate or domesticate plants and animals, nor do any manipulation and exploitation of the natural world. Domestication of animals and agriculture — the basis of Western civilization and progress — were antithetical in their beliefs of the sense of a common consciousness and origin shared by every creature with the Creator. To exploit this integrated world was to do the same to oneself.

The Australian aborigines like the Native Americans, or the Timorese in Indonesia, or most indigenous peoples who consciously have chosen to live harmoniously in relationship to the earth and the cosmos, struggle to hold on to this way of life as much for us, as for themselves. They, like the Navajo and the Huichol of Sonora, Mexico, take seriously the act of welcoming the Sun to another day of life so that all creatures on the earth may continue to live. In their devotion to awaken the earth each day with the return of the sun, they give the generosity of their hearts for all of us.

Our challenge as collective human robots in the Machine is not to throw off our clothes and run off into the wilderness of some National Park. Our challenge, is to rather, enter into our imagination like our indigenous cousins. As we enter our imagination, a future of death and rebirth stretches before us. As the pressure of death and birth grows, individual and collective pain will increase. As a result, more and more of us will make different choices about how to live. Worldwide, traditional people have stories and prophecies of a "cleansing of the earth." Tribal elders are coming forward to publicly describe their secret descriptions of "end times." Although they speak of disaster and cataclysm, they also speak of a return, of an opening of individual hearts to a new-old way of living.

Buck Ghosthorse, a traditional Lakota Sioux elder, has been telling small groups of both Native American and non-native people that the old prophecies from his people are pointing to the years 1993 to 1997 as ones of enormous physical changes on the earth. The Elders, he said, have decided to tell people these teachings to help prepare those who are willing to listen in order that they will make changes in their lives. The Hopi, Navajo and other Native American tribes all have these end-time teachings that are being spoken of publicly. "Public" for these elders means speaking to all peoples who are willing to listen to the Spirit within their hearts, and not just listening to their heads or from a place of fear.

These traditional elders speak directly to the conditions of the Machine world and to us who have created it. They are telling us that it is possible to change our way of life. More importantly they say that it is possible to be initiated again into *remembering* what we've forgotten about living with the earth.

"Remembering" to Be Radical

To *remember* is to begin to enter into the world of imagination. Doing this is a dangerous act. Whatever our method for entering imagination, we open a doorway into ourselves and through ourselves in order to be in contact with another world, another dimension of reality. Remembering is choosing to revalue the natural world through appreciation and respect. Remembering changes our ethics, our politics, and our economic choices. But most of all, this remembering opens up a world within that connects us to a voice that questions the structure and authority of the Machine.

Opening to the voice of the Other, and acting on what it tells us moves us outside the norm. But choosing to experience this voice allows us to become part of an age-old lineage. Through this lineage there are the ancient teachings of the past that are guides for us. But besides the hand of lineage to guide us, we also have to share our own pilot rutters. As we share unique experiences of our inner terrain with each other we can create a clearer and more reliable map for our time and our purposes. As elder-leaders we must be serious and radical about our exploration of learning to bring power and healing from the otherworld into our communities.

To be radical means to go to the roots of our existence. To be radical urges us to formulate alone and with others that which is most important for ourselves and our children's children as well as for the plants, animals and the land that make up our relationship to life. To be radical is to take on the immediate work of voyaging into the inner world of imagination as elders have done and guided people through for ages. This work comes in a variety of ways. It comes through the conscious probing of our dreaming, through silence and isolation, through shared ritual and praying, through the use of sacred plants and meditation, through dialogue and intellectual exploring, and through an opening of our hearts as we serve and help other people.

Radical Acts

Finally, we must make some practical choices about how we live our daily lives. I believe that a significant practical step for each of us will be to *reduce the noise in our lives.* To hear the Otherworld, to remap a larger and more sacred imagination, to become imaginal cells who are growing into some new thing, to be stimulators of epiphanies in our communities of friends and associates, to simply hear our own bodies and minds once again we need quiet. We need to turn off the TV and the stereo. We need to fast for awhile without USA Today or National Public Radio. We need to give ourselves enough time without these stimulators so that we can begin naturally to see, hear and open to a different world that is always waiting for us. These are small steps that we can take. But they are steps that lead us back to our souls, to each other, and to the vast mysterious world of nature and the invisible that lies just beyond us. Emerging out of our own silence and listening to the Voice, this Other, this Logos, will clearly present choices that will change our work, the pace of our lives, the way we spend our money, and where and how we live. Let me present some modest proposals that can begin to change the container of our experience in order to hear this Other more clearly:

1. Do a media fast and join in silence with friends. You can start with a media fast as a kind of purification process. Before vision quests, or significant personal efforts for change, indigenous people prepare themselves by cleansing and refocusing both their body and psyche. They will fast from food for two or three days, do a ritual purification in a sweat-lodge ceremony, or go alone into nature to be silent for a period of days. Each of these acts is a means of opening themselves to hear more clearly their own voice and the voice of the Other in nature. Make a commitment to your spouse or to a friend to not read newspapers, watch television, listen to the radio or stereo for a week or more. Notice the compulsion and addiction you have for the media. Notice what you do with your time when you're not being occupied with the media. Notice the pattern and level of thoughts when you are not taking in all the visual and auditory stimuli and input. During those

hours when you would watch TV or read the paper, go into the yard or to a park — just sit and listen to natural sounds. Unhook from the Machine's world for awhile and notice the wonder of being nourished by the natural world. You could also walk together with family or friends in the woods or park while remaining silent. Or sit as a group with friends or family in silence for 45 minutes to an hour, and then share together what you each "heard."

2. Start a small community by inviting friends for dinner and simply having a self-conscious discussion about the Machine and its effects on your lives. Invite your friends to express their feelings and unspoken desires.

3. Let our individual imaginations join together in creativity. Come together with a small group of friends or work associates and talk about how to live differently. Explore how to perform our work in the Machine in a manner that takes the power back from the Machine's dominance. Focus on ways that use the power in our local environment to create such things as co-housing, a LETSystem, or a neighborhood community.

4. Challenge each other in a spirit of inquiry. Examine each other's beliefs and assumptions and make them a conscious part of any dialogue. Watch for and expand on the epiphanal "aha's" that occur as you converse.

5. Sing and chant with each other. Discover together the power and healing of song in our lives. All ancient people knew this great gift of sound in their lives. Let your unique song, the one that each is asked to sing as death approaches be given to you now so that you can draw upon its power and strength for the days ahead.

6. Learn to pray and be thankful daily for your life. Whatever your conception of the Mystery of life, acknowledge your relationship to it. People that live in balance with the natural world share the value of expressing gratitude and asking for help.

7. Respect the living forms that are all around us. Make relationships to people, animals, plants and physical objects a focus of awareness and respect. This extends to inanimate objects like tools and kitchen utensils. Carl Jung describes how the tools we use take on a life of their own. If we mistreat them they find ways to mistreat us.

8. If you are in your fifties or older, bring together other women and men of your same age and explore with them how to be initiated into a wisdom that can bring healing and balance to your community. Take the initiative as elder-leaders to bring younger people together into communal activities described above.

These are all *radical* acts. They are different from what the Machine has trained us to do. They are a starting point by which the inner Voice can begin to be heard. They are the roots that we once again begin to sink into the earth, into our souls, and into our communities.

The Dance of Mirrors and Shadows

In our arrogance as a nation, we stand smug and proclaim ourselves winners over the Soviet Union in the Cold War. However, given the 45-year dance with the Soviet-Russians, perhaps we are mirrors of each other. The most fundamental mirroring was dancing to the tune of fear and power. Reagan's call to rearm America and to increase the defense budget to record highs in the early 1980's forced the Russians to do the same. The result in both countries was a downward spiraling pattern of enormous debt. The Soviet economic bankruptcy mirrors our huge national debt that is destroying our education, health care, public transportation infrastructure and economic capability. There is also the mutual moral breakdown in both countries with the growing ethnic and racial unrest smoldering just below the surface. As adversaries we attempted to control the world, and as reconciled partners we will try to influence it together. Prophets like Edgar Cayce predicted in the 1930s that Russia and the United States would not only be allies but partners in world politics by the end of the century.

Both the United States and the USSR participated in building the Machine as we know it today. Both economic systems took the path of heavy industrialization in order to build huge military machines. In the determined, grim Soviets and the suspicious and confident Americans a Cold War dance of fear and gamesmanship was undertaken. The Machine didn't grow out of factories and new technologies, it actually grew out of 500 years of our imaginations.

Humankind created tools as a means to make life easier and more creative. These tools evolved into machines, and these extensions of humankind's imagination finally grew to control both the people *and* their imagination. The Machine mirrors dark power and fear from within our own minds. As the machine grew in outward power, the internal shadow of power from our own psyches grew larger. The scientists of the Manhattan project believed, for example, that creating the atom bomb would help humanity. Our desire to evolve genetic engineering or to push into space seems to come from good motives. But it is the power of the destructive shadow in our imagination, wedded to the external power of technology, that is driving the strange apocalyptic horses toward doomsday. The Machine idea that grew out of our imaginations 500 years ago now controls our collective imagination. It attacks that generous, noble part of us and has us imagine the worst in ourselves and each other. The balance between the dark and light of our collective imagining is rooted in the birth of our country.

Our country was founded on freedom of religious beliefs. But the beliefs of the early European settlers were contained in a deep imaging that rejected the culture of Europe. Our founding mothers and fathers came to this country to establish a new Jerusalem, a utopia where heaven would reign on earth. They also brought the eschatological view of the second coming of Christ and the end of the world. They believed that their task was to build a sacred society in the midst of the heathen wilderness and to prepare for the end time. They had a great fear of the wilderness and believed it was their sacred duty to subdue it, to farm it, to take the wildness out of it. And with this dark fear within them, our forefathers killed the wild game, the wild Indians and the wild forests in order for this land to be a servant to them in building their heaven on earth.

Today, we are inheritors of this fearful and hopefilled imagining. Our American Dream is the Utopia on earth. Our machine world is becoming devoid of the sacred wildness. And we face the end of the world as our forebears proclaimed. Within all of us are mixed motives, strong desires, and secret longings. We have become a complicated, unpredictable, and lost society of humans. We hold both nobility and goodness, and at the same time debase ourselves with horrible crimes against each other and our home planet. We are the heirs of those who have tried to build a utopia. And we also seem to have created a doomsday along with it. What we are creating today in the Machine reflects the dark shadow within us, and we dance with it in a hall of mirrors.

In the midst of this hall of mirrors the only metaphysical certitude that can shatter the dance is our capability to make a choice. Many of us don't want to believe that we have choices. We play victims to our situations and circumstances in life, believing that we have no influence or power to make changes. In order for us to be pro-active resources in the world we must choose to be at cause and not at the effect of life's events. This doesn't presuppose some godlike position. Rather it means that in some mysterious way we are connected to all of creation, and what we feel and think and do has influence on what happens in this world. We may not always see the affect, but it will be there.

My argument, then, is that the shadow, as it lays over our world today, is happening because we have made a choice to activate the darker impulses of our collective psyche. The creation of our imagination — the Machine — would have us believe that it is more powerful than we are, the Machine's creators. Our call and challenge today is to reactivate the world of our imagination in a different, more sacred way — in ways that we've forgotten. I believe that our aboriginal sisters and brothers still remember the access point into this other imaginal world. The sacred imagination that comes through the doorway of nature opens to us an inexpressible universe of reality. The *wyrd*, the Dreamtime, songlines, poetry; our night dreams and daytime fantasies are portals into this sacred world. Utopian dreams have always been caught between the imagination and physical expression. Our great experiment with tools and with technology, to build our Machine utopia, has been a game of shadows in a hall of mirrors. As the shadow of the Machine falls increasingly across our lives, we must be willing to walk out of the hall of mirrors and back into the daylight of our imagination. It is here in our imagination, just beyond our present thought that we can reclaim our souls once again.

AFTERWORD

by David Spangler

In the preface to his book *Envisioning a Sustainable Society,* political scientist Lester Milbrath makes the following comment: "Many millions of people now recognize that we must transform society but they have difficulty imagining what a new society, designed to be sustainable, might be like. Envisioning the way we can make the journey from our present society to this new society is even more difficult. Any society, but especially a new society, must first exist in the minds of the people."

One step toward gaining an imaginative vision of a new society is to be honest and clear about the society we now inhabit, appreciating its strengths but also diagnosing what is amiss so that we may accurately see just where changes need to be made. Many authors are providing such diagnoses now, but few as eloquently as David Kyle does in the book you have just read. By highlighting the pervasive character of what he calls the Machine within our society, he challenges us to see the extent to which we acquiesce to and adopt its values and perspectives. Such a critical understanding is important if we are to recognize and free ourselves from its dysfunctional aspects and avoid unconsciously incorporating them into our vision of a new culture, thereby perpetuating the very attitudes and habits we wish to change.

All that I would add to what David has already said so fully and so well is that in the process of disengaging ourselves from the dysfunctional characteristics of the Machine we avoid an adversarial attitude. The Machine is not so much an enemy as it is an exaggeration of certain qualities, talents, and behaviors that are intrinsic to us as human beings. It is a state of imbalance that calls for healing and completeness rather than for eradication.

The society we now live in once existed in our ancestors' imaginations. They dreamed of a world like ours where (at least in Western cultures) the average citizen can live in a manner even an ancient king could not have afforded. Through our achievements in science and technology, we have crafted a culture that would have been considered magical, miraculous, or simply unimaginable two or three centuries ago. We are living in the "new age" of our great-grandparents and great-great-grandparents.

Very few of our ancestors foresaw the shadow side of our miraculous culture: the pollution, the regimentation, the alienation, the reductionism which, as David points out, all make up the unhealthy aspects of the Machine. These dysfunctional manifestations emerged because in creating this Machine culture we exaggerated intellect over feeling, hierarchy over community, mind over body, technology over nature. Now we are trying to redress the balance.

However, in imagining a new kind of society, one that is more holistic, organic, and ecological, we can make the same mistake by rejecting the qualities that created the Machine and by turning exclusively to their opposites. We can exaggerate in the opposite direction, which will only blind us to whatever shadow side the holistic and ecological perspective may have, and create another dysfunctional society that our children or grandchildren will have to confront.

So, in our time, we are called to exercise an inclusive imagination, one that neither surrenders its critical judgment for some kind of pseudo-new-age harmonious mush, in which everything is of equal value (and hence of no value), nor excludes important aspects of human nature and human accomplishment in the name of an equally false "organicism" or "holism" that is considered "holistic" only if it meets some radical, socially determined standard of political correctness. We are simultaneously called to honor the best parts of the Machine and the abilities within us that have created it, while identifying and getting rid of those parts that are destroying us and our world. We are called to an imagination of integration and synthesis, compassion and true wholeness.

In effect, if we are to create a non-Machine culture that nonetheless is served by the best aspects of our human capacity for technological innovation. We cannot use the exclusionary and adversarial techniques of the Machine to do it. In a form of cultural Aikido, we must learn to recreate society through redirection rather than through simple confrontation. The martial art of Aikido is based on a principle of mutual protection: the defender seeks to redirect the energy of the attacker so that neither person is harmed but the attack is disarmed and defused. We are being attacked by ideas, attitudes, and behaviors that threaten us all with grievous harm; David names these attackers collectively as the Machine. But behind the Machine is a creative impulse that can serve us if its energy is redirected and awakened to a new purpose. That is our task.

To succeed at Aikido, a person must stand in a place of inner knowing and balance; there can be no fear in his or her response to the attacker. To succeed at a cultural Aikido, we must stand in a place of cultural knowing and balance, free from the seductions of the Machine but open to its positive elements as well, knowing how they might serve the emergence of a more holistic and compassionate future. David's book gives us insights and strategies that enable us to stand in exactly that place. It is a powerful contribution to the growing literature of liberation and transformation that both enriches and challenges our culture and ourselves.

BIBLIOGRAPHY AND SOURCES

American Psychological Association. *Big World, Small Screen: The Role of Television in American Society*. University of Nebraska Press, Lincoln, 1992.

Baker, Nena. "Nike's World: Power and Profits." *The Oregonian*, August 9, 1992.

Baldwin, Deborah. "The Hard Sell of Advertising". *Common Cause Magazine*, May/June 1991.

Barlett, Donald, Steele, James. *America: What Went Wrong?* Andrews & McMeel, New York, 1992.

Bates, Brian. *The Way of the Wyrd*. Harper & Row, New York, 1983.

Bateson, Gregory. *Steps to an Ecology of Mind*. Ballantine Books, New York, 1972.

Bertalanffy, Ludwig von. *Perspectives on General System Theory*. George Braziller, New York, 1975.

BloomQuist, Randall. "Commercial Brake: Is it time to ban or tax advertising." *City Paper* (Washington DC), May 2, 1991.

Bly, Robert. *Iron John*. Addison Wesley, Menlo Park, 1990.

Bly, Robert. *Selected Poems of Rainer Maria Rilke*. Harper & Row, New York, 1981.

Brand, Stewart. *The Media Lab: Inventing the Future at M.I.T.* Penguin Books, New York, 1987.

Brown, Joseph Epes. *The Sacred Pipe: Black Elk's Account of the Seven Rites of the Oglala Sioux*. University of Oklahoma Press, Norman, 1953.

Brown, Lester, ed. *State of the World 1992*. W.W. Norton & Co. New York, 1992.

Burke, W.K. "On the Air: Dan Quayle's dirty politics are tarnishing the Clean Air Act." pp. 12-13, *In These Times*, July 22-August 4, 1992.

Campbell, Joseph. *Historical Atlas of World Mythology: Part I Mythologies of Primitive Hunters and Gatherers*. Perennial Library, Harper & Row, New York, 1988.

Carlson-Paige, Nancy & Levin, Diane. *Who's Calling the Shots? How to Respond Effectively to Children's Fascination with War Play and War Toys*, New Society Publishers, Philadelphia, 1990.

Castaneda, Carlos. *The Power of Silence: Further Lessons of don Juan..* Simon and Schuster, New York, 1987.

Davis, Wade. *Penan: Voice for the Borneo Rainforest*. Western Canada Wilderness Committee, Vancouver, Canada.

Descartes, Rene. *Philosophical Writings*. Bobbs-Merrill, Indianapolis, 1971.

DeChardin, P.T. *The Phenomenon of Man*. Collins, London, 1959.

Drucker, Peter. *Managing for the Future*. Dutton, New York, 1992.

Drucker, Peter. "How the '90s Changes Will Affect Business". San Francisco Chronicle, March 23,1992.

Eisler, Riane. *The Chalice and the Blade*. Harper & Row, San Francisco, 1988.

Eliade, Mircea. *Rites and Symbols of Initiation*. Harper Torchbooks, New York, 1958.

Ellul, Jacques. *Propaganda: The Formation of Man's Attitudes*. New York, 1965.

Evenson, Laura. "New Age products Thrive in the Midst of Recession". *San Francisco Chronicle*, March 23, 1992.

"Facts out of Context". p. 5, *In Context Magazine*, No.31, 1992.

Fassel, Diane. *Working Ourselves to Death*. Harper Collins, 1990.

Feher, Catherine. *Ravensong*. Northland Publishing, Flagstaff, AZ, 1991.

Forster, E.M. "The Machine Stops" from *Eternal Moments*. Harcourt Brace Jovanovich, New York, 1956.

Frank, Andre Gunder. *World Accumulation*. Monthly Review Press, New York, 1978.

Gardner, John. *No Easy Victories*. Harper & Row, New York, 1968.

Gilman, Robert. "No Simple Answers." pp. 10-13, *In Context Magazine*, No. 31, 1992

Gimbutas, Marija. *The Goddeses and Gods of Old Europe 6500-3500 BC: Myths and Cult Images*. University of California Press, Berkeley, 1982.

Grof, Stanislav. *Beyond the Brain: Birth, Death, and Transcendence in Psychotherapy*. State University of New York Press, New York, 1985.

Hawken, Paul. "The Ecology of Commerce." pp. 93-100, *Inc. Magazine*, April 1992. Excerpt from a speech at the Commonwealth Club of San Francisco.

Hillman, James. *Re-Visioning Psychology*. Harper & Row, New York, 1975.

Hobbes, Thomas. *Leviathan*. (ed) Michael Oakshott. Oxford, 1960.

Huxley, Aldous. *The Doors of Perception*. Harper & Row, New York, 1954.

James, William. *The Varieties of Religious Experience*. Harvard University Press, Cambridge, 1985.

Jones, Michael. Memoranda: "American Indian Religious Rites Threatened by Government Agencies". Cascade Geographical Society, Rhododendron, Oregon, March 1992.

Jung, Carl G. "The Stages of Life", *The Portable Jung*, Joseph Campbell, ed. Viking Press, New York, 1971.

Kimbrell, Andrew. "Body Wars: Can the human body survive the age of technology?" Utne Reader. May/June 1992, pp. 52-64.

Kleiman, Carol. "Women plan to outperform Fortune 500." Chicago Tribune News Service, The Oregonian, April 1, 1992.

Kleiman, Carol. "Economic predicament of older women headed from bad to worse". Chicago Tribune News Service, The Oregonian, August 12, 1992.

Koestler, Arthur. *The Ghost in the Machine*. Macmillan, New York, 1967.

La Chapelle, Dolores. *Sacred Land, Sacred Sex and Rapture of the Deep*. FineHill Arts, Silverton, CO, 1988.

Laing, R.D. *The Politics of Experience*. Ballantine Books, New York, 1967.

Langer, Susanne. *Philosophy in a New Key.* Harvard University Press, Cambridge, 1941.

Lawlor, Robert. *Voices of the First Day.* Inner Traditions, Rochester, Vermont, 1991.

Lewin, Kurt. *Field Theory in Social Science: Selected Theoretical Papers.* Harper, New York, 1951.

Lind-Kyle, Patt. *When Sleeping Beauty Wakes Up: A Woman's Tale of Healing the Immune System and Awakening the Feminine.* Swan•Raven & Company, Portland, OR, 1992.

Living Bible. Tyndale House Publishers, Wheaton, Il, 1971.

Locke, John. *Two Treatises of Government.* Peter Laslett, ed. University Press, Cambridge, 1960.

Lovelock, J. *Gaia: A New Look at Life on Earth.* Oxford University Press, Oxford, 1982.

Mander, Jerry. *In the Absence of the Sacred: The Failure of Technology and the Survival of the Indian Nations.* Sierra Club Books, San Francisco, 1991.

Mander, Jerry. *Four Arguments for the Elimination of Television.* Quill Books, 1977.

Maslow, Abraham. *Eupsychian Management.* Richard Irwin Inc. & Dorsey Press, Homewood, Illinois, 1965.

Maslow, Abraham. *Toward a Psychology of Being.* D. Van Nostrand Co. New York, 1962.

Maugh, Thomas. "Magnetic particles discovered in human brains - but why?" The Oregonian, Tuesday, May 12, 1992. LA Times-Washington Post Service.

Meadows, Donella H., Meadows and Dennis L., Randers, Jorgen. *The Limits to Growth.* Universe Books, New York, 1972.

Meadows, Donella H., Meadows and Dennis L., Randers, Jorgen. *Beyond the Limits: Confronting Global Collapse, Envisioning a Sustainable Future.* Chelsea Green Press, Post Mills, Vermont, 1992.

McCoy, Alfred. *The politics of Heroin: CIA Complicity in the Global Drug Trade.* Lawrence Hill Books, 1991.

McKenna, Terence. *The Archaic Revival.* Harper & Row, San Francisco, 1992.

McKenna, Terence. *Food of the Gods: The Search for the Original Tree of Knowledge.* Bantam, New York, 1992.

McKenna, Dennis and McKenna, Terence. *The Invisible Landscape.* Seabury Press, New York, 1975.

McNeill, Jim. "Back to School," p. 6, *In These Times,* July 22-August 4, 1992.

Meyer, Alfred. "The Rise of the New America." pp. 68-79, *Mother Earth News,* March/April 1988.

Mollner, Terry. "The Third Way is Here" *In Context Magazine,* pp. 54-59. No.19, 1988.

Nixon, Will. "Growing pains: Earth swells Beyond the Limits." *In These Times* Vol. 16 No 25, May 20-26, 1992.

Opheim, Teresa. "Where Were We When East Timor was Invaded?" pp. 24-26, *Utne Reader,* January/February, 1992.

Perot, Ross. Speech at National Press Club, Washington DC, March 18, 1992. Excerpt: *The Oregonian,* March 29, 1992.

Postman, Neil. *Technopoly: The Surrender of Culture to Technology.* Alfred Knopf, New York, 1992.

Power, William; Siconolfi, Michael. "Merrill's Schreyer Gets Fat Pay Package for '91". *The Wall Street Journal*, March 23, 1992.

Rasmussen, Knud. *Intellectual Culture of the Copper Eskimo.* trans. W. Calvert, AMS Press, New York, 1976.

Rasmussen, Knud. *Across Arctic America.* Greenwood Press, Westport Conn, 1968.

Read, Richard. "Fear of Death from Overwork Spreads in Japan's Work Force.". *The Oregonian*, March 22, 1992.

"Report: Ozone Hole Shifts Over A Populated Island", Reuters News Service in *Philadelphia Inquirer*, October 10, 1992.

Riesman, David, with Nathan Glazer and Reuel Denny. *The Lonely Crowd.* Yale University Press, New Haven, 1961.

Robinson, Bryan. *Work Addiction.* Health Communications, Deerfield Beach, Florida, 1989.

Schaef, Anne Wilson. *Women's Reality: An Emerging Female System in a White Male Society.* Harper & Row, San Francisco, 1981,1985.

Schaef, Anne Wilson, Fassel, Diane. *The Addictive Organization.* Harper & Row, 1988.

Schein, Edgar H. *Organizational Psychology, 3rd ed.,* Prentice-Hall, Englewood Cliffs, N.J., 1980.

Schneider, Stephen H. *Global Warming: Are we Entering the Greenhouse Century?* Sierra Club Books, San Francisco, 1989.

"Sears Cutting Back 2,000 More Jobs Primarily Among Middle Managers". Associated Press, *The Oregonian*, April 1, 1992.

Senge, Peter. *The Fifth Discipline: The Art & Practice of the Learning Organization.* Doubleday, New York, 1990.

Silverman, Julian. "Shamans and Acute Schizophrenia." *American Anthropologist* (1961).

Sklar, Holly, Ed. *Trilateralism: The Trilateral Commission and Elite Planning for World Management.* South End Press, Boston, 1980.

Spangler, David. *Emergence: The Rebirth of the Sacred.* Dell Publishing, New York, 1984.

Spangler, David and Thompson, Irwin William. *Re-imagination of the World: A Critique of the New Age Popular Scienc Culture."* Bear & Co. 1991, Santa Fe.

Sterngold, James. "Floodtide of Japanese Money Ebbs." New York Times News Service, *The Oregonian*, March 22, 1992.

Snyder, Gary. *The Old Ways.* City Lights Books, San Francisco, 1977.

Tooker, Elisabeth, ed. *Native North American Spirituality of the Eastern Woodlands.* Paulist Press, Mahwalh, New Jersey, 1979.

Tuchman, Barbara. *A Distant Mirror: The Calamitous 14th Century.* Knopf, New York, 1978.

Turner, Victor. *The Ritual Process: Structure and Anti-Structure.* Cornell Paperbacks, Ithaca, New York, 1977.

"White House, Congress See No End to Big Deficits." *New York Times*, March 23, 1992

Whyte, William Foote, Whyte, Kathleen King. *Making Mondragon: The Growth and Dynamics of the Worker Cooperative Complex.* ILR Press, Cornell University, Ithica, 1991.

Woiwode, Larry. "The Cyclops that Eats Books." *The Orange Country Register*, March 8, 1992. Originally given as an address, February 1992 at Hillsdale College (Michigan) in the seminar: "Freedom, Responsibility, and the American Literary Tradition."

Woodman, Marion. *Addiction to Perfection*. Inner City Books, Toronto, Canada, 1982

Woodman, Marion. *The Pregnant Virgin*. Inner City Books, Toronto, Canada, 1985.

Woodman, Marion. *The Ravaged Bridegroom: Masculinity in Women*. Inner City Books, Toronto, Canada, 1990.

Verity, John. "The Tyranny of Technology." *Business Week*, March 23, 1992.

INDEX

aboriginals, 152, 169, 201, 256, 257, 271
Addiction to Perfection, 239
addiction, 69, 73, 74, 84, 86, 89, 90, 93, 111, 274
Addictive Organization, The, 42
adrenaline, 73, 74, 91
Africa, 83-85, 161, 164, 169, 221, 222, 225, 229, 242, 252, 271
"aha" conversations, 133, 136, 137, 140, 142, 145, 147-151, 164, 165, 275
AIDS, 161
Aikido, 283
Alaska, 33, 34, 131
alcohol, 69, 74, 88, 93, 105, 120, 209
Alcoholics Anonymous, 73
alienation, 24, 91, 128, 218, 282
American Association for World Health, 88
American dream, 104-108, 111, 199, 215, 278
American Psychological Association, 91
American Revolution, 85
Amish, 194
ancestral world, 242
Anderson, Arthur, 65
Anglo-Saxon sorcerer, 256
Antarctic ozone hole, 167
Apache, 211, 212
Apple, 33, 109
archaic revival, 169, 202
Arizona, 211, 212
Australia, 22, 179, 180, 224
Australian aborigines, 152, 169, 201, 256, 257, 271

Babel, 205
Bacon, Francis, 80, 259, 269
Bacon, Roger, 82
Baldwin, Deborah, 40
bandit organizations, 140-145, 150
Bangkok, 159
Bank of International Settlements, 45
Bank of the People's Labor, 177
Bantu, 169
Barlett, Donald, 106

Basque Spain, 176-178
Bates, Brian, 255
BCCI, 88
Bear Sterns Cos., 38
Benedictine monks, 80
Berkeley, 111
Beyond the Limits, 156
Bhopal, India, 34
Bighorn National Forest, 211
biosignals, 71
biotechnologies, 30
Black Elk, 240
Black Madonna, 239, 240
Black Plague, 83
Blackfeet, 211
Blanchard, Ken, 63
Bly, Robert, 233, 234, 237-239, 242-244
Bohm, David, 146, 147, 149
Booz, Allen, 65
Borneo, 210
Boston Consulting Group, 65
Bourne, Dr. Peter, 88
Brower, David, 194
Brand, Stewart, 55
Brandeis University, 222
Brazil, 56, 84
Britain, 84-86
British Columbia, 196
Brown, Lester, 158, 162, 163, 269
Buddhism, 138
Burkina Faso, 222
Bush administration, 34-36, 88

Cal Tech, 257
California, 26, 42, 104-106, 136, 167, 170, 211, 212, 264
Cambodia, 87
Campbell, Joseph, 202, 205
Canada, 52, 103, 179
capitalism, 46, 47, 50, 86, 127-131, 176
carbon dioxide, 159
Caribbean, 84, 85, 121
Carlson-Paige, Nancy, 35
carpal tunnel syndrome, 71
cartoon commercials, 34, 40, 91
Cascade Geographic Society, 211

292

Catholic Church, 82, 83, 211
Cayce, Edgar, 277
Cayuga, 213
Center for the Study of
     Commercialism, 40
Center on Budget Policy, 107
Central Union, 177
CEO, 38, 39, 75, 117, 125, 142
CFIDS, 74, 115, 237
Chalice and the Blade, The, 194
chaos, 54, 63, 67, 255
Chicago Democratic Convention, 111
chief executive officer, 38, 39, 75,
     117, 125, 142
China, 49, 88, 164
Chinese, 257
chocolate, 93
Christian fundamentalism, 54
Christians, 138, 168, 268
Christic Institute, 87
Chronic Fatigue Immune
     Dysfunction Syndrome, 74, 115,
     237
chronobiology, 71
CIA, 87, 88
cigarettes, 89
Civil War, 106
Clean Air Act, 35, 36,
coaggregating, 56
Coca Cola, 214
cocaine, 73, 87, 88, 93
coffee, 49, 93
Cognetics Inc., 75
co-housing, 175, 176, 275
colonialism, 84
Columbus, Christopher, 83
Common Market, 51, 52
communication control, 61
communism, 47, 50, 51, 111, 128-131
Communist dogma, 49
community, 13, 14, 16, 35, 38, 48, 50,
     66, 108, 110, 128, 134, 136, 140,
     141, 144, 145, 158, 164, 174,
     176, 178, 180-183, 193, 202, 206,
     216, 218, 224, 227, 240-242, 246,
     268, 275, 276
competition, 47, 84, 119, 127, 128,
     130, 176
conflict-resolution, 59, 63, 136
confluence in the '80s, 136
Congressional Budget Office, 171
consultant, 14, 24, 43, 59, 60, 62, 65,
     66, 68, 108, 145, 236

consumerism, 32, 40, 46, 47, 52-54,
     111, 222
consumption age, 199, 200
conversations of possibilities and
     action, 150
Coronado National Forest, 212
corporation-economy, 14, 15, 24, 35,
     36, 38, 45, 46, 52-54, 57, 60, 68,
     74, 80, 93, 155, 171, 180, 208,
     209
Council on Competitiveness, 36
Crack in the Cosmic Egg, 91
Crandall, Robert L., 118
credit collapse, 56
crone, 238, 239
curanderos, 253

Dagara, 9, 221, 222, 242, 252, 271
Davis, Wade, 210
de Chardin, Teilhard, 165, 168, 169,
     269
de Tocqueville, Alex, 32
deep ecologist, 79
Denmark, 71, 175
Denny, Reuel, 199
Department of Brain Evolution and
     Behavior, 92
Descartes, René, 81
designer drug, 93
developed nations, 53
dominator, 120, 232
doomsday, 16, 170, 277, 278
Doors of Perception, 254
Dreamtime, 152, 256-259, 271, 279
Drucker, Peter, 109
drugs, 69, 86-88, 120, 227
Dryer, Alan, 47
dysfunctionality, 42, 60, 71, 281, 282

Earth First!, 194
earthquakes, 161, 166
Eastern Europe, 47, 51, 173
Excellence, 67
ecology, 259
ecosystem, 33, 152, 156
Eisenhower, 107
Eisler, Riane, 194, 195
elder, 16, 182, 188, 210, 215, 216,
     218, 220-223, 227-229, 240, 244,
     262, 272, 273
elder initiators, 242, 243

elder-leaders, 16, 188, 215, 216, 218, 220, 226-230, 244, 273, 276
eldering, 181, 182
Eliade, Mircea, 224
Ellul, Jacques, 157
Emerson, Ralph Waldo, 111
employees, 37, 45, 63, 64, 71, 74, 76, 117, 144
England, 31, 84, 85, 192
Enola Hill, 210
environmental allergies, 74
Environmental Protection Agency, 36
EPA, 36
epiphanal action, 150
epiphanal community, 135, 137, 138, 141, 144, 145, 164
epiphany, 135, 137, 138, 141, 142, 145-148, 151
Erie Railroad, 61
Eupsychian Management, 42
Eurasia, 245
Europe, 29, 31, 33, 47, 50-52, 80, 82-85, 109, 172, 173, 199, 201, 207, 277
Exxon, 33, 34, 52
Exxon Valdez, 34

fascism, 37, 54
FCC, 34
Federal Communications Commission, 34
Federal Reserve,173
Feher, Catherine, 196
feminine, 123, 169, 191, 194, 195, 239
feminine values, 76, 120, 195
Fifth Discipline, The, 146
Figgie, Harry E. Jr., 118
film industry, 40, 41, 69
Findhorn Community, 246
Flathead Indian, 226
folk healers, 49, 50
folk medicine, 49
Forster, E.M., 21, 23, 24, 57, 157, 269
Fortune 500 companies, 75, 162, 173
Fortune magazine, 117
Four Arguments for the Elimination of Television, 207
Four Corners, 210
Frank, Andre Gunder, 82

Franklin, Benjamin, 212
"free" money, 55
Freedom of Information Act, 87
French Revolution, 85
Fuller, Buckminster, 139, 140, 150, 151

Galileo, 82
Gardner, John W., 227
General Motors, 52
genes, 30
Genesis, 196
genetic engineering, 30, 277
geobiologist, 257
geomancy, 257, 258
Germans, 50, 52
Ghandi, 191
Ghosthorse, Buck, 272
Gilman, Robert, 154, 156, 157
Glazer, Nathan, 199
goddess, 69, 82, 169, 201, 239
golden age, 169
Golden Triangle, 87
Gould, James, 257
Great Spirit, 169, 196, 239
Greeks, 202
Gross Domestic Product, 70
Gross National Product, 55
Guatemala, 196
Gurdjieff, G.I., 245

Haida, 196, 197
hallucinogens, 254
Hard Sell of Advertising, The, 40
Harlem Globetrotters, 104
Harman, Willis, 136, 137
Hazard Block Company, 104
health-care system, 49
Hearthstone Village, 180-182
Heisenberg, Werner, 60
heroin, 87, 88
Hersey, Dr. Rexford, 71
hierarchy of needs, 43, 63
Hindus, 169, 240, 269, 270
hippies, 72, 192
Hobbes, Thomas, 79, 81, 128
holism, 209, 282
holographic, 263
Holy Spirit, 138

holy mechanics, 21, 99, 100, 133, 135, 140, 141, 145, 150, 151, 155, 187, 188
Hopi, 169, 212, 213, 269, 272
Huichol, 271
human resources, 75, 76
human-interaction strategies, 64
hunger, 53, 64, 130, 156, 270
Huxley, Aldous, 252
Hyper-Dimensional Object, 169

IBM, 33, 109
Illich, Ivan, 157
"imaginal" cells, 262, 263, 274, 279
imagination, 15, 16, 25, 29, 100, 133, 136, 137, 140, 155, 175, 178, 187, 188, 193, 201-203, 248, 251, 252, 256, 259, 262-264, 269, 271-275, 277-279, 281, 282
IMF, 46, 50, 51
In The Absence of the Sacred, 207, 208
India, 34, 83-85, 161, 164, 196
indigenous people, 16, 25, 26, 28, 53, 83, 84, 86, 166, 188, 196, 208-210, 212, 214, 220-223, 226, 234, 246, 251, 254, 256, 258, 262, 270-272, 274
Indonesia, 33, 52, 53, 110, 210, 271
Industrial Revolution, 31, 84, 162, 205
Information Age, 109
inner-directed, 32, 199
inspiration, 136-140, 145, 150, 202
International Monetary Fund, 45, 46, 50, 51
IQ test, 152
Iran-Contra, 55, 87, 88
Ireland, 47
Iron John, 237
Iroquois confederacy, 212
Islam, 54, 169
Israel, 54

Jackson, Michael, 38
Jacobson, Michael, 40
Japan, 31, 33, 47, 51-54, 71, 73, 74, 172, 173, 177, 207
Jaynes, Julian, 28, 29, 251, 252
Jesus, 100, 138, 170, 243

Jews, 83
Jones, Michael, 211
Judaism, 169
Judgment Day, 169
Jung, Carl, 220, 221, 274

Kali, 240, 269, 270
karoshi, 73, 74
Kennedy, John F., 111
King, Martin Luther Jr., 111
Kirschvink, Joseph, 257
Kupers, Terry, 71
La Chapelle, Dolores, 79, 86
Lake Baikal, 202
Lakota Sioux, 240, 272
Lama Foundation Community, 246
Lascaux, 200
Latin America, 43, 45
Lawlor, Robert, 271
LETS, 179
Levin, Diane, 35
Lewin, Kurt, 62
Liberia, 35
"Limits to Growth, The," 156
Linton, Michael, 179
Locke, John, 79, 128
Logos, 146, 248, 251, 252, 267, 274
London, 33, 82
London Stock Exchange, 55
Lonely Crowd, The, 32, 199, 200
Lorenzo, Frank A., 118
Los Angeles Times, 88
loving resistance fighter, 149, 152, 153
Lud, Ned, 193
Luddites, 193, 194

"Machine Stops, The," 21, 23, 157
Madison Avenue, 40
Magical Child, The, 91
Mahoney, Richard J., 117
Malaysia, 210
male role, 120
Malveaux, Julianne, 74, 75
man-made woman, 121-123
management, 38, 39, 42-45, 60, 61, 63-65, 67, 108, 109, 119, 141, 144, 178
management hierarchy, 60, 142, 178
management technology, 63

Managing for the Future, 109

Mander, Jerry, 90, 151, 207, 208, 213, 224

Marx, Karl, 128

Maslow, Abraham, 42-44, 62, 63

mass media, 32, 39, 172

materialism, 47, 69, 93, 111, 187, 222

Mayan, 169, 170, 196

MBAs, 39, 64

McCallum, Daniel, 60, 61

McColl, Hugh L. Jr., 117

McCoy, Alfred, 87

McGregor, Douglas, 62, 63

McKenna, Terance, 162, 169, 202

McKinnsy & Co., 65

Mclean, Paul, 92

Media Lab, The, 55

medicine wheel, 25, 26, 211

megatechnology, 170, 208

Merrill Lynch & Co., 37

Mexico, 52, 110, 159, 264, 271

micro-computer chips, 28

Microsoft, 33

middle management, 64

Mirabai, 238

mirrored greatness, 242, 243

mobile telephones, 23

Mohawk, 213

Mollner, Terry, 176, 177

monarch butterfly, 261, 264

Mondragon, 174, 176-178

money game, 54-57

Montana, 211

Moors, 83

Mother Nature, 9, 91

Mount Graham, 210

Mount Hood, 211

Mount Shasta, 212

Mumford, Lewis, 157

music, 22, 27-29, 46, 52, 68, 191, 225, 248, 262

myth, 122, 124, 140, 196, 200, 205, 210, 224, 225, 229, 257, 270

nanomachines, 30

nanotechnology, 23, 28, 30, 31

National Forest Service, 211

National Foundation for Women Business Owners, 75

National Institute of Mental Health, 92

National Press Club, 171

National Register, 211

Native American, 26, 53, 181, 195, 196, 209, 210, 212, 213, 224, 240, 267, 272

Navajo, 169, 212, 271, 272

nazism, 80

neocortex, 92

neural structure, 92

New Age, 69, 280

New Mexico, 212, 246

New World, 50, 80, 83, 84, 192

new world order, 51, 52, 191, 192, 227

New York City, 52

New York Times, 67

Newton, Isaac, 82, 269

Nicaragua, 87

Ninja Turtle, 34, 91

Nintendo, 90

No Easy Victories, 227

"No Simple Answers," 156

Noriega, 87

North Dakota, 103, 104, 106

North Korea, 49

Northern California, 26, 210, 264

Northern China, 49

nuclear waste, 131, 158, 160

Nulty, Peter, 118, 119

occultists, 49

ochre, 258

Office of Management and Budget, 36

oiler, 47, 60, 233

Oklahoma, 103

Old Testament, 196

OMB, 36

Omega Point, 165, 168

One Hundred Years War, 83

Oneida, 213

Onondagas, 213

Ontara, 235, 237, 238

opium, 84, 87, 88

Oregon, 104, 167, 210, 211

organicism, 282

organizational consulting, 24, 65

Origins of Consciousness in the Breakdown of the Bicameral Mind, The, 28

other-directed, 32, 199, 200

Otherworld, 16, 130, 137, 139, 169, 193, 201, 208, 214, 215, 221-224, 234, 239, 242-244, 246, 252-254, 256, 258, 267, 273
overpopulation, 53
Oversoul, 169, 233-235
ozone, 35, 166-168, 214

Panama, 87
Parabola, 226
Paris, 55, 222
Passage to India, 21
patriarchal society, 194, 196, 205
peace, 52, 53, 138, 238
Peace Corps, 111, 190
Pearce, Joseph Chilton, 91-93
Penan: Voice for the Borneo Rainforest, 210
Penatuba volcano, 166
Perot, H. Ross, 171
Philippines, 166
pilot rutter, 259, 260, 262, 273
pneuma, 138
Pol, Pot, 87
Poland, 177
political alignment, 51
Politics of Heroin, The , 87
pollution, 156, 282
Popol Vuh, 196
Portuguese, 84
Postman, Neil, 151, 152
Pregnant Virgin, The , 237
primary language, 223, 252
Princeton University, 257
progress, 21, 33, 34, 52, 105, 106, 108, 158, 194, 207, 226, 271
psychedelic, 27, 108, 111, 191, 192
pupa, 263, 264

Quayle, Dan, 34, 36

racism, 37, 46, 191
radical, 272, 273, 282
radical acts, 272, 273, 276
Rasmussen, Knud, 253
raven, 196, 197, 245, 255
Ravensong, 196
Reagan, Ronald, 106, 107, 276

Reagan-Bush administration, 34, 35, 55
reality, 14-16, 23-25, 28, 29, 47, 55, 57, 75, 79, 81, 105, 123, 124, 128, 130, 131, 135, 187, 191, 195, 196, 206, 214, 221, 223, 227, 245, 251, 256, 259-262, 269, 272, 279
recession, 37, 169, 172
reductionism, 282
regimentation, 282
Rembrandt, 238
Renaissance, 202, 205
reptilian brain, 92
Republic of Russia, 47, 49-51, 276, 277
resource depletion, 53, 164, 168, 214
Riesman, David, 32, 199
Rifkin, Jeremy, 71, 72
Rilke, Rainer Maria, 262, 264
Rio conference, 158
Rio de Janeiro, 158
Rio Grande Basin, 246
ritual, 26, 28, 130, 200, 223-225, 227, 229, 240, 241, 273, 274
Robinson, Bryan, 73
rock'n'roll, 52
Romans, 202
Royal Dutch Shell, 52, 55
Royal Society of London, 82
Russian Republic, 47, 49-51, 276, 277

Sacred, 14-17, 25, 26, 28, 29, 137-140, 173, 188, 189, 195, 196, 200-203, 206, 208-212, 214, 215, 221, 225, 229, 248, 252, 253, 259, 260, 268, 270
Sacred Land, Sacred Sex and Rapture of the Deep, 79
Sacred Other, 188
Sacred Sound, 248, 252
sacred plants, 273
Sangre de Cristo, 246
Sanskrit, 235
satellite transmission, 23
Scandinavian, 175
scarcity, 128-131
scarcity assumption, 128
Schaef, Ann Wilson, 123, 124
Schelz, J'aime, 260-262

Schreyer, William, 37
Schumacher, E.F., 194
Schwartz, Peter, 55, 56
Scotland, 246
Sears, Roebuck and Co., 41
Seneca, 213
Senge, Peter, 146, 148
shadow, 276-279, 282
shaman, 253, 262
shamanic ritual, 26, 69, 209
Sheen, Daniel, 87
Siberia, 33, 202
Sierra Nevada Mountains, 26
Sikh, 54
sitcoms, 52, 91, 192, 218, 228, 243
Sklar, Holly, 46
skunk works, 43
Smith, Adam, 128
social behavioral model, 62
socialism, 128, 129, 176
Somé, Malidoma, 221-223, 242, 262
songlines, 255, 257, 258, 279
Sophia, 239
Sorbonne, 222
South America, 80, 87, 130, 167, 195,
    225, 253
South Pacific, 225
Southeast Asia, 31, 87, 110
Soviet Union, 47, 49-52, 127, 136,
    173, 174, 276
Spain, 83, 177, 178
speed junkie, 91
Spirit, 138, 169, 196, 213, 215, 220,
    221, 223, 225, 241, 272
spiritual healing, 49, 224
"Stages of Life, The," 220
"State of the World," 158, 163, 270
Steele, James, 106
stock market, 56
stress-management, 42, 59, 71-73
Sufi, 245
sugar, 84, 85, 93
Sugar and Stamp Acts, 85
sustainability, 129, 130

Tannenbaum, Robert, 62, 63
Tasmania, 167, 257
Taylor, Frederick, 61
*Technopoly: The Surrender of Culture
    to Technology*, 151, 152
telecommunications, 55

television, 21, 32, 34, 35, 39, 52, 69,
    72, 89-93, 100, 104, 106, 107,
    122, 152, 200, 208, 214, 226,
    234, 245, 251, 274
theory of indeterminacy, 60
Third Way Economics, 176
Third World, 35, 51, 53, 56, 88, 109,
    110, 115, 160, 162, 164, 173
Thoreau, Henry David, 191
Thriving on Chaos, 63, 67
Time Wars, 71
Timorese, 271
tobacco, 84, 88, 89
Tokyo, 33, 55
topography, 16, 201, 256, 257, 259,
    260
trance dancing, 254
Transcendental Object, 169, 269
transcendentalism, 111
Triangle Trade, 85, 86
Trilateral Commission, 46
Trilateralism, 46
Trusteeship Institute, 176
TV, 22, 24, 32, 35, 40, 52, 69, 70, 89-
    93, 100, 120, 151, 155, 192, 226,
    272, 275
TV violence, 91

U.S. AID, 46
UCLA, 63
underdeveloped nations, 53,
Union Carbide, 33, 34
unionism, 44, 45
unions, 44, 45, 61
United Nations, 47
United Nations Conference on
    Environment and Development,
    158
United States, 31, 33, 35, 40, 46, 47,
    49-57, 65, 68, 87, 88, 90, 107,
    161, 164, 167, 171, 172, 175,
    207, 277
University of Arizona, 211
University of Minnesota, 104
Upanishads, 196
USSR, 275
Uvavnuk, 253, 254

Vanderburg, Agnes, 226, 228
VCRs, 52, 69, 214

Vedic, 169
virtual reality, 23
Vladivostok, 49, 50
Voice, 140, 153, 209, 224, 248, 250,
    252, 260, 274, 276
Voices of the First Day, 271
volcanic eruptions, 160, 166

Wakan-Tanka, 241
Walden Pond, 191
Wall Street, 37
Wall Street Journal, 38
war machine, 53
Warhol, Andy, 200
Way of the Wyrd, The, 255
Wellness programs, 59
West Africa, 221, 252
White Madonna, 240
White Male System, 123, 124, 240
Whitman, Walt, 111
*Who's calling the Shots? How to
    Respond Effectively to Children's
    Fascination with War Play and
    War Toys*, 35
Whole Earth Review, 208
Wintu, 210
women executives, 121
Women's Reality, 123
Woodman, Marion, 239, 240, 244
Work Addiction, 42, 73
Workaholics Anonymous, 73
World Accumulation, 82
World Bank, 45, 46
World Business Academy, 135
World Watch Institute, 156
Wyoming, 211
wyrd, 254-256, 259, 260, 279

"X" theory, 63

"Y" theory, 63

ECHOES OF THE ANCESTORS

The African Shaman Series

RITUAL
Power, Healing and Community

BY MALIDOMA SOMÉ

(THE FIRST IN THE SERIES COMING IN FEBRUARY 1993)

Each book in the series, *Echoes of the Ancestors*, presents an aspect of the Dagara teaching and its application and usefulness to us in our modern Western world.

Ritual describes the kinds of expected interactions between the ancestral spiritual world and this one, the uses and dangers of traditional ritual practice and how it is performed. The grief rituals are used as an example of communal ritual and its healing power for us today.

Malidoma Somé, spokesman for the Dagara Ancestors, lives in three worlds: the world of his village, the world of the Ancestors and the modern Western world. Holder of two Ph.D.s, he considers his traditional initiation into ancestral knowledge his true education. Told by the elders of his village that the Ancestors wanted him to go to the West, he immersed himself in Western culture. Malidoma now acts as a bridge between these three worlds, bringing the teachings of the Ancestors to echo within our own souls.

ISBN 0-9632310-3-0
Paper, 150 pages
Retail $12.95

SWAN•RAVEN & COMPANY
1427 N.W. 23rd Ave., Suite 8
Portland - OR 97210
Fax (503) 274-1044
(800) 499-4849

RITUAL

Power, Healing and Community

FROM THE AFRICAN
SHAMAN SERIES

ECHOES OF THE ANCESTORS

About Malidoma Somé

Malidoma Somé was raised in a village in Burkina Faso, West Africa. He is initiated in the ancestral tribal traditions and is a medicine man and diviner in the Dagara pattern. He holds three masters and two Ph.D. degrees from the Sorbonne and Brandeis University. He has taught at the University of Michigan, leads groups throughout the United States and teaches with Robert Bly and Michael Meade in men's conferences.

Each book in the series presents an aspect of the Dagara teaching and its application and usefulness to us in our modern world.

"Malidoma Somé is a remarkable and uniquely talented man. rarely can one person carry both the ancient ways of tribal Africa and the ways of Western thought and psychology. Malidoma not only carries these, he combines them, separates them, dances with them."

— Michael Meade

Coming in 1993

RITUAL: Power, Healing and
    Community

COWRIE SHELL DIVINATION:
    Listening to the Spirit Guides

MEDICINES AND SPIRITUAL
    PRACTICES: Living with the
    Otherworld

Coming in 1994

TRAVELING TO THE OTHERWORLD:
    going Through the Gateway

INITIATING THE ELDERS: Using the
    Powers from the Ancestors

ELDER LEADERSHIP: A New
    Model for Our Day

When Sleeping Beauty Wakes Up

A Woman's Tale of Healing the Immune System and Awakening the Feminine

BY PAT LIND-KYLE

The story of a near-death journey of emotional healing and spiritual awakening through a long illness with Chronic Fatigue Syndrome. By going through a life and death process, the author uncovered a new path to a woman's feminine strength, and discovered a simple healing system. Her research with professional women presents the loss of true feminine experience in our culture, and how women can return to an inward presence to have stronger self-esteem, self-image and knowledge of the transforming feminine.

"Hers is not only a literal story of her battle with a 'Woman's Disease,' but also a metaphorical telling about the condition of many American women today, whose efforts toward healing are really attempts to reclaim their power in a subtly but insidiously male-dominated culture."

> — Laurie Wimmer
> Executive Director
> Oregon Commission on Women

ISBN 0-9632310-3-0
Paper, 256 pages
Retail $14.95

SWAN•RAVEN & COMPANY
1427 N.W. 23rd Ave., Suite 8
Portland - OR 97210
Fax (503) 274-1044
(800) 499-4849

When Sleeping Beauty Wakes Up

A Woman's Tale of Healing
the Immune System and
Awakening the Feminine

About Patt-Lind Kyle

Patt Lind-Kyle is a psychologist who has taught and consulted in the business community, and has a private practice whose focus is with professional women. She received a BS in biology from the University of Southern California and an MA in psychology from the California Institute of Integral Studies. She is founder of the Swan Institute for the Emerging Woman Leader.

Patt Lind-Kyle gives speeches, presents seminars to women's groups, and talks to Chronic Fatigue Syndrome symposiums using the themes of her book. Patt gives a unique and refreshing presentation on awakening women to the feminine perspective in order to understand how they live and work in a man's world and how it affects their health, relationships, career and self-esteem. Patt uses song, vignettes, story and group participation in her presentations.

"In this book, the author intimately shares her healing journey with us, leading us down through the Seven States of Death, to emerge through the Seven States of Rebirth. In the end she provides a structure for seeing ourselves — a clear and simple system to map out our own healing paths. There is pain in these pages. But above all this is a testimony to the healing power of the human spirit."

— Hal Zina Bennet, Ph.D.
Author: *Follow Your Bliss*,
and The *Well Body Book*,